The Darien Gap

THE DARIEN GAP

TRAVELS IN THE
RAINFOREST OF PANAMA

MARTIN MITCHINSON

HARBOUR PUBLISHING

Copyright © 2008 Martin Mitchinson
2 3 4 5 — 12 11 10 09

All rights reserved. No part of this publication may be reproduced, stored in a retrieval system or transmitted, in any form or by any means, without prior permission of the publisher or, in the case of photocopying or other reprographic copying, a licence from Access Copyright, www.accesscopyright.ca, 1-800-893-5777, info@accesscopyright.ca.

Harbour Publishing Co. Ltd
P.O. Box 219, Madeira Park, BC, V0N 2H0
www.harbourpublishing.com

Front cover photograph by Katharine Ramirez, all other photographs by the author.
Edited by Meg Taylor
Map design by John Lightfoot
Cover and text design by Anna Comfort
Printed in Canada

Harbour Publishing acknowledges financial support from the Government of Canada through the Book Publishing Industry Development Program and the Canada Council for the Arts, and from the Province of British Columbia through the BC Arts Council and the Book Publishing Tax Credit.

Library and Archives Canada Cataloguing in Publication

Mitchinson, Martin, 1961-
    The Darien Gap : travels in the rainforest of Panama / Martin Mitchinson.

ISBN 978-1-55017-421-2

    1. Mitchinson, Martin, 1961- —Travel—Darien (Panama and Colombia).
2. Darien (Panama and Colombia)—Description and travel. 3. Balboa, Vasco Núñez de, 1475-1519. 4. Darien (Panama and Colombia)—History. I. Title.

F1569.D3M58 2008   917.287'780454   C2008-900009-9

For Gordy

CONTENTS

Map .... *viii*
Preface .... *xi*

In the Beginning 1
A New Year 33
Rio Balsas 69
Carajo! 97
The New Politics 109
Butterflies 127
Rio Tuira 139
Afraid of the Dark 171
Caledonia 189
Across the Divide 217

Epilogue *265*
Acknowledgments *271*
Glossary *275*
Selected Sources *281*
About the Author *284*

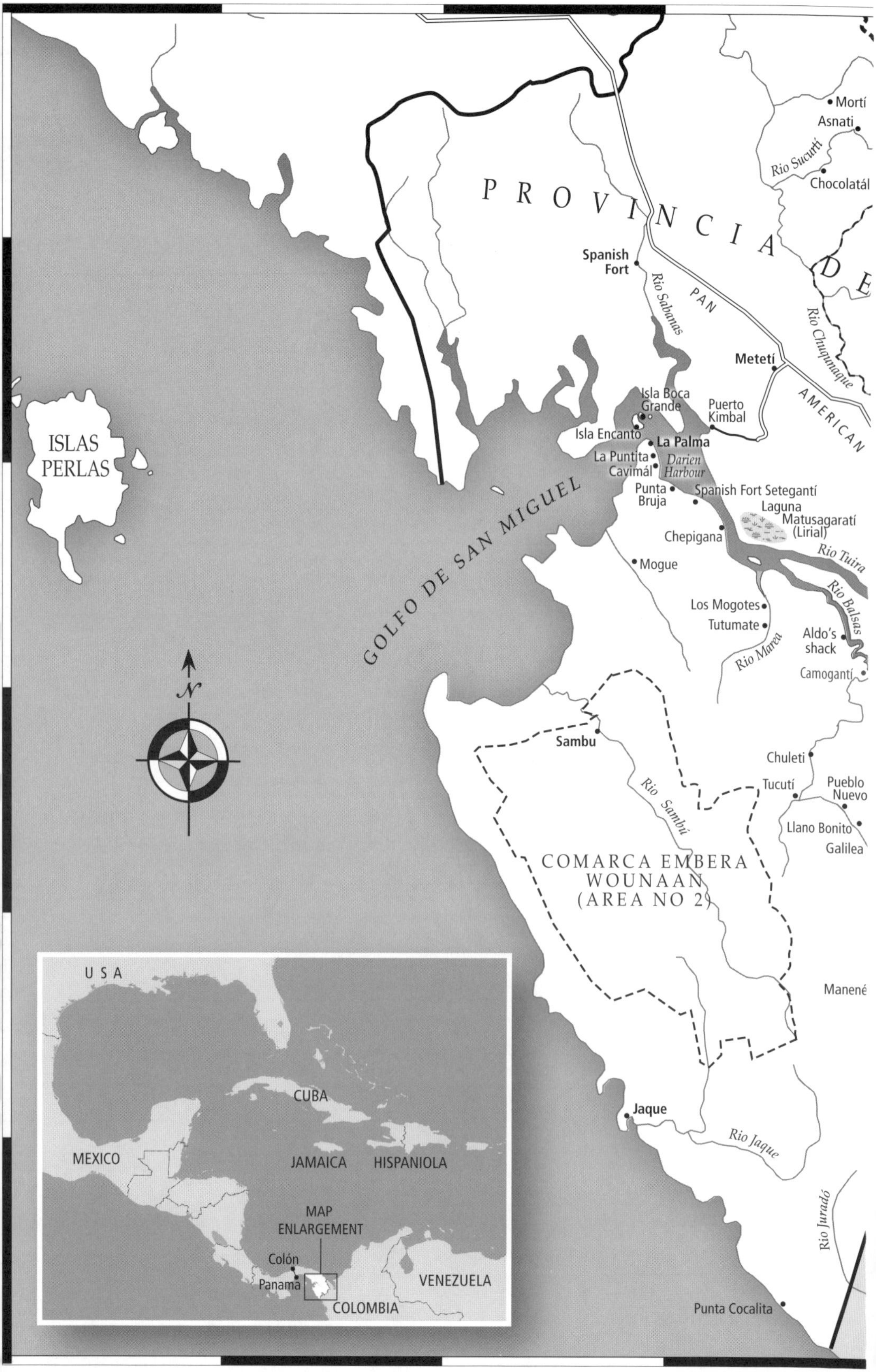

PROVINCIA DE
PAN AMERICAN
Mortí
Asnati
Rio Sucutí
Chocolatál
Spanish Fort
Rio Sabanas
Rio Chuqunaque
Metetí
Isla Boca Grande
Puerto Kimbal
Isla Encanto
La Palma
La Puntita
Cavimál
Darien Harbour
Punta Bruja
Spanish Fort Seteganti
Laguna Matusagaratí (Lirial)
Chepigana
Rio Tuira
Mogue
Rio Balsas
Los Mogotes
Tutumate
Aldo's shack
Rio Marea
Camoganti
ISLAS PERLAS
GOLFO DE SAN MIGUEL
N
Sambu
Rio Sambú
Chuleti
Tucutí
Pueblo Nuevo
Llano Bonito
Galilea
COMARCA EMBERA WOUNAAN (AREA NO 2)
Manené
Jaque
Rio Jaque
Rio Juradó
Punta Cocalita
USA
MEXICO
CUBA
JAMAICA
HISPANIOLA
MAP ENLARGEMENT
Colón
Panama
VENEZUELA
COLOMBIA

DARIEN PROVINCE
PANAMA

PREFACE

Gringo backpackers refer to the region as the Darien Gap. The forbidden link between Panama and Colombia. Panamanians simply call it *El Tapón*. The Plug.

If you want to drive from North America down to South America, you'll have a hard time when you reach Panama's Darien province. There's still no road pushed through between the continents and there's no way around. Darien's dense jungle spans the entire isthmus from the Caribbean to the Pacific where Central America's narrow wrist connects with Colombia. It's the only missing link in what would otherwise be sixteen thousand miles of uninterrupted highway from Alaska to Tierra del Fuego.

From Panama City, a daily Darien-bound bus rattles and pounds for six hours and a hundred miles of potholes to the frontier town of Metetí. From there the road deteriorates, and during the rainy season it becomes an empty ribbon of bottomless mud through forests and flooded fields. The largest three-axle-drive trucks bury themselves, and a driver is lucky if he can crawl away on his belly through the slop.

At the town of Yaviza, still sixty miles short of the Colombian border, the road disappears altogether. Two rutted tracks descend the west bank of the Chuqunaque River, but they don't start up again on the far side. A Chocó native unloads his cargo of plantains from a dugout canoe. A cable footbridge stretches across the river, and a rusty cargo boat leans helplessly against the dock at low tide. From here, standing tall and thick and tangled green beyond the village, the rainforest begins in earnest.

To fully experience Darien you'll have to paddle its rivers in a dugout canoe, or pull on a pair of rubber boots and push through the initial wall of dense undergrowth. Without a road your progress will slow dramatically, but for the first time on your journey you'll really taste and smell the jungle with its cycle of decay and new growth. You'll hear the shrill cicada and the croaking toucan. You'll smell the musk of a bristly peccary, and notice low clouds shrouding the mountain shoulders and snaking through the lowlands at the break of day. You'll stop looking through a windshield or scanning the blur of scenery as you speed by in a motorized boat. Travelling in this way, the world arrives at a walker's pace, at a paddler's slow rhythm. The next river becomes a land far away, or a setting for the creation story, the ruins of an ancient flood or the site of buried gold hidden from the Spaniards.

By foot and paddle, Darien becomes much larger than its size.

IN THE BEGINNING

1

Los Mogotes is a crumbling village in a mangrove swamp. The air is thick with the perfume of organic rot. Deep mud rolls on and on when the tide flows out.

2

Alejandro is in his sixties and has a mouth full of gold. Gold crowns and caps, and an inlaid star on his front tooth.

"I killed a jaguar with a stick," he tells me in the afternoon, describing his hike across the mountains from Colombia.

"I walked from Medellín to Juradó. From Juradó to La Chunga on the Rio Sambú. From Sambú across to Balsas River, then down the Balsas and over to Mogotes," he says. "Everything I've done for this," he tells me, pointing at his mouth.

He's small and wiry, and he has light skin, white hair and bare feet. He leans on a walking stick while he talks.

"For your teeth?" I ask.

"For the gold," he answers.

I might be able to trace his route with my finger on a topographic map, but I'd never survive the trip.

The locals on the porch are laughing at him. They're embarrassed

Near the Marea River is Los Mogotes, a village built in a mangrove swamp.

for me because I'm listening to his stories. Earlier in the afternoon they invited me to sit in the shade on their porch, but he has to stand outside with the sun beating down on his back.

A big black woman stamps her foot on the planks. Kids throw pebbles at his back before they turn and run away.

"Go away, Alejandro," Ovidio says. "Leave the stranger alone."

Ovidio gestures for me to look at him. He draws circles around his ear with his index finger while pointing at Alejandro with the other hand.

"*El es loco,*" he says.

I'm caught in the middle. Even a tiny village with only five houses chooses someone to ridicule. I don't know these people, and I like Alejandro. He just wants to talk with a stranger for a while.

"You people know nothing!" he shouts at them.

"But this man," he says, pointing at me. "He knows what I'm talking about."

And he's right. I do understand.

"He knows," Alejandro says. "He travels."

Alejandro saw my sailboat anchored on the Marea River. Now he wants to leave with me on *Ishmael*.

"People that travel, know," he says.

No one answers. The porch is quiet.

I think he realizes I can't take him with me. What does he imagine we would do together? Two misfits with a small boat on the ocean.

Alejandro whispers, "People that don't travel…"

He says this last part so that only I can hear. "These people … they'll never know."

3

I travel. But I've never killed a jaguar with a stick.

I want to ask Alejandro if he's afraid to be alone in the forest at night.

4

A rainforest without roads is the perfect place for someone who wants to disappear for a time. It's a good place to hide. When I push through the front wall of foliage and walk under the thick canopy, I'm swallowed whole. It feels like anything could happen here and no one outside this world would ever know.

Sweat trickles down my neck and back. I hear cicadas, and water flowing through mangrove roots.

Darien might be a good setting for a novel or an adventure movie, but it isn't really a great location for a writer. There's no dome of blue sky overhead, no open fields. There is seclusion, but not the liberating emptiness of deserts and prairies.

Saint Exupéry never came here. Neither did Rimbaud or Maupassant. Paul Gauguin stopped briefly in Panama, but the heat, humidity and mosquitoes drove him on to Martinique. For their pilgrimages, most expatriate artists prefer vast deserts or tropical islands with an endless ocean.

A rainforest closes in. Mangroves swallow you. Mud sucks the boots from your feet and everything thrives and grows.

Why does that frighten me?

I have to keep beating back the grass and hacking away at vines with my machete just to have a little room to breathe.

When a tree collapses in a rainforest, it crashes down to the floor and opens a small patch of ground to sunlight. If you sit down in that clearing and you're armed with intent and melancholia, and with a store of snacks and a cup to collect rainwater, then bole-climber vines will seek you out. They'll follow the shade lines from your body and twist over and between your legs. Grasses and bromeliads will push up from the ground beside you. Lianas and strangler vines will drop down from neighbouring trees and encase you. They'll draw the moisture from your body, winding around your torso, climbing onto your head and squeezing tight. Epiphytes will perch on your shoulders, and tiny lizards will take refuge under your knees and in your hair. An adaptive crab might even girdle the skin from your ankles.

In less than a year you will be lost to sight. I guarantee that.

5

Kathy and I sailed out of Panama City in the afternoon to time our arrival at the mouth of the Gulf of San Miguel for the day's first light. Our first glimpse of Darien was the Pacific coastal hills against the faintest bands of grey. We steered *Ishmael* between islands and shoals as the warm oranges began, followed by the greens of the forests and then the details of the shaded mangrove shorelines. We rode the currents and boils through a fast, narrow passage where Balboa explored and pirates once sailed, and we reached La Palma just before noon, dropping *Ishmael*'s sails and setting the anchor in front of La Puntita.

We'd sailed all night without sleep, and the tropical sun was beating down on our backs and shoulders. We didn't speak. We just sat for an hour or longer in the cockpit. Brown pelicans fished around us, dropping from the sky with their wings bent, awkward and lopsided.

"What are you thinking about?" Kathy asked me.

For twenty years I'd been trying to reach Darien. On earlier trips I left Canada and drove south with a collection of surfboards on the roof of my Volkswagen. For various reasons—car breakdowns, my wallet stolen, a side trip with a Honduran circus—I never reached Panama on those first attempts. I don't know what I would have done if I'd arrived by car. I don't think that I fully believed the guidebook's warning that the road stopped short of Colombia. *It must be a misprint*, I thought. *This is an old book, and the last few miles are probably built by now.* I'm sure that I would have insisted on dragging my Beetle to Yaviza before I was convinced.

Two decades had gone by since then, and arriving in Darien, I wasn't the same traveller as I was when I first set out. For a twenty-year-old with a backpack, the words "impassable," "roadless" and "dangerous" read like invitations. The need for adventure and physical challenge is important at that age. The desire to be the first, or the strongest, or to be the only foreigner to visit a remote community can be equally compelling when you're young. Maybe it always will be for some. But as Kathy and I sat in *Ishmael*'s cockpit at La Puntita, I realized that this early stage of life was coming to an end. Everything that had once seemed important, everything I'd done until then, the waves and mountains and the physical work on drilling rigs and construction sites that had defined me and had given me strength and pride—none of it felt fresh or vital anymore.

At Tutumate, near Los Mogotes, villagers have built a sidewalk from the mangrove channel to their village. "I'm swallowed whole. It feels like anything could happen here and no one outside this world will ever know."

Something had changed, and for the first time in my life it felt as though I had nothing in my hands, nothing to offer, and little to show for all those years.

On that first afternoon in Darien, even through my tangled thoughts, the sky was still a tropical blue, and the sun baked our skin brown while Kathy waited for an answer. I could see thatched-roof houses built above the water on posts. I could smell the mud and the forest. I heard two dolphins puff as they swam past *Ishmael*.

"I'm wondering how different it would have been twenty years ago when I first tried to come here," I answered after a long pause.

I can't remember her exact words. She said something about keeping my head in the present rather than wishing for the past.

Ishmael tugged on its anchor and faced the last of a flooding tide. I could hear a steady hum from the town's diesel generator. I heard children laughing onshore. They pushed a dugout into the water and paddled toward us.

6

There are three native tribes living in the Darien rainforest today. All of them are believed to have emigrated at different times from the area that is now called Colombia.

On the Caribbean coast and San Blas Islands, the Kuna people have secured an autonomous zone they call the Kuna Yala.

Their former archrivals and Colombian neighbours, the Emberá and Wounaan tribes—collectively known as the Chocó—moved into Darien more recently. When they arrived, they forced the Kuna from most of their interior locations and claimed the Darien lands south of the San Blas Mountains for their own.

7

The Emberá creation story:

Ankoré is the creator of the Emberá world. He's a con man and a bit of a fumbler. In Emberá stories he comes off to be an approachable sort of fellow. A hard-working guy you would like for a neighbour.

In the beginning of time, Ankoré made man out of sticks and branches until he cut himself with his carving knife. These first men were perfect. They would never die. They would go to the other world where the sun shines only at night. And they didn't have to eat. Their mouths were so small that they nourished themselves just by smelling plates of food.

After the carving accident, Ankoré shied away from using wood. He began shaping man out of clay and earth because it was an easier material to work.

Today's men are mortals. They grow old and die. Their bodies become dust and they return to the soil.

Emberá say that if we weren't made of clay we would live forever, shedding our skin like snakes and lobsters.

8

There is another story that goes like this…

Panama and, in particular, Darien are two of the world's most recent arrivals. They're late bloomers. Darien is the newest significant dry land on earth. When it moved into the American neighbourhood, it blocked the last passage between two great seas and it changed the planet forever.

On a timeline map of world history painted onto a canvas the size of a football field, Panama doesn't even appear until the final yard. Darien debuts just inches from the end zone. Of the earth's 4.6 billion years, they miss out completely on the first 4 billion 535 million of those.

The first hint of western Panama appeared sixty-five million years ago, far from its present location. According to the geological theory of mantle plumes, a series of eruptions occurred over the Galapagos hot spot in the Pacific Ocean and formed a chain of volcanic peaks.

At that same geological moment, an undefined, cataclysmic event—a severe climate change or a giant asteroid colliding with earth—wiped out the world's dinosaur population. However, moths and butterflies survived and flourished. Flowering plants appeared and began using insects for pollination. The new Galapagos volcanoes started their long journey riding on the back of a giant basalt slab as it crept over the ocean floor. They scraped east-northeast at the rate of four inches a year for fifty million years until the plate collided with the Bahamian platform. The basalt base became the Caribbean Sea floor, and the piggyback volcanoes sat as islands between the Americas.

At sixteen million years ago, Darien was still nowhere to be found. A series of islands stretched across parts of present-day Panama, but Darien's location was an ocean passage more than six thousand feet deep between Atlantic and Pacific.

Early horses, cattle and deer evolved. Ants and bees developed.

Starlings and penguins, camels, rabbits, bears and parrots. Chimpanzee-type apes appeared in Africa and crossed over to Asia and Europe.

Still no Darien.

Late in the Miocene period, only seven million years ago, the ocean plate under the Darien site buckled against pressure from South America's northwest drift. It began forcing up the ocean floor. The peaks of today's San Blas, Sapo, and Majé ranges surfaced in what was once open water. The Darien passage was now spotted with islands. Water channels were only five hundred feet deep and becoming shallower with sediment.

When the cold California Current temporarily moved south as far as Ecuador, world temperatures grew colder. The Antarctic ice cap spread, causing sea levels to drop, and the two oceans began to evolve separately in their distinct conditions.

By this time, both gorillas and chimpanzees had diverged from the evolutionary line leading to humans. Australopithecus ("southern ape") had evolved, with his slightly larger brain and his grinding teeth for eating plants and fruits.

During the final stretch of time before the passage closed, the Andes and surrounding mountains were forced higher still. Thousands of feet of sediment washed downriver into the inter-island basins. Up to thirty thousand feet accumulated in parts of the Chuqunaque and Atrato valleys. Water passages filled until the Tuira and Atrato rivers were the last connection between Caribbean and Pacific.

Darien was now in place. Mountains blocked the final water passage around three million years ago and formed a land bridge between the Americas.

Initially the terrain was open grassland. Grazing ungulates migrated from both continents. Horses, llamas and deer moved down from North America accompanied by jaguars and pumas.

From South America, large rhinoceros-like toxodons travelled north. Bear-sized and elephant-sized sloths made the journey. Tank-like armadillos with four-foot-diameter shells, giant carnivorous birds almost twelve feet tall with meat-cleaver beaks ... all of these moved north along with smaller species such as opossums, anteaters and guinea pigs.

When forests replaced the savannahs, a second migration took place. Animals from the Amazon Basin extended their range into the new tropical forests as far north as Veracruz in Mexico. Parrots arrived. Toucans, Morpho and Heliconius butterflies, tree sloths, monkeys and two types of rodents—agoutis and pacas—all made the journey.

Man had passed through the *Homo habilis* ("handyman") period and into *Homo erectus*. He was taller now: five feet six inches. His brain was much larger, and he spread from South Africa through Europe and into China.

In the Americas there was still no human population.

Then *Homo sapiens* appeared in Africa. Neanderthal humans were living in Europe seventy thousand years ago, and when modern men (*Homo sapiens sapiens*) evolved, they began travelling to all parts of the world. They arrived in Australia fifty thousand years ago but didn't begin crossing the Bering Strait from Siberia to Alaska until forty thousand years later.

Arrival of modern man in the Americas is so recent that it isn't visible on the great football-field canvas of history.

Groups descending from Alaska by sea or land ten thousand years ago populated the northern continent and passed through Mexico and Darien into South America. Based on discoveries at a few South American sites, archaeologists believe that another migration might have preceded the main flood flowing south from the Arctic. Some speculate that these were ocean travellers from Asia, while others point to possible contacts from South Pacific peoples.

The Darien forest provided game meat, fish in the rivers, land to plant, and materials for clothing, medicine, tools, shelter and canoes.

These early Darien residents were nomads. They didn't build pyramids. There weren't any massive irrigation projects or temples to study astronomy or mathematics. Their tools and shelter were from the forest. They took what they needed to live and then moved on to let the land recover. When a family changed location, insects and rot consumed the abandoned home and left next to nothing for an archaeologist to discover.

This is the story that we hear today. It's a patchwork history made from information scraps all sewn together with science and an academic's imagination.

Manuel Ortega, a Darien Emberá, has heard this version before.

"If we all came across at the same time and travelled all this way overland, then why do we look so different from other Indians? There would be Kunas and Emberá here and up in Alaska too," he says. "Why do we speak different languages?

"How do they know what happened a million years ago … or a billion years ago?" he asks.

Manuel isn't really looking for an answer. I start to tell him the little bit I know about geology, fossils, carbon and radioisotope dating, but he shakes his head and he laughs through his nose. It's more like a snort than a real laugh.

"Who was writing these things down a million years ago?" he asks. "Who was taking all the pictures?"

9

With such a rich history and prehistory, you would assume that Darien has been overrun with scientists, anthropologists and historians, but that isn't the case. The pre-Columbian part of Darien's story is based on clues from all regions except Darien. From digs in Alaska through North America and on down to Mexico and Central America, archaeologists have found evidence of a steady southward migration of people. They've unearthed identical-style spearheads dating back to 9500–8500 BC on both sides of Darien, but from the province itself there is very little. There hasn't been any significant archaeological work here for the last hundred years.

Largely it is Darien's notoriety as a haven for Colombian guerrillas, right-wing paramilitaries and narco-traffickers that has kept researchers out of Darien. Universities don't want to fund a project where their staff could be murdered or kidnapped.

One of the few projects completed in the region involved drilling into a Darien lake basin to extract sediment samples. The results suggest that there was continuous, but irregular, slash-and-burn agriculture in the area between 2000 BC until the arrival of the conquistadors.

The story only begins to take on detail with the first Spaniards reaching Darien around AD 1500.

10

Kathy and I aren't doing well together. Last month *Ishmael's* bowsprit broke in a storm while we were sailing to Panama from Costa Rica. In port we argued over every tiny detail, from epoxy bonding and groceries to commitment and responsibility. Now, in Darien, we're just trying to survive, choosing our words carefully, working on opposite ends of the boat and still feeling crowded.

It doesn't get any easier for us after reaching Darien. During our first week, we run *Ishmael* aground on a sandbar. In the mangroves, mosquitoes swarm over us at sunset. We sink in the mud and lose our boots. When we kayak back to the boat at night through a narrow channel, we have to hold the flashlights clenched between our teeth. Spiders drop down from overhead branches. Shrimp and small fish leap toward the light and land between our legs.

"Look at that neon frog on the left," I call back after taking the flashlight out of my mouth.

"Shut up and paddle," Kathy answers. Shrimp nip at our thighs, and our kayaks collide, the hollow thud echoing in the mangrove dark.

I can hear a native family laughing at the village landing somewhere behind us.

11

Darien is flooded with water. Pacific tides push inland until they are only thirty-seven miles from the Caribbean Sea. Navigable rivers spread out into every corner of the province. A boat is definitely the most efficient way to travel here.

However, for a couple of reasons, a cruising sailboat isn't the right choice. Our six-foot keel is always tripping over shallow logs or grounding on sandbars, and even though *Ishmael* is stained and ragged by yachting standards, it is the only sailboat in Darien. It stands out like a floating billboard invitation for thieves and kidnappers.

When we first arrived and I registered my paperwork at the La Palma police base, I asked the sergeant about problem areas that we should avoid.

"There are no problems in Darien," he answered. His black arms were crossed in front of his chest.

"I've just heard about some attacks and a kidnapping at…" I started to question him, but he interrupted.

"No problems," he said again, this time with more finality. There was nothing more to discuss. He stood at the gate with a rifle slung on one shoulder, his revolver on his hip, and biceps the size of my thighs.

No problem for you, I thought.

Whenever possible, we anchor far enough from shore that it would be a long swim for an intruder. We keep a flare gun and machete on deck, and I sleep very lightly. The turning tides wake me at night when the boat slowly swings around. A falling branch on shore wakes me. Strange bird calls or the shifting current changing the gurgle against the hull. I climb into the cockpit and scan the surrounding water before pissing over the side and falling back into a thin sleep.

We travel as far up the Rio Sabanas as *Ishmael's* keel allows and anchor in a narrow stretch with a light breeze at sunset. As daylight fades, a troop of howler monkeys begins to roar. They can be heard for miles. They shake the forest, sounding more like giant beasts than small primates. Nighthawks and bats dart in and out through the rigging chasing insects. We wrap warm rice in lettuce leaves and sauté the shrimp a native fisherman gave us in the afternoon as he paddled by.

After dusk, the ebb current races out of the basin and drops the river twenty-two feet in six hours. Inside the cabin we can hear the current rushing past the hull, and when I go out on the deck at midnight, *Ishmael's* keel is just touching the soft river bottom. Where earlier we were floating in deep water, the river is now only a narrow stream through a winding ribbon of mud. *Ishmael* is floating in a puddle the size of its hull, and gently sloped mudbanks roll upward all around us.

12

Vasco Núñez de Balboa sailed from Spain as a common seaman in 1500 with the expedition led by Rodrigo de Bastidas and Juan de la Cosa. After reaching the north coast of Panama, they began sailing eastward, exploring and trading in Darien's Gulf of Urabá and on to present-day Colombia and Venezuela. On their return voyage, Balboa disembarked at the Caribbean island of Hispaniola (formerly La Española). Over the next eight years he failed as a farmer, losing all of his earnings and amassing a large debt.

In 1509, the king of Spain granted two contracts for expeditions to return to Tierra Firme, the mainland earlier explored by Columbus and Bastidas. By this time, Balboa was thirty-five years old and his future looked dismal if he stayed on Hispaniola. He used all of his contacts, but even with his New World experience no ship captain was willing to hire him. By the laws of Spain, they would have been responsible for his debts if he died on the expedition or never returned.

In desperation, Balboa started the expedition as a stowaway aboard a supply ship. Depending on which of the colonial chroniclers

A sailboat with a fixed keel isn't the right boat for exploring Darien rivers, which rise and fall with the tides. On the Marea River, Ishmael *lies on its side in the muddy river bottom. Six hours later, the flooding tide floated us free again.*

you trust, he either hid in an empty barrel or in the folds of a sail. The ship followed the path of the first fleet, and when the expedition captain—the lawyer Enciso—discovered his extra passenger, he threatened to abandon Balboa on a deserted island.

Legally, Balboa's crime could have been punished by death, and Enciso didn't want to be held responsible for Balboa's debts. However after the crew protested, Enciso backed down on his threat. Months later he likely regretted not having followed through with his plan.

The lead group of men who had departed months before Enciso's ship were having a terrible time up to that point. Their ships had become separated from each other. They navigated poorly and missed their destinations. Natives attacked them with poisoned arrows and killed hundreds of expedition members, including the most experienced leader. Even more men died from starvation and disease.

Enciso's ship met up with them just as they were trying to sail back to Hispaniola. The survivors from the first group offered the

For sailors accustomed to saltwater baths, travelling farther up Darien's rivers offers certain luxuries. Kathy rinses off with fresh water at the end of a tropical day while we're anchored on the Sabanas River.

lawyer a bribe to let them leave, but Enciso, who had invested his own money in the trip, ordered them to follow him.

Balboa had sailed through these waters on an earlier expedition and now his experience became invaluable. He remembered a location on the Gulf of Urabá where the natives didn't use poison on their arrows. In this new location, the Spaniards' body armour, their mastiffs, crossbows and muskets gave the expedition enough advantage to take control of a land position where they built a settlement and a small chapel. They called the village Santa Maria la Antigua del Darien.

There isn't any clear description of Balboa left by the chroniclers. They wrote in minute detail about the plants, animals and indigenous people of the region, but the Balboa statues that are scattered around Panama City today are based mostly on an artist's imagination.

We do know that expedition members respected Balboa. He had Darien experience and he was a natural leader. Enciso had neither of these qualities and the men didn't trust his judgment. In an attempt to save the expedition, the men sent the king's representatives to sea on two worm-riddled ships and then elected Balboa and one other man as the new mayors for the community. The first ship was lost during the voyage. The second ship with the exiled Enciso wasn't much better, but eventually he reached Spain and went directly to the Court to place charges against Balboa.

Balboa's role in Enciso's expulsion verged on treason, and it isn't clear how he planned to deal with the political fallout. Maybe he thought the second ship would also sink, drowning the lawyer. Or perhaps Balboa was relying on the slow pace of shipping and communication in the 1500s, and hoping that he could collect enough gold that King Ferdinand would forgive the part he had played.

His only intention, he later wrote to the king in a letter, was to save the failed expedition and establish Spain's rule in the New World.

13

While listening one evening to my radio in Darien, I tune into a CBC shortwave broadcast of a Canadian First Nations comedian re-examining the "discovery" of America.

He says that it's as if you were sitting down for dinner in your family condo when a group of armed strangers barges in. They announce that they've just discovered your home. After discussing the situation amongst themselves, they raise a flag and declare that it now belongs to them.

However (and this is the sweetener), out of fairness and Christian charity—*and only if you first concede defeat*—the intruders offer to reserve a small space for you and your family.

In the back room. By the Kitty Litter box.

Books and articles describing Balboa usually use *discoverer* or *conqueror* in the title. One author, appearing late in the titling game and realizing that the two best descriptive nouns were already taken, settled on *Balboa: Finder of the Pacific*.

14

When Balboa set off from Santa Maria la Antigua in August of 1513, he took 190 volunteers. They travelled by boat up the coast and connected with their native allies at Carreto near what is now Caledonia Bay.

August in Darien is the start of the wet season. When it isn't raining, the air around you is dead calm. You can hear canopy trees swaying in an overhead breeze, but nothing reaches you on the ground. If you wipe the sweat from your eyes, it begins dripping again without a pause. On top of the heat, Balboa and his men were weighed down with swords, armour, shields, breastplates, muskets and crossbows. It made for the worst conditions for a crossing.

In the five-hundred-year history of foreign expeditions through

Darien, there is one common theme. Expeditions that ally with natives do well. American, British and French. Pirates, scientists, travellers and writers. In contrast, explorers who set out on their own and ignore native advice do very poorly indeed.

Balboa was shrewd enough to confront one clan at a time. First he threatened and intimidated. Then, if that didn't work, he unleashed his weapons, soldiers and mastiff dogs against them. Later, when he had taken control, he offered gifts and a type of earned friendship in exchange for thousands of natives for guides, porters and warriors.

His first confrontation was really none at all. The entire village population hid in the forest and couldn't be found.

The second confrontation was more of a capitulation, and Balboa showed mercy in exchange for gold and new recruits.

In the third battle at Quarecua, a ruler named Torecha and his men stood up against the Spaniards and their allies. Torecha's men attacked the invaders with arrows, spears and swords made of palm wood hardened in fire.

When Balboa responded with musket fire and set loose his dogs, the native courage turned to panic. They ran for the forest, but it was too late. The Spaniards killed Torecha and six hundred of his men. On top of that, Balboa's men gathered up the surviving tribal leaders. Judging them to be transvestites and homosexuals because of their ceremonial cotton dresses, Balboa threw them to his mastiffs to be torn to pieces.

From the present-day town of La Palma where *Ishmael* is anchored, I can see the hills where Balboa and sixty-seven of his men first caught sight of the South Sea on September 25, 1513. Until that moment, Spain couldn't fully discard Columbus's claim to have reached China and the east coast of the Malay Peninsula.

Balboa's men carved the king's name in tree trunks. They built a cairn and prayed to the Virgin Mary while the priest led them in chanting the *Te Deum*.

All of this ceremony must have puzzled their native guides. Did they understand that the Spaniards had just *discovered* the South Sea and claimed it for their own?

Balboa's men made one attempt to sail on the Pacific Ocean to the Perlas Islands, but after a near capsize they turned around to start a wide loop back to their allies on the Caribbean coast.

A four-month loop through Darien in the rainy season. Constant war. Mud, diseases and the natural dangers of a rainforest. Yet not one Spaniard died.

Even without battles and hostile natives, few expeditions during the next five centuries have had such success.

15

Today, a lot of travel dilemmas revolve around finding a balance between speed and depth. Do we spread ourselves far and wide, or slow our restless spirit to understand a particular moment and space? Do we make the journey focussed on conquest and our role in the expedition, or can it be more about the land and people that live there?

When travellers have a two-week vacation, they sometimes try to make up for the brevity by hitting a dozen highlights. I have a hard time doing that. If I meet a circus on a roadside, I want to paint my face and join them. If I talk with a Mayan family on a bus ride in Guatemala, my natural tendency is to pitch in and help them clear a field, haul firewood, and bathe with them in their communal sauna before I ride a truck out of the village. And even then it isn't enough.

Modern travel journals from Darien usually feature the extreme risks that the writer has to survive. A recent Darien adventurer wrote in *National Geographic Adventure* magazine that the region's reputation as a "no-go" zone rife with violence and danger attracted him. Before kidnapping by Colombian guerrillas became

Travelling in this way, the world arrives at a walker's pace, at a paddler's slow rhythm. The next river becomes a land far away, or a setting for the creation story, the ruins of an ancient flood or the site of buried gold hidden from the Spaniards. By foot and paddle, Darien becomes much larger than its size.

so prevalent, other adventurers created their own hardships by driving trucks across the roadless jungle. The sponsored vehicle expeditions have taken between three months and 741 days. All of them have hired large work-gangs of natives to machete a swath through the forest and help push and pry the trucks over Darien's mountains and float them on canoes across its rivers.

Many of these groups claim to be the first to have crossed the isthmus. Sometimes it's just wishful thinking, but usually you'll find a few lines of small print explaining how their journey differs from all those that have come before.

The common element in all of these claims is that they ignore the history of Darien natives who have been quietly walking and paddling back and forth across for generations.

16

Excerpt of a letter from Vasco Núñez de Balboa to the king of Spain:

> January 1513
>
> Most puissant Lord. I desire to ask a favour of your Highness, for I have done much in your service. It is that your Highness will command that no bachelor of laws nor of anything else, unless it be of medicine, shall come to this part of the Indies on pain of heavy punishment which your Highness shall order to be inflicted, for no bachelor has ever come here who is not a devil, and who does not lead the life of devils. And not only are they themselves evil, but they give rise to a thousand lawsuits and quarrels. This order would be greatly to the advantage of your Highness's service...

17

From the beginning of the colonial era, Spain couldn't control Darien. It's just too expensive to govern a jungle of semi-nomadic peoples. Colonial invaders would have to burn down the forests, kill all the wildlife and poison the waters to enforce their rule. And then, rule over whom? And over what?

The king's newly appointed governor Pedrarias Dávila arrived in Darien with 1,700 recruits shortly after Balboa's expedition. These new immigrants weren't farmers and workers. They didn't come to homestead or to plant corn and *yuca*. They had read reports that natives were harvesting gold nuggets by stretching nets across a flowing stream. They wanted to fill their pockets and sail back to Spain.

Unfortunately, no one was fishing gold out of the river with nets. Even worse, the village at Santa Maria la Antigua didn't have enough shelter for the population explosion. There wasn't even a proper supply of food. After four months, half of the recruits were dead from hunger and *modorra*—a type of sleeping sickness that attacked new arrivals but didn't touch Balboa's acclimatized group of men.

The governor had planned to put Balboa in irons and ship him back to Spain for his role in Enciso's expulsion, but Balboa's popularity intimidated Pedrarias. The success of the South Sea expedition only complicated matters. After the governor absorbed what information he could from Balboa, he placed his rival under house arrest for more than a year.

The cross-isthmus expedition was supposed to be Pedrarias's prize. Balboa had stolen it. Frustrated, the governor sent out his own men to plunder whatever they could in all corners of Darien.

Historians describe Balboa as a kinder, gentler conquistador. While mastiff dogs and murder for gold are hardly a gentle touch, the men that followed in his wake for the next decade made Balboa look like a Boy Scout.

18

In 1514 when Pedrarias arrived at Santa Maria la Antigua, he brought with him a new Royal Order that required all Spanish conquistadors to offer one opportunity for redemption to the natives before coming down and crushing them with all the force and fury of the Lord. However the Order, *El Requerimiento*, was less concerned with delivering salvation for Darien natives than it was with justifying every manner of violence against them.

To fulfill their obligation, a group of Spaniards would assemble on a hillside with their weapons in hand. Usually they would demand gold—often more gold than the natives could possibly produce. One member would read aloud the document in Spanish to the natives who were hiding somewhere in the distant forest while a scribe watched over to certify that the duty was performed.

If, on a rare occasion, the *Requerimiento* was read in a language the natives could understand, the text informed them that the Pope—St. Peter's successor—had donated all the islands and Tierra Firme to the king and queen of Spain, as written in documents that they could see if they desired. The Order required the natives to accept Christianity and acknowledge the king and queen of Spain as their supreme overlords. If they agreed to this they would do well, and would be received in love and charity. However,

> If you don't, and if you maliciously delay following these orders, I certify that with the help of God I will come down mightily against you, and I'll make war in all parts and manners that I can, and subject you to the yoke and obedience of the Church and her high representatives, and I will take you and your women and children, and I'll make them slaves, and as such I will sell them and dispose of them as the Representatives order. And I'll take all of your possessions, and I will do every evil and injury possible to you, as we do to all slaves that resist and disobey their master.

19

An Emberá account, as recorded by anthropologist Stephanie Kane in *The Phantom Gringo Boat*:

> The Spanish came and captured many men, women, and children. They kept them in a round house closed in by high walls to await slaughter. The people inside wondered if they might escape out of a small opening at the top. They thought of using the wrapped bark of women's skirts. These were tied together for a rope, leaving the women nude. They began climbing out one by one. Amongst those inside was a shaman, a *haimbaná*. Furious with the Spaniards, he caused a great storm to come. Heavy rains, thunder and lightning filled the night. But when about half the people had climbed out, a tremendous bolt of lightning lit the sky, revealing the escape to the guards. The natives still inside were killed, including the *haimbaná*.
>
> Those who got free went far upriver and became *cimarrónes* with long hair down to their calves and white skin. For fear, the *cimarrónes* never came downriver again, not even for salt.

20

Cimarrón: (si-ma-rrón) adj., *Amer.* wild; untamed.

In Panama, *cimarrón* can historically refer to either an escaped black slave who has fled from his Spanish overlord and hides in the mountains to live with others of his group, or a Chocó native who turns his back on everything civilized. In the latter case, the native abandons even his tribal people downriver. He moves into the darkest forests, the most isolated regions, and he never returns again. He lives by his wits and his knowledge of forests and the natural world.

26 | THE DARIEN GAP

Over generations his family becomes a blend of man and animal.

Geronimo is an Emberá elder living on the Balsas River. He wears a red *guayuco*—a loincloth draping down from a waist cord. When he was a boy, he lost his right hand and part of his arm from a dynamite explosion while he was fishing.

Geronimo used to see the footprints of *cimarrónes* in the upriver forests, but he says that they've now gone into Colombia, into the densest forests around Rio Sucio.

Geronimo and his wife Ester in Manené tell me stories about cimarrónes—*natives who lived in the most isolated regions of the forest—and about General Torrijos when he visited Darien by helicopter.*

His wife Ester tells me this story:

She says, "When I was a young girl our family went to the *cabecera*, to the headwaters, to hunt. I travelled upriver and stayed overnight with my father while the others waited at the base camp. When we returned to the boat in the morning, the machetes and bags were gone.

"Two strange men had arrived at the lower camp on that same night," Ester tells me. "They wanted to sleep with the women because they knew the men were gone. These were *cimarrónes*," she says.

21

Balboa's final days in Darien were a sad finale for a powerful man.

Near the end of 1516, Pedrarias allowed Balboa eighteen months to build three ships and explore the South Sea. Balboa's men cut all of the timbers on the Caribbean side and hauled them over the mountains into Darien. They built two ships at the river headwaters and floated them down to the Gulf of San Miguel. However, the wood they'd used was full of worms and began to rot. Without pausing for a rest, the carpenters cut new wood on the gulf, but a high tide surprised them, burying some of the timbers in mud and sweeping the rest away. After they managed to float two ships, they sailed to the Perlas Islands where the boats fell apart completely.

Once again they cut timbers and built three new ships. They had just transferred their camp to the Tortugas Islands and were finishing the final preparations when a message came from the governor ordering Balboa to travel back to Acla.

He set off unsuspecting. Since Balboa had agreed to marry Pedrarias's oldest daughter who was arriving from Spain, there was a fragile peace between the two rival leaders. It wasn't until Balboa's former companion Francisco Pizarro arrested him along the trail that Balboa saw the ambush closing in.

Pedrarias's charge of treason against Balboa was a flimsy case based mostly on a single, overheard, incomplete conversation that took place while a rainstorm was drumming down.

The judge recommended leniency or mercy, but Pedrarias overruled. "Those who sin must die for it," he told his appointed judge.

Balboa asked for a chance to appeal, arguing that with his title as governor of the South Sea and the provinces of Panama and Coiba he was entitled to present his case to the Royal Council of the Indies in Spain.

Pedrarias denied that request as well.

Balboa sat in shackles. In eight years he had evolved from a debt-burdened farmer, to a stowaway, to an explorer and charismatic leader in Spain's conquest of the New World. He had avoided death in battle only to be sucked into a political free fall. There was nothing he could do to save himself.

The court found him guilty without opportunity for appeal. Judge Espinosa, pressured by Governor Pedrarias, condemned Balboa to die and the executioner completed the sentence without delay.

There are many versions of that final moment, and the writers doubtless used a number of source texts. In one account, Balboa was strangled by the executioner. Many others say he was hanged. One book states that they left Balboa's body dangling for almost a week to satisfy the governor's thirst for vengeance. But I think that I would trust Pascual de Andagoya, who was an officer with Pedrarias and also a member of Balboa's final expedition.

Andagoya writes that, like many other enemies of the Crown, Balboa was beheaded.

And perhaps the chronicler Fernández de Oviedo is also accurate (although he was in Spain at the time) when he insists that Pedrarias watched the execution from between the reeds of a wall near the platform.

After the execution, Pedrarias marched across the isthmus with all the troops available from Acla. He stepped into Balboa's empty boots, taking charge of the men and ships waiting at Isla Tortuga, and he founded the city of Panama as his new seat of government.

Nothing of the first wave from Europe was left in Darien. By 1519, only five years after the governor's arrival, Darien's native population was dead or had disappeared. All of the easy gold had been collected, and now the Spaniards heard a rumour of even greater treasures in the Inca world of Peru.

Save for the call of songbirds and the crash from rotting trees collapsing in the forest, when the conquistadors left, a sad silence was all that lingered in Darien.

22

My boat is falling apart. I can't keep up with the maintenance. I don't have the money, or time, or strength or desire.

It's such a relief when an American in Panama City offers to buy *Ishmael*. I've lived on my boat for seven years, but in some ways a boat separates a sailor from the rest of the world. When you're tied to your boat, you can't smell and taste the village at night. You miss out on the land experience. The textures. Good and bad. Bugs and snakes and such. You miss the whispers as the cooking fire dies. You don't hear the clatter of pots and pans, a baby crying, someone splitting wood, someone telling stories.

Sailors tend to remember a port by its welding shops and hardware stores, and they spend much of their life rebuilding pumps and valves and rigging. You have to really want to be a sailor. It can't be just about travelling.

Kathy cries when the deal to sell *Ishmael* closes. She still wants to sail but I know I can't go any farther. We haven't been happy together for a while. I think that both of us suspect that our relationship is over, but neither of us has the courage to speak.

We pack our clothes and tools into duffel bags and return to Darien on a cargo boat. We move in with a Wounaan family and slash a clearing in the forest to plant rice. We use our tools to finish a dugout canoe. We plant vegetables, sew a fishnet, and we stop sleeping together.

"Why are we doing this?" she asks one night, tears streaming down her cheeks.

I can't answer. I don't have an answer. I want to explain everything but I know that I'll never get it right.

I need to just stop for a while. It feels as though I'm stuck between a past life that has lost its meaning and the emptiness of the unknown ahead. I want to hide in the rainforest and sort through the confusion. I want to lose myself in a world of strangers and live with no one who needs me, or cares for me, or counts on me for love.

There is a candle burning on the porch. I stand with my arms hanging by my sides, and my hands empty.

Leafcutter ants strip the beautiful tomato plants we started. Chickens get into our cucumber patch. They tear out the roots and burrow hollow beds in the soil. By the time we hear their happy clucking, it's already too late. The destruction sickens me. It devastates Kathy. I hold her in my arms and rock her gently.

She cries, but she also laughs. I think she's the strongest woman I know.

Once we finally begin to talk, our days are better. We finish the dugout and begin fishing with the family. We work together in the garden and we repair the roof and floor of our hut. I tell Kathy that I'm going to stay here for a while. For a long while. I think that slowing down and learning to understand and tell Darien's long story well is a part of what I need to do.

Kathy is physically capable of hiking or paddling anywhere I want to go, but she doesn't want to be here. This isn't *her* dream. I'm not sure if I would have reached Darien without her help, but if I'm going to risk paddling further upriver and hiking through the mountains to gather Darien's histories and stories, then I'm going to do it on my own.

After two months, Kathy leaves me and flies north. My sailboat is gone so I can't sail back to the ocean. In some ways, I'm alone. I have no history and no companion, and no one is waiting for me at home.

23

When telling stories, Emberá elders sometimes say, "But that was at a time when animals were people too."

I like that idea. The fuzzy line between man and animal.

Caragabí, son of Tatzitzetze, overpowers his father and becomes master and supreme god of the Emberá world. He does the best he can for his people. Often he stays in the periphery, stepping in to lend a hand only when he sees a problem.

In the beginning of time, Caragabí notices that man has no water to bathe in or to drink. After he sends out scouts to look for a source, one messenger returns and reports an indigenous woman, Gentserá, still wet from bathing, cleaning a basket of river fish in front of the giant *jenjené* tree where she lives.

For almost a year Caragabí's group of workers chop and chop with a stone axe at the *jenjené* tree. Each day they cut almost completely through, but when they return in the morning, the tree is healed.

In one version it is the frog—still a man at that time—who has been repairing the wood with the touch of his hand. When Caragabí discovers the culprit, he tramples on the frog/man and changes him into an animal.

In another version, Caragabí knocks three times on Gentserá's door. At first she refuses to answer. On the fourth knock she calls out from inside.

"Who is it?" she says.

But of course she already knows.

When he demands that she open the door and share her water, she refuses and tells him to go away. In a rage—and he loses his temper on many occasions—Caragabí breaks down her door. He grabs her tight by the belt. He squeezes until it cuts her in two and turns her into a large black ant that the Chocó today call the *gentserá*.

After that they are able to fell the tree.

When it crashes down, the trunk becomes the open sea. The branches are now rivers and streams. The leaves turn to fish, and all the loose cuttings become caimans, iguanas, turtles and lizards.

A NEW YEAR

24

If we listen to our friends and advisers, we'll never get out the door. We won't hitchhike, or travel alone or sail single-handed. We'll start a family of our own and shoulder an enormous debt to buy a house. It will be obvious how ridiculous it is to paddle upriver in a dugout canoe with only a basket of food, a machete and a mosquito net for sleeping.

My father is taking an interest in my trip this year. He used to ignore them. When I was working on a story in El Salvador, he would ask how things were in Costa Rica. When I was in Costa Rica, he would think Guatemala. Now, for some reason, he's following my Darien trip. It feels as though, late in life, we are closer than we have ever been. On the phone he tells me that he bought a good map of Panama and he went to the library to read about Darien.

When I talk to him later, he says that ignorance was bliss.

Central American guidebooks warn travellers against going to Darien. US and Canadian embassies tell their nationals to stay out of the area east of Yaviza, saying that Colombian terrorist groups and drug traffickers frequent the region and that foreign nationals have been victims of violent crime, kidnapping and murder.

On top of that, other websites list the risk of chloroquine-resistant malaria, yellow fever, dengue fever and tropical parasites. There are still cases of tuberculosis in outlying villages. At one time there was leprosy. Once you start looking there is no end to the warnings.

But that's the funny thing about a danger line. Once you actually start on your way, the frontier keeps moving on just slightly ahead of you.

"It's safe here," a Chocó Indian at Puerto Indio tells me when the cargo boat anchors on the Rio Sambú during my first trip to Darien. "But where you're going ... to Yaviza and the Rio Tuira ... they'll kill you up there," he says, drawing his finger across his neck. "They'll cut your throat," he says in case I missed the point.

It goes that way for much of the trip. I'm safe where I am, but just over the hill or around the next river bend is certain death—especially for a gringo. It makes no sense to them. I'm a fool to continue.

25

I'm tempted to call La Palma the provincial armpit, but maybe I just don't understand it. It looked inviting months ago when I first approached by sail. Up close it has lost some of its charm.

Pastel houses cling to the hillside, porches sagging and laundry dripping from the railings. On the main street there is a bakery, nine cantinas, four hotels, two cockfighting rings and as many churches perched on concrete pilings and wood posts over the Gulf of San Miguel.

Even though it's the provincial capital, there's still no road to La Palma. To make the trip from Panama City a traveller has to ride the bus six hours to Metetí, transfer to a pickup truck for a short ride to Puerto Kimbal, and then it's still another half-hour in an open boat with a 75-horsepower outboard pounding against the wind and chop across the gulf. A faster route is to buy a seat on the commercial flight from the capital's municipal airport. Alternatively, the cheapest method is a cargo boat from Panama City, although that could take three days, or a week or even longer with all the groundings, mechanical breakdowns and stops along the way.

In La Palma, there is only one paved road. It is a noisy road, three blocks long with narrow sidewalks branching off between the buildings. In the daytime, food stalls crowd the street. Pedestrians weave and squeeze past each other, and the music from stereo speakers echoes from one end to the other, cantina jukeboxes competing with the evangelical church.

When I think of that street, I see a tall black woman selling chicken feet from a ten-gallon tub in the sun. I see children in school uniforms, a drunken Asian man living in a cardboard box on the dock and huge-assed women wearing stretch pants and tank tops, pink curlers in their hair. I think of the boat ramp where Emberá and Wounaan Indians pull their dugout canoes to the tide line and park for days until they've sold all five thousand plantains at a nickel apiece. I see garbage floating on the tide, the muddy current dragging back and forth with plastic bags and bleach bottles.

26

Walking east along the shore from La Palma, I follow a footpath and climb the steps carved into a clay embankment. Crossing over the hill, the track drops down to La Puntita on the other side.

The first house on the left is white with green shutters, and it belongs to the carpenter Rufino Gomez and his wife Poncha.

"Be careful who you trust here," Rufino warns me.

Rufino is a craftsman who can carve complex curving blocks for boat repairs using only his handsaw and a razor-sharp axe. He has slender, strong hands but a soft handshake. It's the opposite of our North American powergrip, look'em-in-the-eye tradition. Rufino's light touch says, *You are welcome here. You are with a friend. All is safe in my home and shop.*

"Don't ever lend anyone money in Darien," he warns me. "You'll never get it back. And if you sell your outboard motor, make sure you have every last penny before you hand it over."

It's good advice, but I don't follow it as well as I should.

"I've always wondered…" Rufino says to me later in the afternoon, "When I'm working on *guayacan* (ironwood), I have to keep sharpening my chisels to finish the job. But I've watched a woodpecker go on for hours and hours, pecking into the same type of tree, deeper and deeper. And so I wonder how he keeps his beak so sharp."

Rufino also tells me that if you capture a small monkey and put it under a washtub with a heavy rock on top, the monkey will be gone when you come back. The pail will still be in place and the rock on top, but the monkey has escaped. This has happened to him a number of times. Rufino would like to know how they do it.

He asks a couple more questions, but I don't have any answers.

In Darien, when a foreigner arrives, people take the time to ask a lot of questions in case he happens to know about these things.

27

My new home with Otilio Tovar's family in Cavimál is a twenty-minute paddle from La Puntita.

The *bohio*, the tiny shack, is built on a hillside so that while the front porch is six feet above ground, the back is only a foot above. Including an L-shaped porch that runs four feet wide on two sides, the floor is twelve feet square. It was built for shorter people, so I bump my head on the crossbeams until I learn to walk doubled-over while at home.

On my first day at Cavimál, I sweep out the largest spiders and the mounds of termite dust. Autemio Tovar tells me that a boa uses the house when it's empty. At night, geckos flit in and out of the thatched roof. They drop onto the wall and fight amongst themselves like prehistoric dinosaurs while they wait for insects to land in the glow of the kerosene lantern.

In my new home, when I'm standing to cook, my ear is level with a four-inch cross pole. I can hear termites moving inside, gnawing and marching. That's how I imagine it. They're eating away the house from under me.

I sleep outside on the porch on planks I bought to replace the damaged ones. With my head down at the end of the day, I can hear insects inside these boards as well.

They're the music that lulls me to sleep at night.

28

Otilio Tovar and his grown sons and daughter are Wounaan Indians. They trace their lineage from a tribe that until recent times hunted and fought with blowguns and poison-tipped darts.

I can tell you that the face of a Wounaan is more severe and angular than that of an Emberá. Wounaan men are more serious and the women's faces don't have the happy roundness of an Emberá face. If I was going to risk a generalization, that's what I would say.

On New Year's Eve, ten days after moving to Cavimál, I paddle back to La Puntita to the fuel dock and house owned by Otilio's eldest son, the one they call Tovar.

Everyone is missing teeth in Tovar's family. His older sister Ester has the fewest teeth of all. Ester's husband, Hualajo, hasn't fared much better. Even Tovar's thirteen-year-old daughter has a gap where her upper front four teeth should be. It might be a gum disease. Maybe too much sugar. When they have money, Chocó natives like to buy a soda or bags of sweet frozen juice to suck on. They also put a lot of sugar in their coffee and lemonade. That might be part of the problem.

At Tovar's home, with a half-hour left before midnight and empty bottles scattered on the floor, Hualajo corners me at the party. He looks more *cimarrón* than the others. He has an injured eye, always bloodshot and wandering, and his splayed feet are thick pads of leather with calluses wrapping around the sides.

Hualajo grabs my arm and leans in close to my face. He keeps his one good eye on me and he starts to sing in a high, falsetto voice.

From my home at Cavimál I can see the hills where Balboa first glimpsed the South Sea. I sleep on the floor at night, listening to termites as they chew through the wood planks and to the soft thud of ripe mangoes dropping to the ground beneath the surrounding trees.

"This next one is about my village in Colombia," he says, and he sings again.

"This one is about my fifth son…" And another: "This is how I used to travel with my father," he tells me, tugging at my arm when he wants me to concentrate and understand. But the songs are all in Wounaan dialect, and I can hear only the music.

When he comes to the end of a stanza he pauses, and if I smile and nod he seems pleased. He believes that by sheer intent he's made me understand.

His mouth shapes Wounaan sounds. His lips and his smoky cheeks form a hollow O with no complete teeth visible.

He is a beautiful man with a loving face.

In Darien I learn something unexpected about appearance and perception … that men and women, even young boys and girls, might have no teeth at all or only a row of rotting stumps, and yet they can still be beautiful. Even their smiles. Especially their smiles.

29

At midnight, Hualajo dances in Tovar's fuel shed where a portable cassette stereo plays Colombian music through tinny speakers.

"*Mi patria*," he cries out, half-mad on alcohol. His head rolls back. He closes his eyes and throws his arms wide open until his legs give out and he crashes down and cuts his head on a fuel drum.

"*Tengo fuego, mujer!*" he yells at Ester when she calls for him to sit by her.

I'm on fire, woman! I can't stop!

30

I can tell by the way Tovar runs the outboard and dugout up onto the mud flats the next morning that he is still drunk from his New Year's party.

40 | THE DARIEN GAP

Hualajo and his family live more simply than most Chocó families near La Palma. He speaks almost no Spanish. Whenever he catches a few large fish, he takes them in his boat to La Palma. There, he stands patiently at the edge of the main street with his cooler of fish until he sells the day's fresh catch.

I don't get along very well with him. He's drunk and aggressive most of the time.

At the party, when he wasn't pushing the bottle into my hand, he told me stories about "good" gringos. *Gringos buenos.* Extraordinary characters who have passed through his life. People who have "helped" him in the past. And he, in turn, has been good and honest to them.

When I go down to the beach, he's struggling out of the boat. He sees me and he collapses against the dugout, luckily landing with his seat on the gunwale.

"Autemio?" he asks.

Tovar's lips are sloppy. His shirt is torn from a fight last night with Hualajo. He moves his right hand forward and rotates it outward so that the palm faces upward with the fingers loosely spread. In Darien, the gesture signifies a question mark.

"He went to your sister's house … to Hualajo's," I tell him.

Tovar decides to make the best of our privacy. He returns to his story from last night, about a wealthy gringo who arrived in La Palma and entrusted Tovar to guard five thousand dollars (earlier it was three thousand) while the gringo travelled through Darien.

In the story, when the foreigner returned after months of travelling, Tovar handed him the bundle of money. The stranger counted it and found everything in order.

"Tovar," the stranger said. "You are an honest man."

And with that verified, the gringo gave the five thousand dollars (last night it was one thousand of the three thousand) to Tovar in appreciation.

"Tovar," I say, "You're not only honest, but you're also a lucky man. I'd like to earn five thousand dollars without doing any work."

He thinks I'm thick-headed. I just don't get it.

During my trip, other Chocó Indians tell me variations of this same story.

There must have been a lot of gringos wandering around Darien with duffel bags of cash during the last dozen years. They invariably arrive in need of a safe place to store their money. Then, when they are ready to leave, they are so overwhelmed with the native's integrity that they just give it all away.

I assume that this is a storyteller's attempt to influence me by example. Maybe an episode of generosity did happen at some point in history, somewhere in Darien, for some quantity of money. And now people reflect on it.

What if a gringo arrived with his bag full of money?

It must be similar to our lottery fantasies. *What would I do with a million dollars?*

"Martin, I need a lot of help," Tovar says finally. "Things are bad."

I tell him that if the fishing goes well for Autemio and me, maybe we'll be able to do something for him.

"Not like that!" he says, spitting on the ground. He's disgusted with my stinginess. He's sure I have millions.

"I need a *lot* of help. Now. I have *serious* problems," he says. "I'm going to lose the fuel-dock business."

I tell him that we'll do what we can.

He turns away and stumbles down the beach to look for Autemio.

I worry that Tovar will try to stir up trouble for me with the rest of the family.

At the start of this trip when Kathy was here, she said she thought we should leave.

"Do you wonder if you do more harm than good by being here?" she asked.

31

While Cavimál looks like mainland, it's actually an island. The Gulf of San Miguel borders the front, and the other sides are flooded by mangrove channels that fill and empty with Pacific tides. Yet somehow leafcutter ants have managed the crossing and have multiplied. I love watching them but I wish they weren't here. They attack fruit trees and vegetables and leave nothing behind. I go to bed with bushy, healthy, four-foot tomato plants. When I wake the next morning there are only bare sticks.

Now the ants are in the mango trees on the front slope. They devastate two orange trees I brought from a nursery but they leave the lime trees alone. A week later they return for another attack on my cucumbers, and they eat most of the early corn I planted around the house.

I'm becoming desperate. I'm getting nothing from my garden and I'm even losing sleep. In the middle of the night I sometimes walk out in the moonlight to check on the plants. But Otilio, the Tovar patriarch, tells me that *la arriera* is mostly unstoppable. He tells me to buy Baygon or any of the chemical pesticides.

"And get a gallon of gasoline," he says.

He wants to kill them. He says we should spread the chemical poison along their pathways, then blow the nest to the sky with a fuel bomb.

When I asked him for advice, I was hoping for some ancient wisdom. An Indian solution, a special plant that drops a bitter residue that the ants can't tolerate. Maybe even a story about Caragabí. Something like that.

Leafcutters never play. They serve the colony in whatever way their queen commands, including licking her and grooming her. She produces a new egg every two minutes, and workers carry the eggs out to various chambers where they manipulate the incubation temperatures to propagate seven castes of ants, each with its own size and responsibilities. Garden workers might be as small as a sixteenth of an inch while the largest soldier can be almost thirty times that size.

All day long female worker ants march back and forth in front of my porch, following a path to a plant selected and tested earlier by scouts. A worker uses her serrated mandibles to cut out a leaf section that might weigh as much as six times her body weight. Normally she grips the load with her clenched teeth and carries it on her back, but at times they also use a leg to steady an unusually large load even though it forces them to limp and hobble on the return trip.

In the nest, leafcutters chew the plants into a soft pulp before using the material to cultivate a fungus garden. The worker defecates on the new plant medium to initiate the chemical balance before she places it on the garden. Other gardening ants might add more fecal droplets while still others work in the garden weeding growth from other unwanted fungal species. It's a delicate recipe of foliage interacting with feces and saliva, and it's their sole food. If they decide to move the colony, the final ceremony involves transferring the solitary queen with a morsel of existing fungus stored in her mouth to establish a new garden.

When I interrupt their pathway by flooding a section with a bucket of water, or pissing on the trail, or squirting out a line of liquid soap, there's an immediate uproar amongst the ants. An emergency response goes into action.

After the initial panic a heated discussion ensues. A few of the alpha-type ants (my term) start directing the others. They charge at different groups and gesture this way and that. They just want to get back to work. Even during a long delay, the workers rarely set their cuttings down to rest.

A few scouts hike off in either direction to find alternative routes while one or two of the young reckless ones try to rush the line and push through. However, because they don't want to contaminate the fungus garden in their nest, they usually retreat when they feel soap under their feet.

Otilio loves the liquid soap method. He takes my bottle and puts a ring around the base of each orange tree and all of the mango trees where the ants are already working. Then he walks from one location to another, nodding his head and talking to himself while he monitors the barricades for the rest of the afternoon.

Wounaan dialect often sounds like the speaker's voice is breaking. If you listen to just the music of his words, you'd think he was heartbroken and that he was scolding the ants.

"I warned you, but you wouldn't listen. Now you'll have to pay the price."

32

After the Emberá god Caragabí squeezed Gentserá in two and turned her into an ant, he ordered his workers to cut down the tree of life and give water to everyone. To ensure that the tree wouldn't take root and recover, Caragabí commanded that monkeys, ants and sparrow hawks be responsible for eating any new buds, shoots and saplings.

I've watched monkeys sit in fruit trees, taking a single bite from each mango before throwing the fruit to the ground. And sparrow hawks swoop down in the afternoons to steal the tiny chicks that Autemio and his wife Diana have just bought for twenty-five cents each.

But the ants—these leafcutters in particular—have taken Caragabí's command to heart. They work night and day, and my soap barrier will last only until the next rain washes it away or a fallen leaf creates a bridge. They'll be back. They'll wait for my tomatoes to recover and the next corn to be planted. They don't care about my plans and prayers. They'll devour it all over again.

33

This morning I used a three-corner file to put a fine edge on my machete before I paddled with Diana and Autemio to the mangroves. We spread out under the canopy to look for building materials for their new home, rafters, large corner posts and floor beams. We walked from one aerial root to the next over the mud and standing pools of water. I was working barefoot in a tree when I slipped and fell to the ground. I didn't actually see my foot hit the machete blade. It might have happened while I was falling through the air or at the moment I landed on my back. But now, as I lie on the ground, I can feel the sting from mud entering the wound.

I always cut my feet.

"*Cuidado!*" Autemio calls out.

I've never understood why people tell you to be careful *after* you fall, and I wonder if Wounaan natives learned this annoying habit from the Europeans or if it naturally occurs in all cultures independently.

I wrap a T-shirt around my foot and paddle to Cavimál, then to La Palma, and then I walk over two hills to the clinic for stitches and a shot of antibiotics.

34

During Balboa's crossing of the isthmus, a man named Nuflo de Olano marched with the expedition. He was one of the volunteers on the hilltop when Balboa claimed the Pacific coast of Darien and all of the South Sea for the king of Spain.

Nuflo was a black man in the new American world. However, he wasn't the first black man to arrive on Tierra Firme.

Alonso Prieto sailed along the coast almost twenty years earlier. Prieto worked as the pilot aboard the *Niña* on Columbus's second voyage in 1493. He might have been the first, but there are rumours of even earlier arrivals.

During Balboa's crossing, the Spanish defeated a tribe at Quarecua that used black slaves captured from another Darien tribe two days' march away.

In the following year, natives from the Gulf of San Miguel gave the conquistador Francisco Becerra still another report: "… how canoes came by sea, manned by black men, large of stature and great bellies, with long beards and curly or frizzy hair, who were held in great fear because they killed and ate the natives, and they fought with lances and clubs…"

Were these warriors part of that earlier pre-Bering Strait migration of people? Ocean travellers from Melanesia or other parts of the South Pacific?

35

Who owns the land in Darien? Who has the right to claim it for their own? These are good questions to raise in Panama today if you want an argument.

There has been a cycling pattern of people through Darien during the last five hundred years or longer. Each rotation begins with one group immigrating to an empty patch of forest. They clear land, plant crops and raise a family. A decade or a century later, another group arrives and forces out the earlier one.

During the first wave from Europe, Spaniards killed thousands, even tens of thousands, of Darien's native Cueva population. Even more died from European diseases. Although the Cueva were considered second-rate slaves, they were forced to work in Darien's gold mines or were sent to the new mines in Peru.

Cuevan men didn't last long as slaves. Some hanged themselves. While some died from diseases, others died from a broken spirit. They wandered into the forest and poisoned themselves with toxic roots. Cuevan women used other plants to induce miscarriages. They didn't want to bring more life into this world of misery. Within ten years of the Spaniards' arrival in Darien, all that remained of the original native population were a few pockets of Cuevan families hiding in remote forests.

The Spaniards moved on to more lucrative locations, but Darien was still a rich land. The rivers were full of fish. Wild game thrived in the forest.

At first, escaped slaves filled the void. As early as 1505, Spanish ships were sailing from Seville's slave market with black Africans bought and sold to work gold mines in the Indies. Imported slaves were more resilient than the Cueva, but almost a third of them broke free once they reached the colonies. According to an early account, three hundred of every thousand African slaves escaped into the forest. Eventually they organized into communities. They developed their own hierarchy of *cimarrón* kings, bishops and warriors and took control of Darien province.

36

The black *cimarrón*.

The English shortened the name to *maroon*, likely following the lead from the French *marron*. Later, after publication of the pirate William Dampier's *A New Voyage Round the World* in 1697, it became more common as a verb: "I began to find that I was (as we call it, I suppose from the Spaniards) Morooned, or Lost, and quite out of the Hearing of my Comrades Guns."

Spain completely lost control of Darien for most of the mid- to late 1500s. Panama's black *cimarrónes* built at least three hidden cities with as many as 1,700 men in the largest one. They collaborated with English and French pirates making raids on the mainland. They took what they wanted and then disappeared again. Any Spaniard was their enemy. Any enemy of Spain was their ally.

Government militias tracked them through the forests but with only sporadic success. Captain Francisco Carreño captured a group of slaves that had earlier escaped from the Perlas Islands. The soldiers publicly quartered one *cimarrón*, carving him into pieces as an example to any others that might be planning to escape.

Their next military assault against the *cimarrón* leader, King Bayano, was a total failure and only four men from the Spanish detachment survived. On the following excursion, led again by Carreño, the Spaniards finally captured Bayano.

Upon the militia's return to Panama City, Governor Alvaro de Sosa decided that with so many of Bayano's men still in the forest, instead of hanging the prisoner he would negotiate a lasting peace with the *cimarrónes*. While Bayano responded with conciliatory motions, silently he had adopted a defence strategy that, centuries later, Kuna Indians would use even more effectively.

Simply stated: *Agree to everything. Comply with nothing.*

After Sosa and the *cimarrón* king signed the peace accord, Bayano returned to his forest. He was wiser now than before. His men rebuilt their city and then began attacking the Spaniards more successfully than ever.

37

During the 1550s, Bayano and his followers terrorized much of Darien and Panama. However, during a *cimarrón* raid on Nombre de Dios in 1556, the Spaniards captured one of the attackers and forced him to guide Captain Pedro de Ursúa with his soldiers and volunteers back to Bayano's fortress.

They set up camp in an opening across from the hilltop city. Cliffs surrounded the site on all sides with only a few narrow footpaths leading up to fortified entries.

Ursúa invited Bayano for peace negotiations only after first sending his field marshal Francisco Gutiérrez back to Nombre de Dios for machetes, knives, cotton shirts and hats with which to bribe the *cimarrónes*. He also ordered earthen jars full of wine. Some filled with good wine, others laced with a mild poison.

In their meetings, Ursúa assured Bayano that Spain wanted a peace agreement that would guarantee the blacks' freedom while also allowing other groups to live and travel safely in the province. By today's standards it sounds like a reasonable proposal, but considering their history of broken promises it's hard to understand why Bayano trusted Ursúa. After several days of discussions, they finally agreed to the terms of the accord and Bayano, with forty of his men, arrived for a planned celebration and their promised gifts. The rest of his men stayed behind, suspicious of this new friendship with their enemy.

By the time Bayano arrived, Ursúa had already positioned his men for an ambush. He ordered a few men with weapons to hide in his tent while the others strolled around unarmed to ease suspicion. Two soldiers walked from table to table, serving wine from clay jugs. One offered poisoned wine to the guests, while the other poured good wine mostly to Spaniards. By the end of the meal, the blacks were either drunk or feeling very sick.

One by one the former slaves entered the tent. Each chose a shirt, a hat, a machete or another of the offered gifts, until only four of Bayano's men were still sitting with him at the table. When the next man entered the backroom, Gutiérrez reached forward holding a shirt with a dagger hidden in the folds of cotton. He buried the knife into the man's left side, plunging it into his heart before he could make a sound. The *cimarrón* died instantly, but the next man walked in just as they were pulling the body from the room. He tried to warn Bayano, but it was too late. Soldiers grabbed the three remaining *cimarrónes* before they could escape.

At Bayano's camp, his men heard the shouting. They could see bodies collapsed on the ground, the Spaniards leading Bayano away and a group of soldiers charging up the pathway toward them.

Instead of fighting from the safety of their fort, the men panicked and ran out along another path and into the forest with the soldiers close behind. When they reached a swollen river, some of them turned and fought. Others tried to swim but they were dragged away in the current. Only a handful of *cimarrónes* reached the far side.

At his base camp, Ursúa persuaded Bayano to call back his escaped warriors, promising that he would arrange for a *cimarrón* homeland along the Rio Francisco. They would be allowed to live and hunt and plant on their own land. The only concession he demanded was that any newly escaped slaves arriving thereafter would be delivered back to their masters within three days.

They waited for fifty days until all of Bayano's men returned. Then they marched as a group toward Nombre de Dios. Along the way the soldiers removed Bayano's shackles but when they arrived, other Spanish authorities put him immediately in jail.

King Bayano was burned at his own game. They sent him to Peru for trial. From there he was delivered to Spain where he disappeared forever in their prison and court system labyrinth. The rest of his men were sold as slaves. They were shipped out of the country and never returned.

In Nombre de Dios and throughout Darien, Spanish residents celebrated Bayano's capture, believing that the worst of the violence was over. However it wasn't very long before another *cimarrón* community moved into the opening. They were equally disruptive. They guided and protected the British corsair Captain Francis Drake in 1573 when he raided a shipment of thirty tons of silver and gold on the *Camino Royal*, the king's Royal Road that ran from Nombre de Dios to Panama.

It wasn't until 1581 that the largest Darien community of *cimarrónes* (188 native Africans, over 400 hundred people of mixed blood and a few dozen Cuevan slaves and concubines) finally reached an acceptable settlement with the colonial government.

38

It's impossible for my foot to heal at Cavimál. Salt water keeps the cut open. Humidity doesn't help. Mud oozes in and no-see-ums feed on the blood. The dog wants to lick my wound clean but he's a diseased, mangy, tick-infested mutt and I'm afraid of his saliva and of becoming more like him.

To kill time at Cavimál, I talk with Otilio and read history books. I cook and I garden. I drape an old fishnet around the newly replanted vegetable rows to keep dogs and chickens and pigs out of the topsoil. Why do these animals love to dig and sleep in my raised cucumber patch?

Diana and Autemio watch amazed when I clean the weeds from the garden. They prefer to just throw seeds off the side of their hut and hope that they'll grow on their own. Only the strongest strains survive.

When I stop by to visit, I see they have a cluster of seedy tomatoes growing beside their *bohio*.

Why do the leafcutters love my tomato plants and avoid the ones at Autemio's place? I wonder about that.

I pick one of their tomatoes and I start the seeds in my own garden.

39

In a short essay, Canadian writer Margaret Atwood describes a man in a restaurant sitting across from a woman and facing her.

He plants his feet wide apart under the table as he talks to her, as if bracing himself on a ship's deck at sea. "His eyes roll wildly." He knows that this woman will never understand what it is a man has to be: "to navigate, to sail ... sizing the bastard up ... the knife to the gut ... all muscles bulge together."

It's only later in the evening, when the woman looks around at other couples seated in the restaurant, that she realizes the room is full of these men-at-sea. Waves swelling beneath the carpet. "Wind freshens amongst the tablecloths."

Why do we push our lovers away? Who do we think we are? What battle do we imagine in front of us that we choose to sequester ourselves? To steel ourselves? Telling our women and friends to leave us behind and to never look back.

On the night before I took Kathy to the airport in Panama City, I told her that I didn't see us living together again. In the morning I walked with her to the security gate and I waited by the window, but she didn't look back.

For fifteen minutes I stood there alone, feeling the change inside, my hands clasped behind my back.

40

The machete wound on my foot is still red and swollen. It leaks a little every day—sometimes blood, sometimes a thin pus. But the skin is closing over the stitches and I'm tired of waiting. When Autemio invites me for a trip to Diana's home village, I clip the threads and remove them, cleaning the wound the best I can.

Mogue is a tidy Emberá village with a clear river running along the edge. Thatched-roof homes sit high above ground on corner posts. Twenty men are playing soccer in the sun while I stand with a group of Emberá in a shade pocket of mango and avocado trees.

Other Chocó communities envy Mogue's deep-river access to the gulf, where small cruise ships can anchor and ferry a hundred tourists in small boats to the village. When they arrive, Mogue's residents paint their bodies with a natural dye from the *jagua* fruit. They pound on drums and dance. Local children lead visitors by the hand through town. At the village centre, after a guide from the cruise ship talks about Emberá culture for fifteen minutes, local women sell their woven baskets and animal carvings. The entire visit lasts about an hour and a half before the tourists return to the boats and back to their ship.

After selling *Ishmael*, I bought an unfinished dugout and a brand new outboard motor. Autemio tells me that he wants to buy them from me before I leave. He says that the money is no problem. Right now he doesn't have a dollar to buy a pound of chicken feet. Sometimes he borrows a dime for a bouillon cube. However, he tells me the fishing will improve and that soon we'll be making a lot of money.

On the trip to Mogue, Autemio insisted on driving. When we beached the boat on the river bend at Diana's family home, he lifted the motor onto his shoulder and carried it to their house. He rinsed it with fresh water and he said that I should go with the family rather than help him store the boat.

We haven't hammered out a deal yet over the price and terms, but I'm wondering if he's already told her family that the boat and motor are his.

Rufino warned me not to sell the motor this way. No money down. Just promises followed by excuses, and later topped off with an arrangement for another payment that will never materialize. Rufino described all of this quite clearly. Real money never changes hands, he said.

Wounaan Autemio Tovar and his Emberá wife Diana are my young hosts for fifteen months in Darien.

I can still see Rufino's thin hand gesturing, his long index finger pointing at me while he gave me advice on people and money.

And he's right. I don't know why I do these things. For some reason I always want to believe that I'm the exception to the rule ... that local knowledge and historic tendencies don't apply in my world.

The deal that Autemio and I make is a one-sided agreement. For the next year, it's a pain in my side.

41

Because there is no electricity in Mogue, when one family decided to turn their home into a bar they had to buy a generator for the stereo and a propane fridge for beer. For the first two months they served liquor and played loud music all night. It became the place for Mogue's men, both young and old, to spend the few dollars they had. It caused a lot of problems for the village while making a decent profit for the owner. But then the generator malfunctioned one night. Maybe it was a poorly made generator, or it had been left out in the rain ... some villagers say it was the hand of God. The power surge destroyed the stereo and caused an electrical fire in the generator. Now a curtain of darkness descends in the evenings and everything is quiet and peaceful again at night.

I prefer this to the *cantina* noise at La Palma. But Autemio is younger. He thinks that Mogue is a sad place. He lived for a year in Panama City, and this village life is too tame for him. Now he wants an outboard motor, a rifle, a chainsaw, a television and a stereo. He has been asking me about solar panels. He wants some noise around and a few light bulbs burning in his house at Cavimál.

When he builds their new home, Autemio tells me, he'll use wood planks ripped down with a chainsaw rather than splitting open the shell of a *gira* tree for the floor.

He doesn't own a chainsaw or have the money to rent one. I tell him that I like the feel of a *gira* floor. It has a soft give that makes it a comfortable bed.

"Why would you spend a lot of money on planks when the *gira* is free?" I ask.

"I want a solid floor," he says. "The *gira* is more ... well, it's *estilo indio*," he says. Indian style. As if that is reason enough to look elsewhere.

42

"Hey, gringo! You want to know everything? What do you think about this water?" a Mogue villager asks, pointing at a stagnant puddle in the mud.

"Is it good to drink? Should we make it our water source for the village?" he asks.

He's drunk and he sounds angry. I wonder how many aid groups have come here in the past to tell Mogue residents how they are supposed to live.

Thirty Emberá men stand around a rough-hewn dugout in the forest, far from any navigable water. They're clumped in tiny groups of two or three or four, disorganized, arguing over the best method of moving the boat to the river. They've been drinking corn *chicha* since daybreak and their eyes are glassy and unfocussed. Nobody reaches out with a welcoming hand.

Autemio didn't want to hike here with me.

"They already have enough help," he said as we rolled our blankets in the morning. Maybe he'd heard that someone didn't want me around, some anti-gringo mood amongst the men. I tried to reason with him, saying that we would be the only sober workers in the group by now, but he suggested that we should just relax today. It wasn't until I started sulking at breakfast, looking sad and depressed, that he finally gave in. We pulled on our rubber boots and we ran for forty minutes through the forest to reach the group.

As more trees are cut each year, an Emberá has to travel farther and farther from the river to find a mature *espavé* tree for a canoe. This one is for a big dugout. Forty feet or longer, and able to carry 12,000 or 15,000 plantains from village to market.

If the builder knows what he's doing and has a helper and a good axe and an adze, it might take a month or longer for the first stage of carving and shaping. To lighten the log he has to cut away excess wood, both inside and out, but still leave enough to protect it for the overland trip to the river. It could be a mile or even farther along a rough trail. He'll need a big group of men, twenty or more, to drag the partially carved log through the forest.

To lure volunteers, the owner plans ahead. He usually ferments fifteen gallons of corn *chicha*. On the day of the move, it's a balancing act. His goal is to pour enough to satisfy everyone's thirst but not so much that they burn out before the boat reaches the water's edge.

The forest is beautiful above Mogue. It looks as though the large trees on the hillside haven't been cut for a hundred years or more. The owner has at least two more *espavés* that he can use for canoes in the future. He has *chunga* palms to harvest for basket weaving and other palms for roofing material.

Autemio faded away from me after the first confrontation and now I'm standing alone. Is he embarrassed to be with me here? He invited me to spend Easter week with Diana's family in Mogue, but since our arrival he's been avoiding me most of the time.

The men around the dugout don't want to invite me into their circle. This type of exclusion doesn't happen very often when I'm travelling, but I've developed a standard survival response. I keep walking forward. I put one foot in front of the other. Sometimes I pretend I don't understand Spanish and that I can't read body language. I grab a gunwale as they stumble up and down through a gully while carrying two thousand pounds of *espavé* overhead. When I reach out to help, a space opens for my hands. When I lift and push, they can feel the effort. I don't say anything and they don't talk to me.

We're sweating when we reach the trail. They tie an eighty-foot rope to the bow, and most of the group pulls while the others try to steer or push from behind.

58 | THE DARIEN GAP

A carver at Tutumate uses an axe and an adze to shape and thin the walls of a dugout canoe.

The dugout grinds and thuds over roots and scrapes against trees on the curves. Two-thirds of the younger boys are just holding on and doing nothing. Ten minutes later, one of them calls out for *chicha*. Then a dozen more start shouting until everyone stops, collapsing in the dugout or falling on the ground laughing.

The owner makes a great ceremony of unscrewing the lid. He shakes the residue out of the cup and cleans it with his shirt. They pass a full cup to one person at a time so that he has to glug it down while the others wait. By this first *chicha* break, they've already forgotten the grudge against me. They give me three cups in a row to help me catch up with the others. I'm still not Emberá, but I'm happier than I was. I love drinking *chicha*. The corn liquor burns so sweet inside. It fills my heart and head and gives me life and energy and desire. I think that I could live on sweet-corn liquor. I could sit down and drink it all day long for no particular reason at all. Just for the burn and the flavour.

For another two hours we start and stop and drink and start again until we reach the river's edge. A woman appears with another five-gallon jug. A light breeze drifts in from the river. Our sweat smells like hard work and *chicha*.

One young man shoves another man, and he bumps into two others who are easily offended. I think that somebody left someone's hat behind on the trail. The pushing spreads around the circle, but everyone is drunk and I doubt they'll get hurt unless they fall down and thump their head against a tree.

Autemio touches my shoulder and says we should leave. As we approach the village he separates himself from me again. I don't really care. I just let him go. I only wish that I'd stayed behind and fought until I fell down drunk with the others.

When you travel on your own you have to define who you are, or people don't know what to make of you or how to accept you.

At this early point I still haven't fully decided to write about the trip. Writing isn't particularly natural or pleasurable to me, and it's often a lonely journey.

I can't explain to anyone—especially to Autemio—that I'm running away. I'm hiding for a while, cutting my ties and trying to understand what it is that I'm rejecting. And what will replace it. And what is it that I am longing to embrace. Something more loving and human than what I've lived up to now.

What would Autemio think of all this soul-searching?

As a traveller, if you want to push beyond the surface impressions, you have to decide who your friends are and who will be your accomplice and guide. Even if you don't tell these people about their role in your story, you still have to commit to someone or something.

In spite of the head-butting with Tovar, and now Autemio's rejection, I still believe that I'm in the right place. I'm in for the long ride, not just a weekend jaunt. You have to trust your instincts.

In my view, Autemio is young enough to believe he can carve his own path through life. He won't accept that poverty or tradition or family or race can control him. He's old enough to have his own dreams, yet still a respect for others. I think that he'll sort out all the voices around him and then he'll make his own decision. Something good for both of us. That's what my instinct tells me.

43

Last night in Mogue I was lying awake thinking about Autemio's widowed father Otilio. He looked lonely as the rest of us motored away from Cavimál for the trip to Mogue. He's a tiny man with full lips and sad eyes. He isn't sure of the exact year he was born, but he thinks that he's in his late sixties.

When he works in the field, Otilio wears an old straw hat with the top torn out. He spends entire days barefoot, digging out weeds with a steel bar, battling leafcutter ants and throwing rocks at Autemio's pig when it strays into the pineapple field.

When I first arrived at Cavimál, Otilio welcomed me with his arms open wide for an awkward hug.

"Oh Martin, I'm so glad you're here," he said when I stepped onto

Otilio Tovar, the Wounaan family patriarch at Cavimál, sits in the shade on the shoreline while finishing work on a new paddle.

his shoreline. "I'm here to serve you in any way I can ... whatever you ask for I'll be glad to provide ... although we are quite poor ... and I'm still so sad after my wife's death ... too sad to have planted rice this year ... and so we have very little to eat ..."

44

"You must not thank for your meat. It is your right to get parts...With gifts you make slaves, just as with whips you make dogs."
–Eskimo hunter speaking to Arctic explorer Peter Freuchen

Otilio opened his arms and welcomed me from the first day I arrived. Autemio has given me a home to live in. I can eat their food and gather mangoes and pineapples from their fields at Cavimál, and they've asked for nothing in return.

Money and gifts and disparity of wealth, whether real or perceived, can be confusing for a traveller.

Because I'm a gringo, because I'm North American, most people in Darien assume I have more money than can be imagined. They believe that if they coach me (Tovar's stories, for instance) then I might leave a windfall (about five thousand dollars).

This fallacy combines with my own misconceptions. A foreigner's romantic interpretation of events.

When foreigners sail to Darien and drop anchor in front of a village, natives usually offer fruit and coconuts and fish. They often invite the visitors to their homes, and sometimes they feed their guests while they remain anchored. When the visitors set sail the next morning and travel to another port, they believe they understand how the natives live.

They'll say, "There is so much fruit and fish. The natives plant in the forest, or it grows wild. It costs them nothing and they're happy to share it. They're just good people."

I've heard this from a number of sailors after their short visit to La Palma.

In 1924, American adventurer and political meddler Richard Marsh trekked across Darien, attempting to prove the existence of a mythical race of white Indians. He travelled with an entourage of scientists and porters and native guides. Whenever he stopped he would set up a booty tent full of shiny beads, mirrors, mouth organs, balloons, bells and bird whistles. He wanted to awe these twentieth-century "savages" with cheap toys.

At the start of his trip Marsh praised the Chocó. He said they were noble, if perhaps also irresponsible, savages. Later, after the novelty of the trinket tent had worn thin, he reassessed and complained that the Indians "took everything like greedy children, but never offered us anything for nothing."

Anthropologist and writer Peter Farb writes that early Europeans arriving in the Americas were often offended by the lack of acknowledgment of their gifts. Indians didn't have the *courtesy* to thank them.

I wrestle with this concept throughout the trip. Like the Europeans, I'm hobbled with a body of assumptions and preconceived notions of what American natives represent, and how they will respond to my presence. Everything is interpreted through this filter.

Adding to the confusion is the difference in how we acknowledge generosity. When I give a Chocó native a gift—a machete, photos of his family, or a bag of food—he will usually take the item, perhaps offering a nod of his head or a glance at the item, and then he'll place it out of the way in a back corner. It feels as though I've just returned a borrowed item. The gift presentation is finished. If I was expecting a greater response, I'll be disappointed.

The receiver accepts the gift and will look at it later when the giver is no longer there. If the receiver thanked the other person for an item, then he would be acknowledging his indebtedness to the giver. Neither side would be comfortable with that. Instead, by saying nothing, he offers the highest flattery. His silence indicates that the giver is of such a generous character that he offers the gift expecting absolutely nothing in return. Not even thanks.

The truth is that there is still another layer to the transaction. An unspoken understanding. If a relationship is going to continue, then somewhere in the future the recipient will return the favour in one equal form or another. However, this is done without words or promissory gestures. In contrast, so often our North American custom is more of a vocal demonstration of appreciation than a quiet, but tangible, response.

We receive gifts with a thousand thank yous and smiles.

"It's so beautiful! What a wonderful thing you've done!"

We hug them or kiss their hands, or whatever is our custom. And when we do this to Darien natives, we try in our own way to coach them: "You see? This is how you're supposed to receive a gift from a gringo!"

45

When I first came to live at Cavimál, Autemio walked with me to the tiny, abandoned hut. He said I could use it for as long as I wanted. Since his mother's death, he and Diana had moved back into the main house to live with Otilio.

Autemio apologized for the rotting floor and the holes in the roof.

"It's perfect," I said.

He told me that he couldn't accept anything in return. It would be impossible.

"*Ah ho!*" he said, refusing my offer. "Martin, we are friends."

46

At night in Diana's family home in Mogue, we light a diesel candle. Diana's brother Manqueque asks me what time it is in Canada. I tell him something about time zones, and then I have to explain the little I know about longitude.

Autemio asks why God made the world so that the sun comes up at different times in various countries. I draw a crude map of the world on a grapefruit and I use two limes for the sun and the moon. This leads to questions of why there are *manchas* (stains, or shadows) on the moon's face, and where scientists go when they send a space shuttle on a rocket.

When I tell Manqueque that astronauts have walked on the moon, Autemio looks down at the floor. He doesn't say anything, but I can tell that he doesn't believe the astronaut story.

They ask about submarines. How can they dive and surface? How do they generate power? Some of these questions are beyond anything I know. And how does an outboard motor work, or the internal combustion engine in general? Why did the Russians die in the recent submarine accident we heard about on the radio? Did they drown? Freeze to death? And this in turn leads to a discussion about air and oxygen. About inhaling oxygen and exhaling carbon dioxide. How plants in turn produce oxygen with that same carbon dioxide. About the altitude that jets fly at when they pass over. About vapour trails, and why we sometimes see them in the sky and other times we don't. And the difference between gasoline and jet fuel. And whether I can find the Darien wells drilled by Gulf Oil in the 1960s. And can we get unlimited fuel for an outboard motor if we break the padlock on one of those wells?

Using the last of the diesel candle, we set up mosquito nets and we lie down on our blankets. I fall asleep listening to the deep rattle of Diana's niece coughing up phlegm from her lungs.

47

A Kuna story:

Olonitalipipilele (Olon) has no woman, and so he lives in a house with his sister. He has a lot of nephews that are different types of animals, and Olon uses them as his workers. In the early mornings he goes out to the forest to plant and hunt. He returns in the afternoons.

One night while the sister is sleeping, Olon crawls into bed and has sex with her, but she doesn't wake up on that first night. The next night, the same thing, until eventually she becomes pregnant. She realizes then what is happening, but she's such a heavy sleeper that she still doesn't know who is responsible.

At first she trains a *piojo* (louse) to wake her if someone comes to her bed, but she sleeps through that as well. Then she trains a flea, but the insect jumps up and runs away when her brother comes near.

Finally she chooses a *garrapata* (tick). She also prepares a bowl of purplish-black dye (*jagua*) from the *sabdur* plant and hides it under her hammock to paint the face of the unwelcome visitor. As a final preparation, she dries out all of the pools of water around her house.

That night when her brother draws close to her hammock, the tick wakes her with its bite. She grabs the bowl of *jagua* and throws it at the intruder. It stains her brother's face and he runs outside to quickly wash his face with water. He searches in all the usual spots but the puddles are dry.

In the early morning light, the sister calls out and invites her nephews for something to drink before they go to the hills. She inspects their faces, but none of them are stained. Her brother is still sleeping. She tries to wake him but he says that he has a headache.

At the noon hour he's still sleeping. She calls him again to offer something to eat, but he keeps a blanket over his head and says that he can't get up.

Then when she turns the other way, he throws off the cover and runs out of the house before she can stop him.

"Wait!" she calls out as he runs into the forest. "I'll go with you!" she shouts, but he doesn't stop. And even though she runs fast and follows his path for hours, she still can't catch him.

When she reaches a fork in the path, she asks directions from the animals working near the trail. They say they won't help her unless she comes to live with them. And so it goes. She lives a short while with these animals before she's able to continue.

Later the animals show her Olon's trail, and she follows this path until she comes to a river where an old woman named Kabayay lives. The woman has a number of sons, and when Olon's sister arrives— now visibly pregnant—the old woman invites her in.

Before her sons return, the old woman hides her guest in a giant clay jar. On this first occasion, the sons think they smell something sweet in the house.

"Are there candies in the house?" they ask their mother.

"No, nothing like that," the old woman tells them, keeping the visitor a secret from them.

The boys go back to play in the river.

The next time they come home, they find the pregnant woman. They carry her down to the river to kill her, but Kabayay calls out to save the woman's organs to cook in a pot.

Soon after Kabayay starts to boil the organs over a fire, a baby crawls out of the cooking pot. And then another. And another, until eight babies climb out of the soup.

The old woman decides to raise the newborns in her home, telling the eight boys that she is their mother. When they ask Kabayay how it is that they all have noses and she has none, she tries to fool them by going to the river to make a nose out of clay. But the boys see through this trick and they want to know their real mother.

A short while later, Pugazo—one of the eight brothers—goes to the mountains to hunt and he hears a bird singing these lyrics: "The fish have eaten your mother."

He runs all the way back to his house and tells Kabayay what he heard in the forest.

"It appears that the bird is only predicting my death in the future," she tells Pugazo.

The next day, all of the brothers hike out into the same forest and they hear the bird singing the same words. It's then that they understand that their real mother is dead and that the old woman has been lying to them.

"Let's drown her in the river," one brother says. They all agree, and they return to Kabayay's home.

"We're going to wash in the river," they call out to her at the end of the day.

She follows them, and when she's in the middle of the current a rainstorm starts and the water rises. The river grabs hold of her and no one reaches out to help.

She cries out in the darkness.

When she tries to crawl out at the riverbank, the brothers chop off her hands so that she can't save herself, and the spirits turn her into a frog.

The boys say to the frog, "From now on, whenever it is about to rain, you'll start to cry like you're doing right now so that men will know about the coming storm!"

After living many years in this same place, the brothers decide to make a new home in the sky. They live with the moon and become the brightest stars in the night. And for this reason, it is said that Olonitalipipilele is the moon, and that the stains on his face come from the *jagua* thrown by his sister.

RIO BALSAS

48

On a Sunday afternoon as I'm paddling back to Cavimál, Autemio calls me over to Tovar's porch where the brothers are waiting for the lottery numbers to be announced on the radio. It has been almost two months since the New Year's party and Tovar is still drinking. Every time we meet, it's uncomfortable. Sometimes he grabs my arm and says, "Martin, some men in town say that they're going to your place at night to rob you, but I won't let them hurt you. I told them I would defend you."

"Thank you, Tovar," I answer. "I will do the same for you."

But this particular Sunday afternoon is different. He has a specific point he wants to make today.

"*Martin no es gringo*," he announces when I arrive. Martin isn't a gringo.

In most parts of Latin America this would be a compliment. The term "gringo" is usually a derogatory label referring to a rich American who arrives in Latin America, doesn't learn to speak Spanish, tramples on others and flaunts his wealth. However, it doesn't sound as though Tovar wants to flatter me.

"*Martin no es gringo. El es canadiense.*" He says this a few times. Sometimes to Autemio. Sometimes to me.

I thank him again, and I tell him that he is in fact correct.

"…because gringos *help* the Indians," he says. He finally arrives at the central point. "Gringos are good people. They help us poor people," he says. "We are poor, but Martin is a Canadian."

He completes the equation.

I buy a soda for Autemio and another for myself. I offer one to Tovar, but he is brooding in his chair with his head bowed. He pretends that he can't hear me.

49

Autemio wants my Yamaha outboard motor and the twenty-seven-foot dugout I finished with Rufino. He says that once he sets his mind to something it's impossible to stop him. He'll work day and night. I don't have to worry about anything. I just have to give him the equipment to use.

And then he asks to borrow twenty cents to buy two eggs for breakfast.

"This boat and motor are all I have," I tell him. "Do you understand that I need to sell them to buy my ticket home at the end of the trip?"

He doesn't answer. Probably he doesn't believe me. Tovar tells him that gringos have thousands of dollars tucked away in duffel bags.

"Okay," I say.

I'll charge $850 for the motor—half the price I paid two months ago. He can buy the boat for the $250 I've already invested, but if he wants both, he'll owe me a thousand. I tell him he'll have to sell his fish and pay at least a hundred dollars each month so that I'll have the money by December.

I say something about making a payment on the first day of each month, or after each spring tide when the fishing is best, but I don't think he hears anything after the word "okay."

I realize this only afterwards.

And then I give him a quarter to buy the eggs.

50

At the end of the trail through Puntita, there is a shack on the waterfront. It has a short dock with a hand-painted sign advertising diesel and gasoline for sale. The store window is open but the house is silent.

I rap my knuckles on the counter and call out for a soda.

At first no one answers. Then I hear hammock strings stretching and the rafters groan.

"*Que quiere?*" someone calls out from inside. What do you want?

"*Una soda,*" I say.

I hear more shifting and creaking and then bare feet scuffing over the rough-sawn floorboards. As the man enters the room he rubs the afternoon sleep from his eyes. He's surprised to see a gringo.

"Wait here," he says after he takes my dollar and puts a cold bottle on the counter. He owes me three quarters so I'm not planning on going anywhere, but then he opens the side door to hand me the change. I've seen this man before. A stocky Emberá, barefoot with thick legs, torn shorts and his belly hanging over the waistband.

"Come. Come," he says, motioning me to step inside.

The room is empty except for three fuel drums by a door leading to the dock. I sit down on a wood block while he reclaims the hammock.

For the first minute we don't say anything. I sip on my drink and he watches me.

"Do you buy these?" he asks, holding up a peccary tusk.

"No, I don't," I answer. I don't know what I'd do with a peccary tusk.

Silence again.

"Drink. Drink," he motions to me to tip the bottle. He's looking at me as if I have something to explain.

Then he does the hand motion. The question mark. His wrist flops outward so that his palm faces toward the ceiling with his fingers spread loosely but still lightly cupped.

I don't make sense to him.

"Do you buy *artesanía*? Woven baskets?" he asks.

"Very little."

"Then, you're a scientist."

"No, I'm not," I say.

"You buy wood and timber," he guesses.

"No, that's not it," I answer.

"*Ando conociendo*," I tell him, using a Latin American phrase that translates literally as, *I go about knowing*, indicating that this is a pleasure trip. I'm a tourist, and I just want to see and experience something different.

He stares at me. He has seen me motor past his dock with Autemio on our way to sell fish at the market. I paddle back and forth in my dugout, and I've been here for months, so he's not convinced by my explanation. The room is quiet again. Sunlight leaks through in vertical lines between the wall boards.

I finish my soda and I gather up my daypack to leave. When I tell him my name, he says he is Manuel Ortega.

I've heard that name before. At first I think I'm confusing it with Manuel Noriega, but I sift through my mental notebooks until I remember reading that he was formerly an elected leader of the *Tierra Colectiva*, an Emberá/Wounaan land-rights project.

"I've been looking for you," I say.

Manuel's eyes grow round as he sits up straight in his hammock.

51

My first trip to Manené with Manuel takes twelve hours in a motorized *piragua*. During the rainy season the Balsas River floods and it's possible to make the journey in half that time, but in these dry months we have to raise the outboard and drag the boat over long shallow sections.

By the time we arrive it's already dark. I smell food cooking and I hear babies crying, but my night vision is terrible. I can see only the fire glow and silhouettes in each open-walled home, and so I follow close behind Manuel.

He calls out to neighbours as we pass their platforms in the dark.

"Oh, Alonzo!" Manuel says at the first round house.

"Oooo!" they answer. Or sometimes they shout something in Emberá dialect.

Alonzo's children greet Manuel as we walk close by their home. They start to say something and then they stop and run back across the floor to the fire.

"Gringo," I hear them whisper to their parents.

Manené is an upriver village with game meat smoking over cooking fires. It's cool and comfortable here at night. There are coconut palms towering over the Rio Balsas, and avocado, mango, orange, cashew and grapefruit trees growing between the homes. The river runs deep and strong all year through.

In the village, one family has a propane fridge. They sell cookies, cold sodas and vegetable oil. Another family stocks sugar and coffee.

During the rainy season in native villages, boys and girls love to play soccer on a muddy field. "Vamos a jugar sucio!" *they announce.* "Let's play dirty!"

A third home carries one-pound bags of flour and packages of flavoured drink crystals. To make a proper batch of pan bread, you have to stop at all three homes to buy supplies.

52

In Darien, most Emberá and Wounaan natives have animal nicknames. In the village of Manené, thanks to Manuel Ortega, villagers call me *Ansabidá*—a kingfisher, a bird that fishes for sardines in their river. They refer to Ortega as *Coríbe*, though he prefers Ortega.

A *coríbe* is a *poncho*, or capybara. A busybody animal and the world's largest rodent. It has a stocky body, reddish-brown hair, webbed feet and a large boxy head. Day and night the *poncho* pokes its nose everywhere looking for food. To the Emberá, a *coríbe* also represents a teller-of-tales, someone whose stories aren't necessarily true.

Ten years ago, Manuel was *cacique suplente* (second chief) for all the Darien Chocó villages outside of the Emberá-Wounaan *Comarca*. These villages don't have any legal protection or title for their land. With the help of a Danish NGO they organized into a *Tierra Colectiva* project and began to lobby Panama's national government for communal land-title status.

Manuel's elected position lasted for five years. When the *cacique general* was forced to step down partway through the term, Manuel took over those responsibilities as well. During his time in office he addressed Panama's Legislative Assembly, he trekked backed and forth across Darien and he flew to Washington to take part in a Smithsonian festival. His half-brother Clementino Berrugati is the current *cacique general* of the *Tierra Colectiva*.

These aren't paid positions. They're an honour and also a burden. An elected chief rarely has time to return to his village. Clementino hasn't been back to Manené for three years, and while his home by the Rio Balsas has a small padlock on the door, the walls are collapsing from rot.

To buy food for his family, Manuel manages his brother's small store in Puntita. He lives there alone and has only a one-week visit with his family each month.

At night I sleep on the split *gira* floor with Manuel, his wife Tranquilina and their four young boys. We spread our blankets under the palm-thatched roof, the breeze blowing through the open sides. Manuel snores like an unmuffled tractor so that sometimes he shakes himself awake. He and Tranquilina laugh whenever it happens. Ortega quickly falls back asleep and the cycle begins again. After 1 a.m. he quiets to a low rumble. At 2 a.m. he finds his radio and turns the volume up loud for ten minutes of Colombian news. He does it again at 3 a.m. The neighbour's roosters wander over to start crowing under our floor at a little after four, and Manuel rolls out of bed at 4:45.

He lights a candle and immediately looks for something to do. When he sees me stirring in my mosquito tent he hops down to the ground and grabs his machete. He begins slashing at grass and weeds around the house so that he's dripping sweat when I emerge a few minutes later.

It's still pitch black outside.

"Working," Manuel says as a greeting—the first words out of his mouth.

"Working for you," he says.

53

Ortega and I laugh at each other's jokes, but I suspect that the intended punchlines are culturally sensitive. While each of us might find something funny, it may not have been the point of the story.

I notice that a joke doesn't have to offer a clear punchline if instead it delivers either a well-told slapstick scene or a crafty native character who outfoxes an authority figure (preferably a black or a gringo or a government official of any race). They laugh extra hard if the joke combines the two elements.

We've been sitting on the floor all afternoon, tearing thin strips from *chunga* palm fronds. Tranquilina soaks the strips in water and then sun-dries them. She dyes them using plants and roots and seeds so that later she can weave them into watertight, beautiful baskets.

When Ortega decides to tell his joke, he first sets the stage. It feels as though he's about to admit to some dark secret. He pauses in the middle of work and his face becomes grave.

"Martin," he says. He touches my arm to get my attention.

I'm worried that he just heard news that a friend has died. Maybe he wants to ask an enormous favour. He has that look about him. But it's just his way of establishing the full audience concentration for his joke.

He tells it well, and I laugh when he delivers the finale—how the Emberá labourer grabs the extra egg after his Spaniard boss tries to take it for himself. Manuel laughs for a long time at his own story.

"Ooooo, that *ladino* thought he'd tricked the Indian," Manuel

Tranquilina weaves a basket with strips from the chunga *palm, while her youngest son sleeps in the hammock.*

says, shaking his head. He's still laughing. "But somehow the Indian was able to come up with a better story. He tricked the white man out of the egg in the end."

Even though I enjoy most jokes people tell me, I rarely remember them afterwards. But the last time I was back in Canada, a friend on Vancouver Island told me a joke about native land claims. For some reason it stuck in my memory, and it seems appropriate here. In translation for Ortega it might lose some of the subtlety, but with appropriate hand and foot gestures it all comes across.

"A gringo," I begin, "is hunting deer in a government forest outside of the Indian *comarca* when he spots a big buck on the edge of an open meadow. He raises the rifle, looks through the scope to aim, and he shoots and kills that trophy deer. He drops it right where it was standing."

I have his attention.

"Excited, the hunter runs out across the meadow to claim his prize, but just as he's approaching, an Indian steps out of the bush. 'Whoa, gringo,' the Indian says, holding up his hand to stop the hunter. 'Not so fast. You've killed a deer on Indian land. This deer belongs to me.' The gringo can't believe it. He's certain that he's far outside the *comarca*. He argues and argues, but the Indian remains with his arms crossed and one foot on top of the deer. 'Indian land. Indian deer,' is all he says.

"The argument grows wilder and they start shouting back and forth until the Indian proposes a contest. The tougher man will take home the deer. 'Gringo,' he says, 'first I'll kick you in the balls. Then you kick me in the balls. And it can go on from there until only one man is standing. That man wins the deer.'

"The gringo is a big man," I tell Ortega. "And the Indian comes up only to his shoulder. So the white man agrees. He's certain that he's the tougher of the two."

Ortega can't believe what he's hearing.

"It's just a joke," I explain. "A story that's made up."

"Go on," Ortega insists.

"So the Indian winds up and gives a full-swing kick into the

Manuel Ortega sharpens his machete while his wife Tranquilina prepares food on their kitchen platform.

gringo's groin. The hunter doubles over and collapses onto the ground. He's crying and howling."

Ortega explodes laughing. I could finish the joke here and it would be enough for him. A joke well told. But I wait for Ortega to recover and then I continue.

"This gringo is incredibly tough and mean," I say. "And so after almost blacking out from pain, he forces himself back up to his knees, then he grabs hold of a tree and drags his body up. He gets his feet on the ground and leans against the tree. This takes almost twenty minutes. The Indian stands patiently and watches."

While I say all of this, I go through the motions with my feet and hands. Ortega has his right hand over his groin and he's still grimacing.

"'All right, Indian!' the hunter says, tears streaming down his cheeks. 'Now it's my turn.'

"The Indian looks at his opponent sadly. Then, just before he turns to walk away, the Indian says, 'Stupid gringo. This isn't *comarca* land. You can keep your damn deer.'"

Ortega laughs again but not as much as during the actual kick to the balls. He looks a little uncertain as to whether the joke is finished.

"He pretended it was *comarca*," I explain.

"He kicked him good," Ortega says, screwing up his face again in pain. "Oh, god," he laughs. "The Indian sure tricked the white man. Indians are tricky," he says. "He really got the better of him."

"It's just a joke," I explain. "It didn't actually happen."

"That's one smart Indian," Ortega insists.

Later when we visit other families, Ortega asks me to tell the joke again and again. They always laugh at the kick to the groin—their faces contorted in pain. But when I tell the punchline, Ortega has to switch to dialect and give a very involved explanation. The men in the room bow thoughtfully as if they're pondering some philosophical nuance. Sometimes they offer a few more chuckles and maybe a nod my way.

And then Ortega switches back to Spanish. He begins laughing again.

"That's a smart Indian," he says.

54

Even fifty years ago, the village of Manené didn't exist. Emberá and Wounaan were nomads, or semi-nomads. They didn't accept or recognize the border between Colombia and Panama.

What was this *frontera* to them? Just someone's imaginary line drawn through their forests. They carried no identification. They followed rivers and footpaths and they travelled back and forth between the countries. If the soil or game meat or fish was depleted, then the Chocó would walk away from their house and move to another region, letting the forest and river recover for a decade or longer.

Tracing the long history of nomadic people is impossible to do with certainty. It's even more difficult with tropical forest and riverine peoples. There's so little to find. They leave clues but no written texts or permanent structures.

Darien tribes didn't build stone temples or irrigation canals. Their tools and homes collapsed, rotted in the forest and turned into soil and nutrients for new growth.

In Darien, rain pours down and rivers flood. Trees crash to the ground and within a year, vegetation covers anything left behind. You can't find even a trace of surface history after ten years—let alone fifty, five hundred, or a thousand years or more. We have to use Spanish texts and native oral history combined with inference and poetic licence.

Based on language and customs, it appears that today's Darien natives are distinct from those at the initial contact period. Except for a few isolated crossover words used by Kuna and Chocó, the original Cuevan Indian language and culture didn't survive the first few decades of Spanish occupation.

Two boys from the Tovar family laugh while walking through the rain with fat mangoes in their hands. In late April or early May, after the rice has been planted, rain begins to fall again in Darien.

In 1556, after the Spaniards had captured Bayano and shipped the *cimarrón* prisoners to other colonies, Darien was temporarily emptied of its human population again. Before long, native tribes from Colombia began arriving from across the mountains.

A Spanish captain, Trejo, reported meeting groups of Chocó Indians between the Sambú and Balsas rivers in the mid-1500s. In 1572 Father Cristóbal Suarez wrote about a protectorate of Ostio Indians (believed to be Chocó) between the same rivers. As well, the earliest French and English pirates listed both Kuna natives and black *cimarrónes* as their collaborators during raids on Spanish gold mines.

Chocó stories from this period describe their wars against the Kuna in Colombia, attacking and burning their villages in an attempt to exterminate them or drive them from the Atrato Valley. For the next fifty years, Kuna families flooded across the mountains from Colombia's Santa Marta and the Gulf of Urabá. According to Catholic priests, by the early 1600s Kuna made up almost all of Panama's Darien population. They settled along the upper Tuira and Chuqunaque rivers and the Bayano regions. They rarely mixed with other groups, and for the next two hundred years they attacked any group or individual that threatened their independence.

Details of the early Chocó presence are uncertain. The only clues we have to their history are the characteristics they share with Amazonian riverine people in Brazil. Both groups built similar dugouts with standing platforms on either end for spearing fish. They hunted with *cerbatanas* (long, hollow blowguns) and poisoned darts. They also shared the custom of incorporating slaves into their tribe, sometimes forcing prisoners to drink a drugged potion to cause them to forget their place of origin. They sounded shells as a trumpet to call on spirits, and many of their tribal myths and oral histories overlap.

According to English pirate William Dampier, Chocó were solidly entrenched on Colombia's upper Atrato River by the end of the 1600s. He writes that they would come downriver to attack Kuna settlements, and that they had "no business with the

Spaniards or any white man. They use poles almost eight feet long to fire poison darts, and are so silent when attacking their enemies, and retreat quickly afterwards, that the Spanish can never find them."

While the Kuna controlled much of Darien's interior for over two centuries, Chocó groups came and went for most of that time. These tribes had been mortal enemies for generations in Colombia, and when the Chocó finally did decide to stay in Darien, it is likely that they repeated their confrontational history and did so by force. It appears that they immigrated to Darien following Colombia's Juradó River (a Chocó term signifying the "River of the Kunas"), and by the early 1800s the Emberá and Wounaan began attacking Kuna communities and pushing them out of the interior.

In the face of the aggression, the Kuna retreated across the San Blas Mountains and down to the Caribbean coast and San Blas Islands where they still live today. Emberá and Wounaan have remained in the interior, but Darien's cycle of displacement continues to plague them.

The Emberá-Wounaan *Comarca* established in 1983 is much smaller than they had hoped for and it fails to protect almost half of the Chocó people and land. A year after the *comarca's* formation, Panama created Darien National Park and imposed park regulations on the dozen existing native villages, including Manené, lying within the boundaries. In other areas, Colombians escaping civil unrest in their country have fled across the mountains and settled on native land. Small logging companies continue to push roads into what was once inaccessible forest, making it easier for other loggers and ranchers to follow. Immigrant farmers from Panama's western provinces arrive hungry and looking for property to title for their family, and each new cattle rancher can use as much land as an entire native community might need for subsistence farming.

55

In Emberá and Wounaan attacks against the Kunas, the Chocó might have chosen a warrior to lead them. Their ritual ceremonies often relied on a powerful shaman to call upon spirits through songs and incantations. However, the Emberá and Wounaan have never had a clear tradition of chiefs or village leaders. Previously, as independent nomads, their largest recognized political organization had been the immediate or extended family. They continue to be suspicious of any individual—especially another Chocó—who tries to rise above that level and speak for the group at large.

Manuel Ortega and his half-brother Clementino suffer from that tradition even though their own people elected them into the *Tierra Colectiva* positions. Chocó assume that their leaders bend the rules for their personal advantage. And the truth is that any father and husband is going to do what he can to look after his household. If his political position offers him opportunities, then it will be difficult to just turn away from good fortune.

56

At least in theory, nothing moves through the *comarca* or *Tierra Colectiva* without approval from all political levels. To protect their land, the Chocó have gone from having no formal organization to an almost unnavigable labyrinth of politics and bureaucracy.

Every village elects a *dirigente* (director) and a *suplente* (second-in-charge). There are often subcommittees for women's issues, finances, water-system maintenance, artisan marketing, and health programs. Beyond the village level, they choose a regional *cacique* and a regional *suplente* to oversee village decisions throughout the region. Above that level is the *cacique general*: Clementino Berrugati in *Tierra Colectiva* lands and Francisco Agapí in the *comarca*.

These elected and unpaid positions are responsible for native issues, which include almost everything that happens in a native village. Running parallel to and overlapping this hierarchy are the paid Panamanian government positions—representative, legislator and *alcaldía* (mayoral) offices.

When I first arrived in Manené, I had to talk with *Dirigente* Alonzo Guaynora and with his *suplente*, Wilson Carpio.

It feels as if each official is looking for an angle to work on a visitor.

"Why are you here, Martin? What can you offer Manené?"

And sometimes: "How can you benefit me and my family?"

But as with *Cacique* Clementino, when you are a village representative and also the head of a family, then your responsibility is to both.

I planted rice in the hillside fields for two days alongside Wilson Carpio and twenty members of his extended family. Six men pounded holes in the soil using sharpened sticks while the rest of us followed behind dropping rice grains in the holes. They didn't understand why I would want to help plant. This isn't what Carpio and Alonzo intended when they asked me how I might be able to help Manené.

The women wore red, green and yellow rags tied around their heads and draped over their shoulders against the sun. The oldest ones watched me carefully and then whispered amongst themselves. I would bend over to drop in the grains and brush loose dirt over the hole with my fingers. When the women plant, they keep a small basket of rice tied to their waist with a thin vine. For them, it's a simple wrist motion from waist height. They push dirt over the rice with their toes as they step forward to the next hole. They don't bend over, yet every grain finds its target so that birds don't see scattered rice and come to dig out the rest.

I planted another day with Alonzo's family and then I went to work with Ortega. He waited too long before burning his field this year. The rainy season had already started and the wood was damp when he set the fire. Now we have to drag branches off to the side, and all day we climb over partially burned logs and stumps. My back

Manuel Ortega carries his son across the river.

aches and my hands are sore when we start to hike back after the first day.

While we're working, Ortega says, "You learn a lot with me. I'm working for you."

I'm too tired to appreciate his joke. Besides, he's not trying to be funny. I doubt if he understands irony.

"Yes. Thank you," I say.

On our hike back to his home we stop and Ortega fells a fifty-foot tree. After cutting it into seven-foot lengths, we each hoist a section on one shoulder and carry it back for firewood, leaving the rest for future trips.

"I'm your guide," Ortega says to me after our second day working his field.

We're standing in the sun, tired and dirty and exhausted.

"You're lucky to have met me."

His face is serious when he says this. I don't think he understands why I'm smiling.

57

Harold Baker—alias Perú—was a large white man. He dressed in the traditional Emberá loincloth, the *guayuco*, and he painted his body with *jagua* dyes.

Perú arrived on the Rio Balsas in the early 1960s and he stayed in Darien for about ten years. Chocó villagers still talk about him. The Emberá say that his father was an American admiral (it's never just a sailor) and his mother a Peruvian. He spoke nine languages. He lived alone, and ate only vegetables. He knew the Bible from beginning to end, and he studied stars and made complicated mathematical calculations to predict the future.

Harold Baker saw that the road from Panama City was entering Darien. Oil companies began drilling exploration wells. Others came to cut timber, and landless *colonos* followed behind, bringing their cattle to graze on the new clearings. Perú anticipated the growing conflict as land-hungry Panamanians arrived from other provinces and a steady stream of Colombians flowed across the mountains.

The Chocó didn't know how to respond or how to approach government officials for help. Most of them had no education. They couldn't read or write, and they barely spoke Spanish.

Perú encouraged them to move into villages and to demand schools and health services and electricity. He helped the people in Manené to develop a hierarchy of leadership. He told them that they had to join together to protect themselves and their land.

Harold Baker fulfilled the role of the great white foreigner arriving with knowledge, power and influence. Although he didn't have much money of his own, he was somehow able to find supplies for Manené. He is famous for travelling to the city, apparently without a penny on him (travelling "clean" is the local term), and returning to the village with boxes full of medicine, or pallets of cement, or food, or clothing, and even a diesel generator that once worked in the centre of Manené.

"Harold Baker would hook it up to a two-way radio," Manuel tells me. "And he would talk to people and presidents around the world. 'Oh, these Emberá need your help, and Panama's president does nothing for them,'" Manuel says, repeating what he remembers. "And then a helicopter arrived with food and medicine ... everything we needed."

Geronimo, the Emberá elder, is sitting with us.

"These people climbed out of the helicopter, all bent over," Geronimo says, waving his good arm in the air like a helicopter blade turning slow and heavy overhead.

"They started looking for the man that they had talked to on the radio. In their languages. Nine languages he spoke. But we were all standing in a row, and no one said anything until Perú finally stepped forward, wearing the *guayuco* and the necklaces with animal teeth, and his face and body painted with *jagua*."

"Harold Baker?" they asked. "Is that you?"

58

In her book *The Phantom Gringo Boat*, anthropologist Stephanie Kane describes Harold Baker as an "eccentric, former military, missionary, astrologer gone native."

He didn't just come to plant rice and visit. He wanted to live with the natives and enable them to organize and protect their land. In at least two regions, he convinced isolated families to form communities and to demand schools and health clinics.

A village leader told Kane that Panamanian authorities wanted Perú out of Darien, but the Emberá kept watch along the rivers. At the first sound of the National Guard's outboard motor, they would move Baker into the forest until the soldiers were gone.

Cacique Clementino and elders in Manené tell me that after Perú moved to a Chocó village in Colombia, a disgruntled native gave him a slow poison. He died a few months later.

Perú's diesel generator broke down twenty years ago. It sits rusting on a raised concrete slab in front of the school. Villagers sometimes

The diesel generator at the centre of Manené broke down twenty years ago. Now villagers sometimes gather on the platform if the ground is muddy. Often they'll lean on the engine during a long conversation.

gather on the platform if the ground is muddy. They stand barefoot, still holding a machete after working all day in the mountains. Sometimes they lean on the engine during a long conversation.

On one side of the slab, Harold Baker inscribed a passage from the New Testament Book of Luke: "Forgive them, Father, for they know not what they do."

59

In many ways, Darien province doesn't belong to the rest of Panama. The concerns here are distinct from other regions. The Chocó are often more connected with events in Colombia than anything happening in Panama City, and news selection is usually determined by whichever channel they are able to receive on their radio.

Unlike most of the country, the Emberá and Wounaan weren't swept up in General Omar Torrijos's 1968 military coup or in his campaign to repatriate the Canal Zone from the gringos. However, Omar is still the one political name spoken with respect by many natives in the region. Most likely few of them have heard the accusations against Torrijos—that he imprisoned student protestors and tortured them. Or that Father Hector Gallegos was thrown to his death from a government helicopter after organizing a group of peasants. Or that certain dissidents were sent to a penal colony on Coiba Island and beaten daily until they died. Instead, what lingers in Darien is the memory of Omar's charisma. Panama's poor felt that he understood their problems and that he was going to bring about a solution. Twenty-four years after his death, his reputation is still magic in Darien. On billboards, you see him smiling.

When you focus only on the surface events, his thirteen years in power were good ones for the Emberá and Wounaan. Until he arrived, they were losing more and more each year. Torrijos created a national purchasing agreement so that they would have a guaranteed market for their rice and root crops. He pushed ahead with the village formation program, allotting locations for communities along major rivers. He built primary schools, sent teachers to remote villages and introduced a project to train health promoters in each community. Torrijos worked with the Chocó to begin planning their Emberá-Wounaan *Comarca*, and even though it was smaller than they had hoped for and was split into two separate zones, still it helped control the continual loss of land to immigrants.

This year, twenty-four years after a plane crash claimed the life of General Torrijos, his son Martin Torrijos is running for the presidency. Everywhere I travel through *Tierra Colectiva* villages, Chocó residents tell me that this is the man to see their project through. His campaign posters are stapled to the posts of their thatched-roof homes.

When I ask them why they believe in Martin Torrijos, they say, "Like father, like son."

60

Chocó elders often have an Omar Torrijos story to tell. They usually remember meeting the man, shaking his hand, or profiting by one of his programs. When they tell a story about Torrijos, they don't often refer to him as the General, or even as Torrijos. Usually they just say Omar, as if they are referring to an old friend who came to visit their village one day.

"Omar was flying in a helicopter not so far from here," Geronimo tells me one afternoon in Manené.

"In a clearing the pilot saw a group of *cimarrónes*. Well, Omar wanted to land, but they were threatening him, pointing arrows and spears at the open door," Geronimo says. He slides forward on the floor and leans toward me. He loves to tell stories. Some of it he tells in Spanish. When he switches to dialect, Ortega translates.

To win them over, Omar throws out candies until every *cimarrón* has one, and at that point the natives wave him down to land. When he steps out he tries to communicate with them, but they can't understand each other.

"They don't speak," Geronimo says to me.

"They don't speak Emberá?" I ask.

"No. Omar doesn't speak," Ortega says.

I think I understand.

"So the two groups are confused," Geronimo says. "And they get angry and start to threaten the soldiers. Omar digs into his pockets and hands out more and more candies. The pilot has already noticed the problem, and so the blades are turning. When Omar sees a pathway open up, he throws his last handful of sweets into the crowd. Then he runs to the door, and the helicopter lifts off before the *cimarrónes* can reorganize and shoot at him with their arrows."

Isabel whispers something to Geronimo. He nods his head and then turns to ask me something in dialect.

"He wants to know what you would do if you knew where the *cimarrónes* were living," Ortega translates into Spanish.

"I hear it wouldn't be safe for me to go," I say. "That they would want to kill me."

Geronimo nods his head.

"Don't go," he says. "Now they're far from here."

While the Chocó traditionally would stand and fight any tribe that threatened their territory, against the Spaniards they often responded by turning away and abandoning their homes to move even deeper into the forest. This was the start of *cimarronaje*—becoming wild and returning to the forest. It was as if they saw the Spanish scourge as punishment for having accepted European goods into their life. The only way back to freedom was to leave every trace of that evil behind.

By the mid-1900s, Panama's Chocó still talked about *cimarrónes* living at the river headwaters. Some Chocó still do. They point toward the hills on the Colombian border as if it's an impossibly long journey into another world. It looks lush and green and beautiful from here but it isn't very far away. There is really nowhere left for them to run, no wild jungle large enough for a tribe to disappear.

61

When Ortega returns to Puntita, I decide to stay behind and travel a little further upriver. It takes four hours for me to walk from Manené to the last village, Buenos Aires, and when I arrive my shirt and pants are soaked through with sweat. I leave my bag at the home of a man called Chicho, and I go to swim in the river and rinse my clothes.

At Buenos Aires the Rio Balsas is described as *playa*, with just rock and sand on the bottom so that the water is clear and pure. The river is narrow here. It flows over rounded boulders and into back eddies. Canopy trees spread across from both sides and create a pattern of sunshine and shade pockets.

I'm probably the only person in all of Darien who swims so soon after sweating. Locals warn me that it could be fatal. I've heard now eight separate accounts of people who have made this mistake. All of them paid a heavy toll for their foolishness. Usually the cold swim causes permanent paralysis or heart seizure. According to the stories, one man went blind and three others died a short while after the incident.

62

Twelve kids crowd around my hammock in the afternoon, blocking out the cooling breeze. Everyone is coughing. One boy grabs my peeled mango with his dirty hands and takes a bite. Snot rests on the curl of his upper lip. I know he pushed the mango into it. Smiling, he hands back my piece of fruit.

They always thank me. Then they laugh. What am I supposed to do?

From the earliest age, Chocó children can swim like fish. They love to play in fast-moving rivers, even climbing onto drift logs as they float downriver.

63

Chicho is long and thin. His hair is a thick black mop. His brown skin stretches tight so that in the orange glow of a diesel candle I can see shadows under every rib.

At night, his youngest daughter curls up in his lap where he sits on the floor. She brings her school notebook and pencil, and she begins filling the lines with words and letters.

Chicho watches as loops and sticks and crosses appear on her page. Sometimes he'll point at a word. She tells him what it is and he nods his head.

Seven years ago Chicho was sick and dying. He began to cough up blood, and he couldn't get up off the floor. Local teachers and villagers collected money and they sent him first to La Palma and then to Yaviza where he spent nine months receiving treatment for tuberculosis. He's supposed to return every three months.

"But the doctor is gone," Chicho tells me.

"Isn't there another one?" I ask.

"Maybe," he answers, "but we don't have money."

64

If Darien is mentioned in a Panamanian newspaper, it's usually to rehash the story of poverty in the province, or to announce a new development project funded by the United States. During my stay, for instance, the American government provided eighty-two million dollars destined to improve road connections, build a commercial slaughterhouse and encourage business development along the highway.

In a report published by the World Bank, ninety-six percent of Panama's indigenous people live below the study's poverty line. Eighty-six percent of the same group survives in extreme poverty. It states that virtually every indigenous person in a rural indigenous zone lives in poverty.

The formula used to arrive at those numbers states that individuals need a certain monetary wealth to provide the minimum average daily caloric intake in their diet. If individuals living below the study's poverty line were to spend all their available money on necessities, then they might just barely afford sufficient food for themselves and their family, but there wouldn't be enough left for non-food necessities—things such as clothing, shoes and school supplies.

Those people labelled as extremely poor could spend every available penny they had strictly on food and they would still fall short of the minimum intake level. Malnutrition follows, with all the related debilitating effects.

I wonder about those numbers and the story they tell.

Everywhere I travel in Darien I can see that people have no money. They want to buy food and tools and clothing, but there is so little wage work available. When there is work, the pay is impossibly low. If a man works a full physical day for another man, clearing a field with his machete and axe, he'll earn less than what a high school student in Canada is paid for an hour of flipping burgers in a fast-food restaurant.

However, while there is almost no cash work available in the *comarca*, there is food: rice, green plantains and root crops including *ñame*, *yuca*, *ñampi*, and *papa chino*. In season there are oranges, bananas, mangoes, grapefruit, avocados, watermelons and other foods to eat or sell. Some families grow tomatoes or peppers, although most villagers don't seem overly interested in vegetables other than onions. On the lower river reaches, fishing with nets for the fat *corvinas* is good. Higher up, small boys pull out the bony *huakúko* fish, and they hunt for wild game in the mountains.

Sometimes it seems as though the poverty microscope focusses so narrowly on what money can buy that it misses the glaring necessities of life. During the dry season in many isolated villages, potable water becomes more precious than cash and employment. Babies die from water-borne parasites, and communities fight with new immigrants who cut down the protective forest around the only flowing water source. One percent of that eighty-two-million-dollar gift from the US could have guaranteed clean, healthy drinking water to every village and every house in Darien. There would have been plenty of money left over to build the slaughterhouse near the highway.

65

At night when Chicho's family hang their mosquito nets from the rafters in the new house, I set up my tent on the rough-sawn planks that serve as flooring. To cut the floorboards, Chicho bought a used chainsaw with money from his son working in Panama City. The son also sent out thirty-six sheets of zinc roofing.

Like their traditional Emberá home next door, there are no walls on this new one. The floor is built on posts, almost nine feet off the ground. The boards clatter when you walk on them because Chicho doesn't have money for nails. And while metal sheets will last for twenty years, the family still spends their days in the old house because the palm roof keeps the air so much cooler in the afternoon.

A light breeze drifts through the netting tonight. Earlier, the children came over to help me with the tent but now they settle down in their beds. Chicho's home grows quiet. The village is peaceful.

In unison the cicadas stop screaming, and I can hear the croaks of a cane toad (*Bufo marinus*) and the Rio Balsas running fast and clear.

Later, after a *baracoco* bird sings her lonely scale of notes, Chicho begins his hollow, rasping cough that goes on and on through the early part of the night.

CARAJO!

66

A Chocó dugout canoe has the lines of a woman's body with long and slender curves. Otilio tells me that the bow point is the *piragua's* ass. The inner V lining the ass is the vagina. The dugout's flat bottom is its lower back, the sides are the rib cage, and the stern point where the man steers is the boat's nose.

The piragua *dugout is fast and beautiful to paddle.*

Both ends of the hull taper to a rounded point in the water, but the topsides widen and flatten out to form a curled platform at bow and stern. Even tied off to the bank, a *piragua* looks as though it's running fast through the water.

Only ten years ago it was common to paddle and pole a dugout between Manené and La Palma. It took two or three days each way. Now there are only a couple of families in the village who make the trip without an outboard motor. They're considered to be poor and unfortunate rather than purists.

67

When Ortega's wife hears about my plan to paddle from Manené, she tells me that I can't go alone.

A neighbour says that the *piragua* I bought is made for rivers, and that I shouldn't try the final stretch across the gulf to Cavimál. He says that I need a bigger boat and an outboard motor.

One-armed Geronimo looks worried, but he doesn't try to stop me.

"Can you swim?" he asks.

"Like a fish," I lie to him.

He nods his head.

Emberá prefer to stand in a dugout when they paddle, even in the smallest canoes that are as stable as a ten-foot log stripped smooth of its branches.

The floor of my dugout is slick with a film of wet algae. Even when I take a wide stance I can't stop my feet from sliding.

"Maybe I'll try kneeling until we get going," I say over my shoulder to Jesús, a young Emberá who has offered to give me a lesson on the river. But he doesn't hear me. Or it doesn't register. It wouldn't make any sense to him for a man to want to kneel in a *piragua*.

As I turn around to repeat my suggestion, he pushes the boat out of the eddy and into the current. The river grabs the bow and we bank hard to the right. Jesús is expecting this to happen. He's done this since he first learned to walk. My feet slip out and fly into the air, and I crash down on the floor. I drop the pole overboard but recover it before it floats away.

This happens again and again. I fall twice in the boat and four times into the river. I spend less time poling than I do swimming in the rapids. Each time when I look up, Jesús is standing in the stern. He smiles, but he doesn't laugh out loud.

On our return downriver he puts me in the stern to assess my steering skills. I immediately run the canoe onto a shallow boulder where the current shoves the bow up high and swings the dugout around so that we're racing backwards through whitewater. I dig my paddle in and try again and again to pivot the boat, but nothing works. As we slide sideways over a shallow bar of gravel, I hear Jesús laughing out loud. From behind, I can see his body shaking. I don't fully recover control until we enter the deeper section at Manené.

"You'll be fine," he says when we tie off at the village.

The riverbank is lined with spectators. Women are whispering back and forth amongst themselves. They do this a lot.

"No problem," I assure them as I walk by, water dripping from my hair and down my glasses. "Jesús says I'll be fine."

My shorts and T-shirt are soaked through. Manuel's son takes my paddle and we walk together up the pathway to his house.

68

In the morning Jesús joins me for the first leg downriver. His father and two other Emberá men are facing charges for killing twenty mountain pigs in the National Park with the intention of selling the meat in La Palma.

It rains off and on as we paddle past Galilea, Llano Bonito and Pueblo Nuevo, and begins to pour as we reach Tucutí. Jesús's father and the other two Emberá stand under an overhang at the police station, scuffing their feet on the sidewalk outside.

Last night the police captain at Manené coached the Indians to admit to the charges. "Don't try to defend what you did," he said each time they started to slant the telling of their story. "Just ask for leniency," he told them. "Tell them that you don't have any money, and that your family needs you."

But the Chocó are natural storytellers. When we arrive, one man says, "We sure learned our lesson. Everyone is frightened in Manené." (Which means: You don't have to make an example of us.)

He says it loud enough so that everyone at the station can hear.

"We know we made a mistake," the second in line says. "*Now* we know. It's clear," he says, inserting the idea that it might possibly be a case of an honest mistake. A situation in which three illiterate Indians hadn't been able to read the rule book.

The Tucutí police at the station listen to the men, but at first they don't respond.

The third man in line picks up on the new defence angle.

"We know now," he says. Then he adds, "But when you don't know..."

He shrugs his shoulders and opens his hands in a *what-can-you-do?* gesture.

"You knew," the black sergeant from Tucutí says, cutting them off and putting an end to their game. He's easily as big as two of them together.

Manené's police captain doesn't defend the Indians at that moment, but later, thanks to his help, they're sentenced to only fifteen days of community work. The police return their boat and motor and rifles, and a guard rounds up three dull machetes and tells the Indians to start clearing the field around Tucutí's boat landing.

They look like three boys in the school hall after discovering that the strap wasn't such a big deal after all. They don't look up. They're not sure if it's too early to smile. They sharpen the blades by honing them over a large rock and then they spread out on the field and begin long, powerful, arcing strokes so that the grass is floating everywhere, hanging like soft focus and mist overhead.

Jesús's father lets go a throaty whoop that the Emberá use when they're working hard.

He calls out, "Come on, men. Let's clear this field."

They reach out further with each perfect swing of the blade, and I can see the tension melting away.

Up above by the railing, a police officer hands his rifle to a large woman. She props the rifle up so that the stock sits comfortably on her massive hip. What do these guards expect? That someone will try to bust out of community service hours and they'll have to gun the criminal down?

Twenty-five locals from Tucutí spread out along the railing. Other people sit in groups on the hillside like tiny picnic gatherings. They talk amongst themselves and watch the men work.

Jesús frowns, and he hangs his head.

"Why are they all here?" he asks. "Don't they have anything better to do?"

69

I continue alone downriver.

Since Tucutí, my stomach has been churning. I try to ignore it but later I can feel the first flush of a fever. By the afternoon my burps taste like sulphur and I realize that I have stomach parasites.

I also finally realize that the Chocó are right about the standing position in a *piragua*. It is the most comfortable way to travel. Or it would be if my paddle wasn't so short. By the time I reach the Wounaan village, my back and arms ache.

At Chuletí, *Dirigente* Santos insists on calling a village meeting so that I can be formally presented. He uses a piece of rusty rebar to bang on a suspended steel rim. Old women climb down from their homes, and men hike in on the trails. While he waits, Santos puts the finishing touches on a new yellow-pine paddle. By the third call, twenty minutes later, the room is almost full.

I chose the small tributary to Chuletí because I was sick and needed a safe place to sleep. I'm just starting to realize that they expect me to announce a plan for a development project. No foreigner comes to Chuletí to sightsee. They're sure that I must be launching a study of animals or presenting a proposal for a health project, or a potable water system, a co-operative venture or something like that. It doesn't make sense to them that I would be here for pleasure.

Santos turns to me and says, "Okay, Martin, everyone is here. Tell them why you are in Chuletí."

Imagine if this happened every time you felt like going for a drive. You're on a short vacation and you stop for a meal or a room. When you go into a shop to buy ice cream, someone rings the church bell and the entire town gathers to hear your intentions for the weekend.

My fever is rising and my stomach is churning and gurgling. Perspiration rolls down my chest and back, soaking my shirt and pants. I must look desperate. I clench up my loose bowels and I say something about the tourism project I've been discussing with the Emberá in Manené, but that only makes things worse.

"Always Emberá!" the *dirigente* complains. "They run the *Tierra Colectiva*. They control the *comarca*. They get all the projects."

"And our weaving and carving is better than their work. They learn from us!" a woman shouts.

She's right. *Dirigente* Santos is probably right too. I don't really care. I just need to lie down and fall asleep. I have nothing to offer the people of Chuletí.

I buy a *bejuco* basket to carry thirty mangoes and two pineapples and I buy the paddle from Santos. It's over six feet long. It feels good in my hands.

I collapse in a hammock at Santos's house, and I eat their rice and fish.

Santos's wife tells me that her family still paddles to La Palma if they don't have money for gas or if the motor is broken. I think that Chocó women see more clearly than the men what a family sacrifices for the convenience and speed of a motor. I don't want to use my outboard because I like to hear birds singing. I like to surprise a caiman or a peccary or a capybara at the water's edge, but to a Chocó male, a motor is essential. It is a necessary tool and a symbol of his strength and ability. A man will work for years and save every penny that could go toward so many other things. His children might have to move to Panama City to find work and send money home. A father will split up his family to have a motor and a zinc roof. Afterwards, the cost of fuel and maintenance will take up what is needed for flour and oil and clothing and school supplies. But a man feels as though he is a failure if he can't provide his own outboard.

A woman understands all of this.

70

After sunset, Chuletí becomes a nightmare of mosquitoes. They pile thick on the surface of my tent screen. As soon as I lie down, my stomach churns again. Four times that night I have to open the zipper and run through the dark to squat in the bushes.

Bats dart and flit in front of my face. I wrap my head in a shirt and leave my ass out to get chewed. Even worse, I partially soil myself. Then again, there really isn't anything partial about shitting your pants. Either you did or you didn't.

71

Carajo!

I can hear Aldo's voice from a half-mile upriver. To be fair, there's a light breeze helping the sound along. But he never talks. He shouts everything, and it's always with an exclamation mark.

Carajo!

Again. It's the only word I can make out from the distance.

Aldo lives alone in a black shack beside an abandoned sawmill. At least it looks black with the paint peeling off the mouldy walls and porch.

The sun is about to set, and I can barely lift my paddle. My fever swings back and forth so that I'm either shivering or sweating. My bowels are empty. I have nothing left inside.

Carajo! (Ka-rá-xo!) If you want to use the expression on your own, here's how it goes:

The first syllable is a little longer than the others. It's like stretching out a slingshot. Then it explodes with the second syllable. It fires out, hard and aggressive, so that the "r" almost rolls, but then it growls instead—a little bit or a lot, depending on your mood. The last syllable is a super-hard "h" that you force up from down deep, a guttural "h" that verges on the point of coughing up phlegm.

Carajo!

It's like *Damn!* or *Hell!* Or like *Crikey!* if we still used that, but with an edgier feel to it.

By the time I reach Aldo's muddy landing, the daylight is fading. My fingers fumble with the bowline when I tie off to a boulder. Another Latino and his two sons have also stopped at Aldo's to wait for the tide to change and carry them further upriver to Camogantí. I can hear them talking on the lopsided porch where Aldo spends his days watching the Rio Balsas.

A month earlier while I was travelling with a group of Emberá natives, I stayed at Aldo's home. That night he told me he was still holding out for his last paycheque from the sawmill. He's been waiting for two years. He showed me his notebook with the dollar amounts owed to him since the lumber company declared bankruptcy. He knows that if he leaves he'll never get the final payment. At night he chases off thieves with his shotgun. During the day, he calculates the hours spent guarding tools, hoping that the future owners will recognize his time and commitment and, at the very least, pay him his final two weeks' wages.

When I offer a bag of food and provisions to Aldo, he first looks into the bag and then back at me.

"*Y eso?*" he asks, handling the bottle of cooking oil, the bag of rice, the sugar, coffee, onions, garlic and canned sauce.

"It's for you," I say. "To replace the food you cooked for us last month."

For a moment it looks as though he might start to cry. Then he turns and takes the food into his shack where a diesel candle smokes and flickers. Aldo shouts at us while he cooks two cups of rice, three *huakúko* fish and boiled plantains. When he serves it, I can barely manage the bony fish. I'm too sick to eat. I have no appetite and the rice gets stuck in my throat. I'd choke if I tried the plantains.

I really want to fall asleep, but the Latino launches into his stories of conquest.

"That girlfriend was beautiful," he tells Aldo. The Latino is in his late forties and he's talking the same tired machismo stories I hear over and over again.

"I was crazy about her. I put her through high school and bought her a house in La Palma," he says.

"*Carajo!*" says Aldo. "*Bien preparada, ella.*" She's well looked after.

"Yea, but she treated me badly, and she left me in the end."

It's dark on the porch. I sag in my chair with the plate of food resting on my lap. He describes one woman, then another. And they're all *just beautiful.*

"I explained to my wife that she doesn't have to worry about this *calentura*—this fever of mine. I might fuck around, but I'd never leave her," he says.

Maybe because I'm sick tonight, I wish he'd leave and let me listen to the river.

"I'll always have enough money for our sons and her…"

I want to tell him that nobody cares. That he's just a lonely, aging middleweight searching for validation.

His two sons sit in the dark while he drones on until the tide finally turns and begins to flood the river again. I watch the beam of his flashlight as they walk down the path to his boat. I hear the outboard start, and then they disappear in the night.

"You haven't eaten anything," Aldo says as he takes my plate. "And you'll never get across the gulf to La Palma. Your canoe is made for rivers," he says. "Not with a paddle. You won't make it."

"I'll leave around 2:30 in the morning," I tell him. "I'll go out with the tide current."

"No. We'll get some gas," he says. "And I'll fix this motor."

Aldo has an old Evinrude in a hundred pieces. It looks as though it's been dismantled for twenty-five years.

"You can leave your *piragua* here. I'll get someone to tow it down."

I might be tempted to change my plan if I thought there was any possibility that he could reassemble the antique motor, resurrect his leaky boat and conjure up five gallons of gasoline. But I know that won't happen. I tell him that my mind is set on paddling.

In his book about the Sahara, Swedish writer Sven Lindqvist writes that "Decisions are nearly always carried out under different conditions from which they are made. Decisions are made at headquarters. They are carried out in the trenches. Decisions are made in Paris, and then carried out in the Sahara."

He says that by poring over maps, drawing lines and creating schedules, the journey can take on a life of its own. It pushes the traveller forward. Long after the original reason and the passion have been forgotten, and even though the clarity of the mission may be lost, the intention will remain. The traveller continues because sometime earlier in Paris he made a decision. Something seemed important then. In the jungle or desert, it often makes no sense at all.

At Aldo's swampy home site, with my tent set up on his porch, at least I'm safe from mosquitoes. Rain drums hard on the zinc roof. I have a fever again and I lie naked in the tent, feeling bouts of sweat come and go and soak the clothes I use for a mattress.

Aldo lies down on his bed in the shack just before midnight. I try to sleep, but twenty minutes later I hear him rattling cups and spoons in the kitchen.

"Do you want some coffee?" he asks.

"No thanks," I answer. "I think I'll just sleep for a while," I say from the tent.

We go through the same routine at 1:00.

"There's no moon," he says. I don't answer.

A long pause.

"You'd be crazy to go out in this rain at night."

I wish I wasn't sick. I just want to sit up and drink coffee and talk all night with Aldo. This Colombian transplant. This survivor, woodcutter, mechanic, sharpshooter and rainforest raconteur.

He doesn't go back to bed. At 1:30 I accept his third offer of coffee. I crawl out to feed the mosquitoes, and we sit in the dark on his porch.

This is the second time I've stayed in his cabin, but it's the first time in my experience that Aldo isn't shouting.

"I have a girlfriend in La Palma," he tells me.

Silence. We sip our coffee from enamelled tin cups.

"She was supposed to move out here, but someone said that she's burning me."

Silence. Coffee. I can hear the river slowing.

"They say that she's living with Luis … the guy that fishes off Punta Bruja. He stops by here sometimes and gives me fish."

I'm too weak to do anything except listen and drink my coffee.

"It's still a long trip to La Palma," he says.

This shack on the river might be a good place for a writer. It's a wide and open section of the river. There's plenty of space and light, and you can see storms rolling toward you across the hills.

Aldo has at least thirty mango trees, and I love mangoes. They might be my favourite fruit.

I could probably write here. I think about that while I sit with Aldo.

I can't see anything through the blackness tonight. I can't see the river or the trees.

I slip while I'm bailing out the *piragua* and loading my basket and bags. The rain has tapered off but it hasn't stopped. It still comes in shifting mists and light showers so that by the time the boat is ready, my clothes are soaked through. I feel mud squeezing up between my toes at the landing. I'll have to paddle hard at first to warm my body.

Aldo is standing beside me but I can't see him in the dark. He explains how to use a fat balsa pole to spear a crocodile through the mouth if I'm attacked.

"They'll try to knock you out of the dugout," he says.

And then he tells me to hug the shore. And that I should spend tomorrow night at Chepigana. He shares a few other gems of wisdom, but both of us know that the tide has peaked and the river is turning around.

Aldo fills my mug with a sugary coffee that mixes with rainwater as I head out in the current toward the gulf.

PHOTOGRAPHS

Ishmael *lies anchored near Mercadeo on the Tuira River.*

Above: Anchored on the Sabanas River at sunset: the air is still and the roars of howler monkeys echo from the surrounding forest.

Left: Kathy walks under aerial roots in a mangrove swamp.

THE DARIEN GAP

Above: Autemio sets fire to the slashed hillside to prepare the land for planting rice.

Right: A merchant unloads his shipment of new bicycles from a cargo boat on the Sambú River.

PHOTOGRAPHS

The deck crew of the cargo boat Doña Flor *prepares to depart through the surf line at Jaque for their return trip to Panama City.*

Above: After a few days without rain, the Pan-American Highway to Yaviza is open again.

Left: Homes of Latino residents in Yaviza are more enclosed and brightly painted than Chocó homes in Darien.

THE DARIEN GAP

Water arcs from the bow as the outboard motor pushes our dugout up the Balsas River.

PHOTOGRAPHS

For fifteen months my home is in Cavimál, living in a bohio, *a shack built on a hillside covered with corn and pineapples and fronted by mango and coconut trees.*

Above: Autemio and Diana, my Wounaan hosts at Cavimál, fish for corvina *at Punta Bruja.*

Left: The battle with leafcutter ants and other insects that attack my garden is an endless, and often futile, battle.

THE DARIEN GAP

Manuel's wife Tranquilina prepares a meal in her kitchen at the Emberá village of Manené.

Above: Jagua *dyes decorate an Emberá boy at Manené.*

Right: To prepare for a formal photograph, this Emberá woman applied makeup, borrowed a bra and adorned herself and her child with necklaces made from old silver coins.

PHOTOGRAPHS

A quiver of dugout canoes floats in the current on the Tuira River at Capetí.

THE DARIEN GAP

Above: Alfonso paddles from Isla Caledonia to the mainland, where we begin our hike across the continental divide.

Right: Alfonso and Aristotle, the Kuna guides who led me through the mountains, cross the Sucurtí River on a quiet stretch before the flood.

THE NEW POLITICS

72

"Oh, viene Martin!" Martin comes!

I can hear Otilio approaching through the mango trees as I reach the shore with my dugout.

"We heard the news!" He calls out as if I'm a mile away. "We heard the sad news!"

Tomorrow I'll have to hike to the clinic for medicine, but right now I just want to collapse in my hammock. I'm exhausted, and I'm feeling sorry for myself. And what is this sad news that Otilio is moaning about? I know that his son Bill was sick in Panama City. Did he die? Do they need money to go to the city, or to bring the body back, or what? I'm just guessing, but I want to at least touch land before anyone asks me for money.

The tide is at the midpoint and I run aground a hundred feet from the gravel beach. I have to drag my baskets on shore through the deep mud.

"Ai, Martin. Llegaron las noticias tristes." The sad news arrived.

He reaches my pile of bags and baskets.

"Yes, it arrived," I say. "Yes, yes."

I'm just going to carry everything up to the house. I know that any decent human would say, "What news!? What's the sad news!? Tell me!" But I don't. I'm not decent today. I'm tired out. I just want to drag my belongings up the hill.

Otilio tries to show me that he's crying. He starts to rub his eyes whenever I look his way. He does it three times. I pretend not to notice. I don't ask about the sad news. I make three trips up and down the hill for my backpack, the two paddles and my baskets. I dump my muddy bags on the porch and I collapse in the hammock.

I can see that the corn is in worse shape than before. Leafcutter ants never rest and now some sort of aphid is taking a run at my second batch of tomato plants. That's all I notice before I fall asleep in the afternoon.

When I wake I'm sweating from the fever, but the air is cooler. It's still light outside and when I look around I can see that the Tovars have built a new house at the opposite end of the clearing. I see a lot of changes. There are sheets of zinc roofing scattered along the beach. Near the new house I see a fridge and a stove under a tarp. There's at least one new pig wandering around. I've been gone for only three weeks.

Just as the light is fading, I walk to Otilio's hut and join Diana and Autemio for supper. Otilio swings in his hammock. Diana serves me a bowl of fish soup, and Autemio says, "Bill moved back here from Panama City."

"Is he still sick?" I ask.

"No, he's pretty good."

They tell me that Bill and his wife have come to stay. And that another brother, Bernardo, has also arrived with his wife and three kids. If you count the pig, Cavimál's population has tripled in less than a month.

More unexpected news. Tovar has decided to run for La Palma's *representante* nomination in the upcoming Democratic Revolutionary Party (PRD) primaries. Stranger yet, he has stopped drinking. He's been visiting Mogue and other Chocó communities and he says that he has a lot of support.

No one died, I realize. That's a relief.

How can I be so selfish? How can I do that?

"What's the sad news?" I ask Otilio, but he doesn't answer. He's sitting in his hammock, facing away from me.

"We thought you were hurt," Autemio answers. "We thought you were in trouble. While you were away the police came in a boat and asked us questions about you. They wanted to know what you were doing and if you were paying us money."

Kuna and Chocó can be generous and accommodating, but they don't share information unless they have a good reason. Autemio told the police that he didn't know why I was living in Cavimál—which might even be true. He has a hard time understanding why I want to plant rice and corn here when I could earn a decent wage in my own country.

I see Otilio in the dim light from the kerosene lantern. He nods his head. Eventually he turns around to face us.

"They didn't tell us why they wanted to know. They just took pictures of your place, and they went away," Autemio says.

So that was the sad news. That was why Otilio was rubbing the tears from his eyes.

I'm such an ass.

73

Later, on the following day, I ask Autemio if he has made enough money for the first motor payment.

"That's not my business anymore," he tells me.

"But we have an agreement," I say. "You've used the boat and motor for three months of fishing…"

"You have to talk to Bill," Autemio says. "It's his business now." Autemio looks away. I can tell this is uncomfortable so I decide to see how things unfold.

This is the third time Autemio has assured me that he will come through with the first one hundred dollars. I still don't have a penny, and I'm getting worried that at the end of the trip I'll have to unload the boat and motor for a fraction of their worth. I'm counting on that money to pay for my trip home.

The next evening when Bill walks over, we talk about his move to Cavimál. His leg is still swollen. He says that he plans to buy the motor—with or without Autemio's help—for eight hundred dollars before I leave at the end of the year. He assures me that Autemio still wants to buy the boat.

Bill apologizes that they had to spend most of his savings to make the move back to Darien, but he gives me eighty-four dollars—a ten-dollar bill, twenty-one singles, and 212 quarters.

I thank him and we write it down in a notebook. Bill says he'll be selling the fridge and stove, and that if Tovar wins the primary nomination, he'll have extra money to help as well.

Por cierto. For sure. There'll be two hundred dollars when I come back from my next trip.

74

Late one afternoon, I meet Manuel Ortega's stepbrother Clementino, the chief (*cacique general*) of the *Tierra Colectiva* project. He's repairing his dugout on the beach at La Puntita. When I arrive, he sets down his adze and he tells me that a cold soda is a good thing to have on a hot day, if you can afford to buy one.

Two days later I see him again in La Palma. He wants to call his office in Panama City to arrange for a fuel voucher so that he can make a trip to outlying communities, but he doesn't even have coins for the pay phone. Clementino tells me that the problem is that the project has a lot of outstanding debts at fuel docks.

Two days after that, Clementino calls me over as I'm paddling back to Cavimál. I enter his house and he offers me a seat. He has a soft face. His skin is lighter than most Chocó and when we shake hands, I'm surprised at how smooth his palm feels.

Clementino gives me a map outlining the surveyed regions that *Tierra Colectiva* is attempting to protect for the Emberá and Wounaan living outside the *comarca*. He says that the nomadic life is over for the Chocó people and that they have to work together to protect the small parcels of land that they now use for planting,

In the late afternoon at Mercadeo, after our boat trip from La Puntita, Chief Clementino Berrugati (left) bathes in the Tuira River.

hunting and gathering. He wants to hold meetings at a number of villages but his outboard isn't working.

"Our 25-horsepower engine is damaged," he says. He shows me the cost estimate for four hundred dollars of repairs—rings, valves and bearings. "Maybe you can help us with this," he says.

The motor is dismantled on his porch in the same spot it was two months earlier when I first met his half-brother Manuel. The cost estimate is dated from almost a year ago.

"We want to go to Mercadeo for a meeting," he says. "And my friend Mario Cabrera is campaigning for the PRD nominations in that region."

I tell him that I'll go with them. We can use my boat and motor for the week, and while we're gone Autemio can fish with his small dugout. If I stay upriver and travel further, Clementino can come back with the boat and return it to Cavimál.

"Or we can store it here," Clementino suggests.

"No. Autemio will pick it up. He needs it to fish," I say.

Autemio and Otilio don't trust the Emberá natives from Balsas River. They told me not to let them use the outboard. Autemio says that they'll swap the coil and electronic parts for old ones and we'll be left with a used-up motor.

There are so many levels of distrust in the Darien, I'm now developing my own healthy dose of the same. Sometimes I even wonder about Autemio. He asked me once if I was marking the engine parts so that I'd know if they were changed. He said he was looking at them and they all appeared to be marked.

Why was he looking for marked engine parts?

Autemio lived for a year in Panama City. To earn money, he pedalled a three-wheel cycle with a cargo platform carrying two big drink coolers. He spent all day breathing exhaust fumes, riding around Panama's congested streets selling *chicha* for ten cents a glass. Until he had saved enough to buy his own *chicha* cycle, Autemio worked for a middleman who paid him less than five dollars a day. To make ends meet, Autemio sold drugs. He stole things. He helped circulate counterfeit twenty-dollar bills. He says he bought a .38 revolver and had to use it twice.

"We'll also need thirty gallons of gas," Clementino says.

"What about *Tierra Colectiva* funds?" I ask.

"They don't have any money left for fuel," he answers.

I don't know if that's true. I don't imagine that it is. But I want to sit in on his meeting, and it would be good to have a host and guide.

"I'll pay half," I say, and we shake hands again.

75

I have to bail out the boat with a plastic cup as we travel upriver. Water is seeping through pinholes left by wood-boring insects in the hull. By the time we notice the problem, Clementino's bag of clothes is already wet.

"Martin," he asks me after inspecting the wet clothes, "do you like beer?"

"Sometimes," I answer. "I used to like it a lot, but now it's just once in a while."

"I can't work without it," he tells me. "We have to get more in El Real."

The wind flattens Mario's hat brim against his forehead. He has the throttle wide open. They don't care how much fuel we burn.

76

In Mercadeo, we lean our bags against a post and lie down on the floor to sleep through the late afternoon until the villagers begin to arrive.

There aren't any lights in the shelter. When the sun sets and the sky turns dark, someone runs a power cord from a neighbour's generator. They tape the bare wires to a 25-watt bulb, and one by one people begin to appear. By 7 p.m. there are twelve men and two women sitting on the floor. Three more arrive at 7:30, and Clementino decides that we have a quorum.

The *cacique* talks quietly, but Chocó are natural speakers and storytellers. It's a pleasure to hear his voice. He reads verbatim a letter sent to ANAM—the Ministry of Environment—proposing that land title be granted to *Tierra Colectiva* in regions where Chocó villages existed before the National Park was established on top of them. He flips through folders labelled Law #41, Law #2, Law #17 and Law #6. Each one is flagged and highlighted with a yellow marker. He reads passages by the glow of the single light bulb, and then he opens the response letter from ANAM.

Clementino reads this also verbatim. He starts with their home address and the date, the mailing address and the few lines of formal flattery and introduction that preface most letters in Latin America.

More people arrive. They swat at mosquitoes. Women nurse their babies. A man flashes a light at any noise in the forest, but everyone hangs on Clementino's words. When he reads these dry texts from bureaucrats, the Emberá villagers stay focussed. No one is impatient to leave. They listen to the letters written and read in Spanish, which is their second language. These letters come from a world that is so remote from their reality of subsistence fishing and hunting that it is impossible to comprehend. They have sick children at home and there is no money for a visit to the doctor or for medicine. Their rice and plantain crops have been attacked by a plague of insects. Mercadeo doesn't even have a source of potable water.

The *Tierra Colectiva* project has been struggling for twelve years, and while they've surveyed the proposed land parcels, they haven't won anything from the Panamanian government. Still, somehow, the Chocó believe that this is a game they can learn to play and win. This land is all they have. It's their home. It provides their food and ensures their future.

Clementino reads and patiently explains each sentence in the response letter from ANAM. It is nothing but standard governmental rejection. It states that according to Law #41, title for land within National Park boundaries cannot be granted to any individual or group.

There's a loud moan from the listeners.

A *Foiled-again! They-got-us-this-time* sort of moan.

However, *Cacique* Clementino doesn't let the flame die. He tells them that if Law #41 is the problem, then it will have to be modified. The others murmur their agreement. It's the only way. Onward. Next order of business.

Where does their belief come from? I don't know if I've ever seen so much faith in the political process. Maybe it will take another few generations to develop a cynical attitude.

The discussion shifts to how to arrange for identification cards for those natives who still have no documents. Clementino explains that without a government *cédula* they can't vote. They discuss laws governing native rights to cut trees and hunt within Darien National Park for personal use.

When Clementino mentions the Panamanian government's refusal to recognize *Tierra Colectiva* hierarchy, he says, "The president says that she'll communicate directly with each village, but not with the regional or general councils. It's as if Canada's government came to talk politics with the mayor of La Palma," he says, turning to me. "but they refused to respect the country's president."

He doesn't shout. He's quiet and measured. He doesn't have to convince anyone in this group that they're at risk of losing their land and homes. Their situation is more precarious every year. Roads improve. Logging companies make direct deals with small villages and then strip the hillsides clear. The contracts aren't always paid in full, and only rarely do the companies complete their replanting obligations. Villages often squander their money, ending up in the same economic straits as before, only now without their forest.

"They just want to divide us, and bit by bit take the land and resources," he tells the Chocó from Mercadeo. "We have to stick together."

At the meeting a small girl arrives crying. She asks her father to come home and put her to bed. The meeting continues. The father lays her down on the floor and he rolls his shirt under her head. He uses a notebook to fan her and chase the mosquitoes away. He rubs her bare back and shoulders and strokes her hair until she falls asleep.

77

Mario Cabrera speaks at each of the meetings. He's campaigning to represent the PRD for this part of the Tuira and Balsas rivers in the national elections. He has next to nothing to fund his campaign. He asks me if I have any millionaire friends that might be interested in helping him.

One of his front teeth is broken and jagged, but he can't afford to fix it. With the campaign schedule he hasn't had time to clear land

and plant rice this year. I don't know how he'll feed his family if he loses either the primaries or the election.

We stay overnight in Mercadeo. Clementino holds another meeting at a nearby village the next afternoon, but I can barely keep my eyes open in the heat under the metal roof.

Someone kills a snake that is attacking a chicken. A mangy dog with open sores climbs the *tumé* and sits down beside me to lick his wounds.

78

The consensus in Darien is that Martin Torrijos and his PRD party will sweep Panama's upcoming federal elections. The primary runoffs feel more like election day than just a party selection ballot.

In both the *comarca* and *Tierra Colectiva*, Chocó officials are encouraging their people to vote in block for indigenous representatives in the PRD primaries to counter the non-native votes in Camogantí and Tucutí. No one else is going to promote the *Tierra Colectiva* project for them.

In Darien, distrust of others is a defining feature. It divides and debilitates the population along Rio Balsas and all across Darien. And it isn't restricted to Chocó people. It divides along race lines: Chocó vs. *kampunía*, Emberá vs. Wounaan. It pits a family against their neighbour. One village against another. *Comarca* against the *Tierra Colectiva*. It isolates groups based on wealth and language, or political power.

There are always exceptions, but I think that when disparate groups or individuals work together in Darien, a common good is often the secondary goal. That seems to be the situation on the day before the PRD primaries in Manené.

Two local Emberá men are on the ballot for the position of regional *representante*. They both want the position, but if they split the native vote it's unlikely that either of them will win. It isn't until the last minute, as the five native Balsas communities are gathered for their last instructions, that the native pre-candidate named Badillo arrives with a black man from Tucutí and presents him to the group.

Globys Blanco is running *against* the Emberá Mario Cabrera for the *alcaldía* position. Globys stands at least a foot taller than most of the native men at the meeting. Even though his shorts and shirt are old and torn, his flip-flops are falling apart and his teeth look yellow and grungy, he is still able to take control of the meeting. There is an unspoken hierarchy operating in Darien. A black man, often taller and louder and with more money and a larger boat and motor, can usually intimidate a native group.

"Badillo and I have an alliance," Globys tells the group. "I'll deliver the forty votes from my supporters in Tucutí to Badillo," he says. "My supporters will listen to me. But I also need your help for my campaign."

His wife and mother-in-law are giving the same message to his left and right.

"Our voters are serious," his wife says.

"That's politics. That's the way it works," his mother-in-law says, flicking her wrist and hand in the air in a gesture that says, *I've seen it a thousand times before.*

While they spread their message, the sky has opened up and a tropical rain begins pouring down outside our shelter. Everyone is sucking on the homemade popsicles that Globys brought. The kids have started a soccer game in the mud using a grapefruit for a ball. It feels like a party. Badillo smiles. After introducing Globys to the group, he now stands back and lets his partner do the talking. He doesn't interrupt when Globys misquotes and criticizes their native opponents. Badillo looks pretty certain that he's chosen a winning strategy.

Later, when our group is hiking back to Manené, I ask Badillo if he feels right about siphoning off votes from Mario Cabrera to gain more votes for his own campaign.

Badillo shrugs. "The Emberá will vote for Mario," he says. "They only say they'll vote for the *moreno*"—the black man.

Ortega looks at me, then he turns away.

That's one tricky Indian, I'm thinking.

79

Ortega sits on the floor of his house surrounded by monkey skulls and assorted bones. These were part of the traditional costume he used at the Smithsonian event in Washington. He also painted his body and wore a *guayuco* loincloth and a crown woven from *chunga* palm strips.

Ortega and I are awkward around each other on this visit. It feels as though he's intentionally sabotaging any meetings that I arrange with other people in the village. If they talk to me in Spanish, he'll try to take charge of the conversation, speaking only in native dialect and interrupting anyone who answers in Spanish. Sometimes he shouts until everyone shifts to Emberá.

Ortega's half-brother Santos closed the Puntita store last month and Ortega has moved back to Manené, but there's no work for him here. He has no cash income. The rice we planted is growing well, but some of his neighbours' fields are dying. Manuel worries that his crop might be next.

On an earlier trip I brought some *boronjó* fruit and we saved the seeds and cleared a patch of forest to plant them. Now there are three hundred small trees started, but it will be eight years before they produce fruit to sell. Ortega has a case of cooking oil and a large sack of candies. He has a box with damaged bleach bottles that he salvaged from the store. At night he sits on the porch with Tranquilina and they tear off strips from *chunga* palms. They dye them for weaving, and then they send the bundles to a buyer in Panama City.

"*Ansabidá*," he says. Kingfisher.

"Yes, *Coríbe*," I answer.

"How would it be possible to send my son Crispín to school in Canada to learn English?" he asks.

He doesn't mean just for a month, or even a year. He wants to send his twelve-year-old son away through middle school and on through university.

"I don't know, Manuel."

All he wants is something good for his children.

My savings are running out. Manuel is broke. I know I can go home and earn a good living using my hands and tools and the strength of my back. Ortega doesn't know what to do next. He tells me that Clementino has asked him to go to Panama City to address the Legislative Assembly when *Tierra Colectiva* presents its proposal for second debate. Ortega wants to dress the way he did at the Smithsonian ... with the *chunga* crown, body paint, the loincloth and a necklace of bones and monkey skulls.

"When I go to Panama, I'm going to wear all of this, and I'm going to say, 'Indian people in the villages of Manené, Buenos Aires, Galilea, Llano Bonito and Pueblo Nuevo all pay the government's new sales tax,'" Ortega begins.

When he acts out these anticipated moments, he wears a grave facial expression. His words are formal, and he chooses phrases and a pronunciation that lead you to believe that he's hardly able to speak Spanish.

"The indigenous people support the government in all their projects [he's referring to their participation in election voting and the sales tax], and we ask that the government support us in only this one project ... that they give us the land asked for by *Tierra Colectiva*."

Ortega rehearses all the time for moments like this. He listens to radio news and then he revises certain headlines to fit his themes. At the store in Puntita, he practised his delivery on his neighbours and customers until he was convinced he had it right.

"Indians aren't asking for a raise in government salaries." This is in the news right now.

"No. We don't ask for loans for big business." Also in the news.

I just listen tonight. I don't argue or debate like we usually do. He has no money to send his boys to school in La Palma after sixth grade. There's no cash work in Manené or anywhere else in Darien. He just wants what I already have: a few more options.

80

After the votes are counted, Badillo is still smiling. He wins the PRD nomination for the Rio Balsas *representante,* thanks to the forty-four votes from Globys Blanco's supporters in Tucutí. However, Mario Cabrera loses soundly. Apparently twenty-four of Badillo's Emberá didn't realize his manoeuvre was only a trick. They weren't actually supposed to give Mario's vote to the *moreno.*

81

Ortega takes me through the forest to a sixty-year-old cacao tree—a chocolate tree with its branches stretching out and sagging down to the ground. Rolling lines of ants crawl across the limbs, but the fruit is fine.

A cacao fruit looks like a small orange pumpkin with a pulpy shell and hundreds of seeds enveloped in sweet, translucent meat.

In the afternoon Tranquilina serves a cacao *chicha* made from the fruit. Afterwards we suck the seeds clean and then spit them into a common bowl. Tranquilina spreads them on a tarp to sun-dry for three days before roasting them in a pan over a low fire. Then we crush the seeds with our fingers and a rounded wood pin.

Ortega's wife spreads the powder and chips and shells on a large platter so that she can toss it lightly in the air and let the breeze carry away the chaff. Whatever is left on the platter is then worked twice through a grinder until it comes out like coarse-ground coffee.

From the ten fruits we harvested, Tranquilina makes a dozen egg-sized packets, each wrapped in a leaf and tied with a thin vine. They apologize for having no milk and we mix the cacao with hot water. After that, I'm ruined for life. It is the best chocolate I have ever tasted. They tell me to add more sugar, but I love the sharp edge and bitterness and the heaviness that fills my head and leaves me content.

In the early evening at Ortega's home, after we finished preparing chocolate grounds from the cacao, a border police officer arrives to ask about my plans in Manené. While we talk, Tranquilina shapes a small ball of the chocolate in her hands. She folds a leaf around it, ties it with a thin vine, and as the officer turns to go, she gives the gift to him and wishes him well.

Coríbe. I owe him more than I can repay.

When I leave for La Palma, I give him enough money for the round-trip bus ride from Yaviza to Panama City and the *Tierra Colectiva* presentation.

He mentions that hotels also cost money.

"Stay with your brother Clementino," I answer.

Anticipating his next question, I say, "And take along a bag of rice and some smoked meat for your meals."

82

By the time I return to Cavimál I've been gone for over a month. I notice that Bernardo has dismantled his family house and moved to a new location far from his brothers. You can do that with an

Emberá home. Bernardo and his wife unlaced the palms from the roof and stripped off the poles and flooring. They even pulled the posts out of the ground. I find out later that Bernardo and Bill have been fighting and don't want to be near each other.

Little else appears to have changed. The five chickens and two pigs are bigger than before. I visit with Otilio and the others, we pull weeds in the rice field and still, after two days, no one has mentioned anything about the overdue payment for the outboard motor.

Here's my experience of a financial transaction in Cavimál: First, we make an agreement with a specific date and dollar amount. I travel somewhere while the Tovar brothers fish. When I return, nothing happens. The date arrives and passes by. Nothing is mentioned until a few days later when I ask, "How's the fishing?"

"Always a struggle," Autemio answers. That's all he says.

A pause.

"And the money we agreed on?"

"You'll have to ask Bill," Autemio says.

I walk over to Bill's house and he asks, "What did Autemio say?"

There's always a disaster or emergency that has just occurred. A thousand dollars is an overwhelming amount of money for them. They usually don't have coins for coffee or sugar. A dollar feels large in Autemio's pocket.

On this encounter, they finally admit to me that they lent their earnings to Tovar for his PRD campaign.

"If he had won, he was going to pay the motor off," Autemio says.

When the first deadline passes, we set an alternative one. Then that deadline slips by in silence as well. Invariably I lose my patience at that point. I say something about responsibility and about my need to pay for the flight home. Sometimes I tell them that I'll take the boat and motor to town to recover my money, that they might lose some of the money they've already given me.

I feel like such a pushy bastard. Just another gringo lecturing a native. But the promised two hundred dollars has never materialized.

And apparently they didn't catch a single fish for the two weeks since Tovar's loss. They don't even have sugar or coffee or flour at home. Just green plantains, a bag of rice and brackish water in the well.

That's how it goes.

Usually, a few days later, some of the lost money miraculously reappears. It happens again this time. Bill comes to visit at sunset. We talk for a while about small things, and then he pulls out three tens, thirty-seven singles and 152 quarters.

It's less than what I wanted and it's almost a month late. There's still a lot more to go with only a few months remaining. I write it down in the notebook, and Bill and I make another deal for next month.

At night when I'm alone, I stash the money in a plastic jar and bury it under a rock in my garden.

Tovar never really had a chance in the PRD primary. How could they have dreamed he would win? His own family never registered to vote. The blacks and *colonos* in town know him only as the drunken Indian stumbling through the streets begging money for another bottle. They would never vote for him.

Not even the Emberá villages on Mogue River supported Tovar. He made three visits to Mogue. He brought a pig to roast, bottles of liquor and a barrel of gasoline. They ate and drank and promised him their votes. But they were just tricking him. Nobody voted for him anywhere.

After the primaries, Tovar pulled down the PRD banners from his house and dock. He closed the fuel-shed doors because he'd spent all his money on the campaign. Even the front shutter to his store is closed. All the shelves are bare and he can't afford new inventory.

Now, when he comes to Cavimál, he uses the tide current and a paddle instead of his beloved outboard. He's clean-shaven and sober when I see him in the afternoon. He wears a big straw hat, no shoes on his feet. He's very good with a paddle.

He must have believed it was possible.

83

"Martin. Here's a couple coconuts," Autemio says when he stops at my hut in the evening.

He cuts them open to drink. I like it when he visits alone with no reason in particular. Sometimes he talks about fishing, or his plans to build a new house. Sometimes he complains about living with Otilio. But he's always thoughtful.

"You know, Autemio, I'm just trying to get the money to fly home at Christmas," I say to him. "But am I being rude to you and Bill?" I ask. "Are you angry with me?"

When we finish drinking the coconut water, he splits open the shells for the soft meat inside. Then he slices an oval blade from the shell to use as a spoon.

"Things are probably different here than where you are from," he answers. "Here, when two people make a deal … if a person doesn't have the money because there aren't any fish, or something else happens, then the other person sets a new date. That's all."

I have a hundred protests, but instead I just nod. He's right. That is how business is done in Darien.

BUTTERFLIES

84

On four separate days in four Darien towns—La Puntita, La Palma, Tucutí and Yaviza—black men have stopped me on the street or in a bar and said, "Hey, gringo. I know what you're up to."

Some of these men were drinking. They all looked fairly smug, as if they had seen right through my clever disguise.

"So, what am I up to?" I ask each time.

"You're looking for gold."

They say this as if gold was illicit sex or drugs.

"All gringos want gold. You're all looking for it."

"Actually," I answer honestly, "In Darien, it seems like it's mostly black men looking for gold."

"Ah! Ha ha ha ha ha!" The drunken ones always laugh at that. "I know what you're up to," they say again.

How can I argue with five hundred years of precedent? Since the Spanish arrived, Darien has been a revolving door for treasure hunters. English, French and Dutch pirates, Spanish conquistadors and soldiers, international mining companies, petroleum exploration groups, timber companies cutting down forests and leaving the soil to wash away, and fishing fleets dragging their nets back and forth across the Gulf of San Miguel so that nothing is left for the small fisherman.

Outsiders come to plunder Darien. They usually leave when their pockets are full.

85

Paddling alone up the Tuira River sounded like a good idea yesterday when I was looking at maps in the afternoon. I imagined a paddle in my hands, and the muscles in my back and shoulders satisfied after long hours on the river.

86

Floating in my *piragua* at slack tide, only minutes before dawn. I'm still waiting for the day's first light when a *moreno* from Chepigana arrives at Punta Seteganti. He's suspicious to find me on the water so far from any village. Like me, he left home in the dark. A fisherman likes to believe he's the first man on the water.

His dugout is faded and chipped green. It's rotting and patched with rags jammed in the cracks and tin strips nailed down over layers of roofing tar.

"*De donde viene?*" he asks me. Where are you coming from?

I like that question. Especially in Spanish. It can refer to your nationality, or your trip origin several months back, or just your most recent departure point.

I think he wants to know my nationality, but I answer at the local level instead.

"From La Palma," I say. "From Cavimál."

The second half of the answer is confusing for local people. They think of Cavimál as an isolated hill with pineapples growing and a Wounaan family living in poverty.

Who is this gringo?

He stares at me. Then he glances at the bags and the basket of fruit in my *piragua*.

"Where are you going?"

"To the ruins on the hill," I say. "And you? Where are you going?" I ask.

"I'm fishing." He points his paddle at the nets in his boat.

He tells me that there's nothing left of the old Spanish fort. He says I should fish with him instead. I can't tell if he thinks I would be of some help. He likely suspects that I have a metal detector and I'm looking for gold, or else he's worried for my safety.

I decline his invitation and wish him luck with the fishing.

It frustrates locals when a stranger is set on doing things that don't make sense. They think he might get hurt, or that he's up to some sort of trickery. This happens all the time with me.

"It's all gone," he says again as I turn toward the mangrove channel.

I don't say anything. I just wave and begin to paddle.

"There's just a bunch of rocks," he shouts as I reach the channel mouth.

I thank him over my shoulder and, when I shout back to him, six parrots explode into flight from a branch overhead, squawking and creaking with a sound like rusty bicycles riding hard through the sky.

I love these birds. They're comforting to me. They're awkward and inefficient, beating the air so hard with their wings just to stay in flight. Always in pairs. Always in love. Relentlessly hammering out important issues. Yak, yak, yakking all the way to the horizon, as if the conversation can't wait until they land in a tree again.

87

The ruins of Fort Santa Rita stand at the top of the hill at Setegantí Point. There isn't much here except for a good view and a pile of rocks. The *moreno* was right. I can see him fishing below in the shallows.

Last week Autemio mentioned that a group of people—gringos, he said—had come in a boat and cleaned up the trail and the area around the fort.

I imagine that these gringos were a group of light-skinned

Panamanians from the capital. Maybe university students. We all get lumped together.

"They were probably looking for gold," Otilio mumbled.

Autemio agreed.

"What gold?" I asked.

"The gold the Spaniards kept at the fort," Autemio answered.

Otilio bowed his head and nodded. His posture said, "That is the sad and terrible truth, Martin."

88

Spanish forts in Darien were usually ineffective and vulnerable. Most of them were short-lived. The soldiers built three-foot-thick walls with stones and muddy clay, and windows that tapered from wide openings on the inside to narrow slots to fire at the enemy. However, although the structure was solid, the soldiers used white cane and palms to build interior shelters against the sun and rain. Just one burning arrow could set everything on fire.

For three hundred years from the mid-1500s, fort building followed a predictable cycle. Whenever Darien was peaceful, the Crown recalled the soldiers and abandoned the forts, leaving just a small detachment to guard major gold mines. Timber cutters and other businesses had to look after themselves, and usually everything would remain peaceful for a year or a decade or longer.

Eventually, however, Kuna Indians or black *cimarrónes* would attack the intruders, sometimes killing everyone in a work camp or townsite. At other times, pirates hired blacks and natives to help raid the royal gold mines. They would sail to the Caribbean side and cross the isthmus in groups of two hundred men or more.

After each incident, Panama's governor would send a panicky letter to Spain, and Spain would reissue old orders as if they were something new. The king's orders usually included instructions to contain any rebel groups. Initially Spain tried to forcibly convert the Kunas to Catholicism. When that failed, they ordered soldiers to

The ruins of the Spanish fort at Isla Encanto overlook the narrow entrance between the Gulf of San Miguel and the lower Tuira River. Spanish soldiers built a series of forts throughout Darien to block the traffic of British and French pirates and to stop "wild" Kuna from attacking the few natives who chose to live in the Catholic missions.

burn everything Kuna—tools, homes, canoes, crops and any plants used to make weapons. By the late 1700s and early 1800s many government documents recommended extermination of the natives as the only complete solution.

The Spanish built stronger forts at El Real to protect gold shipments arriving from Cana, and at Santa Fe to monitor cross-isthmus traffic on the major travel route. They constructed one at Yaviza to control the movement of "wild" Kuna coming downstream to raid and kill the converted Kuna living in Catholic missions. They erected smaller forts near La Palma—at Isla Encanto, Isla Boca Grande, and this one at Punta Setegantí—to deter pirates from entering on the Pacific side.

At the end of each long period of instability, the opposing sides would sign another treaty and allow Darien to return to a temporary state of calm. After a short pause, the government troops would pack their belongings and destroy the forts. They burned anything that could be used by other groups, and then they sailed out of the province to deal with problems in other parts of Panama.

That history probably explains the crumbled ruins at Setegantí and the larger ones at nearby Isla Encanto and Isla Boca Grande.

89

After lunch at Setegantí, I launch my dugout again and begin to ride with the Pacific tide as it floods into the Tuira Basin.

This is exactly what I'd been dreaming of doing. Paddling Chocó style, standing in the *piragua* through the afternoon, my bare feet planted on the wood floor and my toes curled up the sides.

Fish break the surface. Sunshine bakes my arms and legs. I drink water from coconuts and eat guavas that I picked near the ruins.

I wish I could be travelling with my younger brother Paul on this river. I've been thinking so much about him this afternoon that I start talking to him while I'm paddling.

BUTTERFLIES | 133

A dugout canoe glides through reflections in a mangrove channel.

"Over there. A blue Morpho butterfly," I say. Or, "Wow, listen to those monkeys." Simple things like that.

Whenever I speak out loud to him this afternoon, I'm surprised that he doesn't answer. I wish he could hear the parrots, or watch a keel-billed toucan sprint across a mangrove channel.

I become hypnotized by the rhythm of the paddle, hardly noticing the hours slip away, until early evening arrives and I still have nowhere to land. The lower Tuira isn't like the river headwaters. The shores here are swampy banks and mangrove channels populated by caimans and crocodiles. I haven't seen any high banks with dry ground where it would be safe to camp for the night.

The hills to the east are turning pink as the sun begins to slip behind the horizon. The flooding tide is about to turn around. It still feels as though Paul is in my dugout, so I'm embarrassed at having planned so poorly. I've done this to him so many times before, yet for some reason he still trusts me. He doesn't know that I'm unsure of what to do, that I'm frightened of the night coming on.

I say, "You should spread the tarp and rest for a while on the *piragua* floor."

Paul doesn't answer. I look and he's not there.

The sky is still clear overhead but I can see rain falling in the mountains. I watch the towering cumulus clouds anvilling off on top, and the lightning strikes walking across the hills toward me. When the flood tide peaks, it barely pauses before turning around to empty back to the sea.

I don't remember when it was that I first traced my finger along a map of the Tuira River. I don't know what seemed so important about solitude, and going my own way, and the feel of the paddle in my hands.

I'm sitting in a moment of intense beauty. A brief moment that will slip away and be gone, and I have no one to share it with.

90

The morning after.

I sit in my dugout, holding onto a tree root protruding from the riverbank. I have no strength left in my body. My clothes are soaked. My back and shoulders ache.

A white ibis stands on one leg and floats by on the back of a driftwood log. He passes so close to my boat that I can see the texture of his pink leg and mud stains on his feathers. He pretends I don't frighten him, but if I moved at all he would fly away.

I look into the ibis's eye, and the ibis looks right back.

Last night I tied off to a submerged tree in the river as the day ended and the tide peaked. If I had been travelling with Autemio or Manuel or anyone who knew anything about Darien and rivers, they would have told me I was making a mistake.

On the lower Tuira, the Pacific tide floods in and out twice each day. For six hours it pushes inland, swelling the basin and holding back the river's outflow. When the tide turns around, the river lets go and drops as much as twenty feet in the same amount of time. In both directions the current usually moves slowly for the first hour. It picks up power during the second hour. The third and fourth have the strongest flow, followed by a gradual easing over the next two hours before stalling at slack tide and reversing direction again. But last night was different.

It was raining in the mountains, and the rivers must have flooded. There wasn't the usual slack period between tides. One minute we were still creeping upriver. A moment later the current was in a hurry to empty the flooded basin.

I opened a jar of beans as the sun set. I sliced a fresh tomato, and the sky went dark. As I tore off a piece of bread, I thought of how Paul would appreciate this picnic menu.

By the time I finished eating, downriver logs were bumping and then hammering into the dugout. I couldn't see them coming in the dark. I tied the packs and baskets to the thwarts and I cinched the strap on my glasses so that the frame pressed into my face.

I should have untied the bowline right then, but I didn't want to lose the distance I'd paddled that afternoon. I thought that I could survive the worst of it if I stayed low in the boat. By the time I fully understood my mistake, the river was racing out and the current began dragging the dugout from one side to the other. Barely an hour had passed and I'd already lost control. Uprooted trees hooked onto the bow and then let go with a shudder, and the low branch I'd used to tie the line was already far overhead.

Dragging a machete beside me, I began inching forward on my belly to cut the bowline. As my weight shifted to the left or right it sent the dugout shooting off in one direction and then correcting hard to the other side. When I was still a few feet from the bow, I felt the dugout veer hard to the right, then tip even further, and then further still as the current grabbed the gunwale and water flooded over the bow, forcing the boat completely under the river.

The current washed me back until my feet hit the thwart. Submerged and without a plan, I gripped the sides and waited while the first seconds passed. I thought of my brother again. I thought of the loose paddle and my glasses strapped to my face. And then we levelled off. The boat was filled to the top, the current racing and washing over the gunwales whenever we dipped to one side even slightly.

Sometimes in a moment of crisis, when it's something real that you can see and touch and taste, you can force yourself to focus only on the tiny steps ahead. You don't let the overwhelming entirety destroy you. And just by moving forward, tiny step by tiny step, you find a strength and confidence that might be far beyond what you have any right to feel.

I still had my glasses. I felt the spare paddle strapped to a thwart. I carefully moved one hand behind to find the half-gallon can tied to a string. Balancing the full canoe, I began bailing bit by bit while logs with tangled roots and branches lumbered past at chest height.

Maybe it took a half-hour, or maybe it was more. I just moved and didn't think of anything else until the canoe was empty.

Again I went down on my belly, and this time I came within a machete blade's length from the bow. I cut the line with one swing, and the tail shot off and was gone. In that same second, as the current swept us away, the world went calm. I stopped fighting. The dugout washed downriver while I paddled with steady strokes away from the bank until we ran aground on a sandbar. The tide would be emptying for hours. I heard thunder in the hills, and then the sky opened overhead and rain poured down. I wrapped a tarp around my body and drifted in and out of sleep so that I never noticed when we floated free on the next flood tide.

This morning everything is soaked from the river and rain. I know I have to throw my soggy bundles onshore before the tide turns around again, but I don't have the strength to move. I tell my body to lift, and it responds without me. I crawl onto the bank, but I'm not really here at all.

After swamping my canoe at night, I build a camp the next morning along the Tuira River.

I sit on a log and I watch another bird float by on a balsa log. An egret this time. Black legs and a yellow beak.

I don't do anything else for those first minutes.

When the sun edges over the trees, I take off my shirt to feel the warmth.

I take off all my clothes and I sit on a log.

Then butterflies arrive in twos and threes. They land on my hands and back, and they stroke my skin and tickle me with their antennae. I wonder what they want. I shake my arms and brush them aside, but they fly back and start again, so I leave them to their work. They're my only companions. It's the most intimate touch I've felt in a long time.

91

In Spanish they say, "*Que rico, el sol.*" How rich is the sun.

Why don't we use that expression in English? There is no better way to describe the depth of its warmth and how it heals us when we are weak.

92

My shirts and socks and plastic bags flutter on the clothesline just before noon. I see a storm in the distance, but it looks as though it will miss us.

"The tide will be flooding again in a few hours," I say out loud. "We won't have much time to get upriver to Mercadeo before dark."

And Paul answers, "Let's camp here for the night, brother."

He feels safe because I'm here. That's how it seems. He doesn't know how frightened I am sometimes.

"Okay," I say. I just sit there, naked in the sun, butterflies stroking my arms and back.

RIO TUIRA

93

There's only one phone in Boca de Cupe. I wish it would ring for me.

94

Boca de Cupe is on the Rio Tuira—the Devil's River, according to the Spanish chronicler Gonzalo Fernández de Oviedo in 1526. In translating the indigenous *Tuyra*, Oviedo was attempting to apply his Catholic-Spanish experience to a native term. But the Tuira isn't the devil in the sense of hell and damnation. It is a spirit or force that can do good or evil depending on the shaman's desire.

On the river's lower reaches near Cavimál, Rio Tuira is wide and muddy, with islands and bars at low tide and a dark tangle of mangrove wetlands forming the banks on either side.

Climbing inland, the river narrows. When it takes the sharp turn to the east at the edge of El Real, it changes character, losing most of its tidal force while retaining some of the depth change with each ebb and flow. At Boca de Cupe, at the mouth of the Cupe River, Tuira's water begins to clear. The bottom becomes sand and rocks. The banks tighten together. Trees reach across to each other from either side, and the current froths and tumbles through the shallows.

When the wet-season storms begin in the mountains, the Tuira floods its banks and washes through the trees. It sweeps away loose branches and every fallen log and deadhead. It erodes the banks, moving river bends and cutting new channels.

But I can't see any of this with my own eyes. The police won't let me through. Not with a native guide. Not on my own. The captain at the police base crossed his arms in front of his chest and told me that I might as well go home. He said that I was like a giant white ant walking amongst little black ones and red ones. He wasn't going to allow me to be kidnapped by Colombians and ruin his career.

I'm surprised by his use of similes, and I wonder if he's a frustrated writer trying to block the path for the rest of us who haven't yet given up hope.

The only records of the upper region are historic texts written by French explorers while they searched for a Darien canal route. Or, if I want something more creative, I can rely on the fanatic Richard Marsh, or the reckless tales of the British traveller Karl Bushby, who refused to let Darien thwart his plan to walk around the world.

To reach the upper regions today, I'd probably need to start in Colombia and follow Bushby's path across the border to Darien. Mimicking his technique, I would cloak myself in rags and stain my face with exhaust soot. I would sneak through the Colombian forests by day and hide in thick growth at night until I eventually reached Panama's upper Tuira. At that point, if I wanted to remain true to Bushby's inspiration, I would fill my clothes with empty plastic bottles and float downriver to Boca de Cupe.

95

When I first sailed into Darien, my plan was to stay for three weeks and pay respect to the patch of rainforest that interrupts the Pan-American Highway. I wanted to push upriver as far as *Ishmael* could travel and then write an article for a sailing magazine. That was all I thought I wanted from Panama. After that I would pull up anchor and sail across the Pacific.

When a month was over and I'd written a short article, I realized that Darien was complex, many-sided and confusing. *I'll dig deeper*, I decided. For once in my life I wanted to understand a place down past the scenery. And so I changed my mind.

I won't write at all. I'll just listen and learn. I'll work with my hands and back, and I'll come away knowing something that will stay with me.

"You should write a definitive history," Vance suggests. He's an American working in Panama. He recently finished reading McCullough's hefty *The Path Between the Seas* about the building of the Panama Canal. Now he's ready for his next historical tome. Something that covers everything and chases down every lead. It sounds enticing, and Darien deserves it.

But that's not me. *Just a slender work of poetic prose*, I think to myself. And then again, *I won't write at all*. I'll even stop observing as a writer. I won't jot down notes or keep a journal describing other people living extraordinary lives. I'll start to live my own life, and I'll sleep well at night.

"Don't spend too much time in one place," Jim warns me. "Kidnappers can't organize a plan if they don't know where you'll be."

Jim worked as a Peace Corps volunteer in the 1960s and continues to generate projects in Darien on his own.

"Don't go, Martin," a Colombian tells me when we meet in La Palma. "It's too dangerous. There's nothing in this forest that you can't find in the library at Bogotá. I'll take you there myself."

"Don't talk about your dreams," Hans says in his thick Austrian accent.

Hans and I met at an anchorage in Panama City. He has lived all his life on the sea. Wreck diving, smuggling and trading in Africa and Southeast Asia.

"People will steal your dreams away from you," he says. "Just live them."

Is writing like talking?

Hans gives me a book tracing the history of the "savage" character throughout recorded history.

"Go native, man," Hans advises.

He has a tangle of facial hair below his bottom lip. He tells me that his teeth hurt.

"Go to Madagascar and get a sailing craft. Take a native woman for your own."

Hans also tells me that every time a man ejaculates, he loses a part of his creativity. I think I understood his English.

When I paddle away from Hans's fifty-foot Polynesian-style catamaran, his woman waves goodbye. Their three young boys grab hold of masthead lines and they swing giant overhead circles around and around the deck.

96

In *A New Voyage Round the World,* British pirate William Dampier wrote that the Cana Valley gold mines were the richest yet found in the Americas.

Darien historians tend to confuse the events and dates and nationalities in their telling of the story, but clearly Cana was a favourite target for French and English pirates. Using escaped slaves and Kuna Indians as guides, they attacked the mines in 1684, 1702, 1712, 1724 and again in 1734. As well, they often raided the fort at El Real where gold was stored en route to Panama and Portobelo.

In 1702, four English pirate captains with 272 men took control of the Espíritu Santo Mines at Cana. On the first day, they washed and cleaned five pounds and eleven ounces of gold. On the second day, six pounds. On the third, eight pounds. The fourth, fourteen pounds. After only four working days, they burned the nine hundred houses in town and left with forty-nine pounds and nine ounces of gold.

Most historians agree that it was a French pirate, Carlos Tibón, who ransacked the mines in 1724. (Only one dissenting writer claims Tibón was an Englishman). He marched across the isthmus with three hundred natives that he'd recruited from the Golfo Urabá and eighty Europeans, including a number of French settlers who had moved to Darien and taken Kuna wives. At Cana, Tibón not only stole the Spanish gold and slaves, he also destroyed parts of the mine shaft and left the town in ruins.

This time, Panama's *presidente* of the *audiencia,* Manuel de Alderete, sent out a local half-breed named Luis Garcia and a group of men who knew Darien's forests and pathways. Some sources claim that they killed Tibón, while others write that they took the pirate prisoner. But they all agree that after his victory, Garcia sailed to Panama City to collect his reward. Unfortunately, the president was in Portobelo to welcome the Spanish fleet which had just arrived, and he hadn't left instructions to pay the hired soldiers.

Garcia waited in Panama until he was broke and he could no longer feed his men. Then, sufficiently insulted, he returned to Darien to take what he felt was his reward. Along the way, his plan evolved from simple revenge into an elaborate scheme to take control of the Royal Road and Portobelo before moving on to Panama City and Cartagena. Apparently, Garcia never considered following the Portobelo road to simply collect his payment from the president.

In Darien he connected with *Cacique* Juan de Dios, who had recently been offended by a Catholic priest. Together they assembled an army of two hundred native soldiers armed with seventy shotguns, some pistols, spears and arrows.

They steamrolled through Darien. They started with Yaviza, killing blacks and Spaniards, young and old, male and female. They killed the Spanish priest and all of the converted Kunas living inside his mission. They moved on to El Real and burned the town and the church, destroying sacred objects. They hunted down any villagers who ran into the forest to hide.

The rebels moved on to attack Chepigana, Molineca, Pinogana, Cana, Tucutí and Santo Domingo de Sábalo. They were almost guaranteed success because the Spanish had so few troops to protect their outposts. That was supposed to be Garcia's job.

When *Presidente* Alderete finally returned to Panama, he sent out veteran officers with seventy men. They hiked upriver to the headwaters of the Chuqunaque River where Garcia had built a temporary fort.

At that point, Garcia's plan began to crumble. Government soldiers wounded him during a second attack on El Real. At Chepigana, the soldiers killed *Cacique* Juan de Dios and his lieutenants and captured many of Garcia's soldiers. In the battle that followed, a black miner serving as a soldier cornered Garcia. He grabbed hold of the half-breed leader and killed him with his own hands.

And that's the way it ended, unless you prefer the version by eminent historian Castillero Calvo, who claims Garcia was captured alongside his men and later exiled to Peru. But I doubt that version. Spain wasn't very subtle in responding to pirates and traitors.

The Cana gold mines never fully recovered from Tibón and Garcia. Workers patched and repaired the shafts, but a few years later a tunnel collapsed and buried two miners. After another pirate attack in 1734, Spain decided to close the mines completely. Soldiers destroyed any of the remaining tunnels to discourage outlaws, and they banned all unauthorized traffic on the Rio Atrato and other rivers leading into the interior. Anyone moving through Darien was suspect.

97

One hundred and fifty years later, a British mining company reopened the mines at Cana. They shipped ore to Boca de Cupe on a narrow-gauge railway, and for twenty-five years Colombian immigrants flooded across the border to work. It was only after a series of tunnels collapsed in 1912 that the company closed the mines again.

During the rest of that century and on into the present one, only major catastrophes or acts of violence have brought the Tuira River back into the media spotlight.

January 31, 1993
At night in the Kuna village of Púcuro, guerrillas from the Revolutionary Armed Forces of Colombia, known as FARC, abducted three American missionaries at gunpoint. Their wives and children, along with the rest of the villagers, could only stand by helpless and frightened.

FARC guerrillas demanded a five-million-dollar ransom, but New Tribes Mission has a no-ransom policy.

Three years later, a guerrilla defector led Colombian officials to the site where the three hostages had been held prisoners. He said that during a battle against government soldiers, the guerrilla commander ordered the three men shot rather than risk their escape.

August 7, 1996
A group of twenty armed men and women joined forces with a few local residents to attack Boca de Cupe. They cut off all radio contact, stole what they could from the hospital and stores, and then kidnapped fifty-five-year-old Antonio Ramos, who owned a small store in the village.

There was only one police officer stationed in town at that time. He saved his life by submerging himself and his weapons in a lagoon until the attackers returned to the mountains.

The group initially demanded three million dollars from the Ramos family, but later settled for fifty thousand dollars. They released Antonio in May of 1997 after nine months in captivity.

November 16, 1997
Guerrillas attacked Boca de Cupe again. A tall, good-looking woman with green eyes led a group of M56 Colombian guerrillas on the village raid.

The twenty police officers abandoned the village. Three of them were wounded and one drowned in the river during their escape. The guerrillas burned the police station, damaged the hospital, and carried away supplies, money and weapons.

A week later in Union Chocó. Reported gunshots and guerrilla activity. Police later say that it was a case of two drunken men firing shots in the air during a weekend party.

January 18, 2003
North American writer Robert Young Pelton (*The World's Most Dangerous Places*) arrived in Darien with two young Americans to walk across the roadless rainforest from Panama to Colombia.

In the past, Darien was once a popular backpacker's destination, but due to kidnappings and violence the traffic has stopped almost completely.

Before leaving his home in the US, Pelton sent emails to FARC guerrilla and AUC (United Self-Defence Forces of Colombia) paramilitary websites detailing his plans, but he heard nothing in response. In Darien, the police refused to grant him permission for the trip and Kuna villagers urged the group to turn around, but Pelton found a local guide who agreed to sneak them through to Colombia.

On the eighteenth of January, shortly after the group left from the village of Paya, gunshots shook the forest. AUC members intercepted the Americans and their guide. They shot dead another Kuna who was walking in the same direction, and then they marched the three gringos into Colombia and held them on a farm. They fed the hostages up to five meals a day including box lunches, Gatorade and yogourt. A week later, the AUC released Pelton and his two companions to church leaders in the region.

Meanwhile in Paya, there were no box lunches. Besides the execution of the first Kuna, a coroner's report listed three more deaths:

> *The Saíla* (village leader): A bullet entering his mouth, exiting on the right side of the head. Fractured ribs and contusions over his body.
> *Second Saíla*: Also fractured ribs, his arm pulled almost completely off, and finally he was decapitated.

Saíla Comisario (village representative): Received four bullet holes in his back. Crushed cranium indicating that he was hit repeatedly on the head with a blunt object.

98

I see a storm approaching and I can taste fresh rain in the wind.

I run over the pathway, over mud and chicken manure and the mangy dogs lying on the edge of town.

A police officer in fatigues steps out of the trees as I race by his post.

"Where are you going?" he shouts at me.

"*A bañarme*," I say, for a bath in the river. This control game is starting to irritate me. "I'll be right back," I call over my shoulder, still running, feeling reckless.

This wind makes me crazy.

99

I wait five hours one morning at the side of the river for a boat going downstream to Capetí. Every half-hour, a soldier stops by to ask me when I'm leaving.

"What about you?" I ask the soldier after the fourth hour. "When are you leaving?"

100

At noon, when a boat stops at Boca de Cupe, there really isn't any room for me, but the driver wants the fare. His boat is full of Kuna passengers from Púcuro. Some stare at me. Others ignore me. No one moves to clear a space.

This is something that I've learned in Darien. If you want to hitch a ride on a crowded boat, the trick is to advance without apparent reflection or hesitation. Even while you're asking for a seat you have to be moving toward any hint of an opening. And remember that you're on your own. No one will help you do this. The passengers would rather not have another body crowding the boat.

My standard manoeuvre is to have everything bagged and double-bagged inside my canvas pack because there's going to be water seeping through cracks in any dugout. Everyone will be sitting on the high gunwales or on scraps of wood to avoid the water sloshing around on the floor. They won't expect you to toss your pack directly into the puddle at the low spot. They leave that zone unguarded.

So that is your target. The puddle of water. Continue negotiating with the driver, but now, with your pack suddenly wedged in place and the passengers temporarily startled, you follow right behind. Don't wait for an invitation. Climb on top and sit on your bag.

Often someone will immediately protest the unfair baggage

In the lower reaches of the Balsas River the channel runs deep. The motor easily pushes us against the current until we reach the narrow sections upriver where rocks and rapids make navigation more difficult. During the dry season, we have to cut through logs that have fallen from an eroded riverbank and drag the canoe over sections of shallow gravel and sand.

placement, using the excuse that your clothes will become soaked.

"Don't worry," I say. "It floats. You can use it as a life jacket if we tip."

This surprises them, and usually they just accept my invasion. However, later on they start to examine the pack. The loose flaps, drawstring and plastic clips.

"It doesn't look waterproof."

Someone points at the water flowing in and out of the top flap.

"It floats," I say.

Karl Bushby would love this pack.

The boat wallows with my extra weight. My feet become tangled with Kuna feet. Theirs are the colour of the earth, splayed wide and callused. Mine are white and hairy, with bug bites and an infection where the doctor in Panama City cut out a wart that was taking on a life of its own.

101

Santo Tomás de Capetí was established (or perhaps re-established) in 1638 as a Dominican mission to educate and pacify "wild" Kuna Indians. Prior to that time, in the early 1600s, the Kuna had attacked Chepo and killed the mayor and other officials. They terrorized the province, killed another group of black men cutting timber around Bayano, and drove out any other native groups that were living on the Tuira River and its tributaries.

It wasn't until Father Adrian de Santo Tomás and Julian Carrizolio worked together to broker a peace accord that the quarter-century of violence came to an extended pause. These two—the Flemish missionary and Carrizolio, a shipwreck survivor raised by the Kunas since age fourteen—in the same year also established (or re-established) San Enrique de Pinogana and San Jerónimo de Yaviza as missions to pacify Kuna Indians.

Deciding locations, tribes and founding dates for Darien settlements isn't an easy task. Writing about the province, historian

Mauro Ocharan asks, "What exactly is it to found a village? Don't we see the same village (at least in name) being moved from one place to another like a camping tent?"

Along with Father Adrian's founding ceremonies at these Tuira villages, Ocharan cites a number of previous ceremonies using the same village names: a year earlier with Carrizolio performing the honours himself; a short time later by an Augustín Father from Cartagena; and later still by the Panamanian Augustín Padre Ignacio. However, the Kuna mission established by Father Adrian at Capetí must also have faltered, because five years later the village was refounded as San Sebastian Capetín with a population of Páparo Indians.

When Fray Adrian retired from Darien in 1651, Kuna natives staged a general uprising and attacked the new fort built at El Real. During the next few months, they drove out any settlers and miners who had filtered into the region during the period of peace. They abandoned the Catholic missions and destroyed everything built by Father Adrian's fourteen years of labour.

Today the village has transformed itself yet again and is now the largest Wounaan community in the Emberá-Wounaan Reserve.

102

Some historical sources place the Páparos as a subgroup of the Chocó. Others label them as a Kuna splinter tribe. However, according to Padre Jacobo Walburger, an Austrian Jesuit who dutifully recorded the three miserable years he spent amongst the Kuna at Yaviza, if the latter is true, there must have been some trouble in the family.

> When a Kuna Indian dies, if he's a captain on some river, they perform his funeral honours; and if he had slaves—Páparos or Chocó Indians—they kill them with arrows and spears and bury them with their master so that in heaven he has servants and help for his work. The Páparo Indians live

in the headwaters of the Yape, Pucro, and Capetí rivers … their language is distinct from others … Earlier they were owners of all of this province and were great in number, rich in gold until the beginning of the [1600s], when those that presently possess the land [Kuna] came down from Santa Marta [Colombia].
—Padre Walburger, 1748

Because Páparos refused to make contact with European traders, they didn't have steel tools or firearms. They fought with arrows and spears made from fire-hardened wood. They still used fire and stone tools to shape their canoes. Measles devastated their communities, and they were easy prey for tribes with modern weapons.

In 1713 Spain issued a decree imposing fines on anyone taking Páparo Indians for slaves, but by the middle of the century the tribe had disappeared completely.

103

The concrete slab at Capetí's landing is breaking apart and creeping into the river on the back of an eroding riverbank. Looking up from the dugout I see a woman dumping a basket of garbage into the water where children are playing and swimming. They think it's wonderful. They grab hold of the aluminum cans and empty bleach bottles and throw them back and forth like Fisher-Price toys.

104

I'm always somewhat cautious arriving at a new village. It never really becomes any easier for me. I'm aware how little I have to offer.

Ando conociendo. I travel knowing, wanting to see and listen and learn. But what good is that to my hosts?

The Púcuro Kunas have continued in their boat down the Tuira. I can't leave Capetí even if I want to. There's no bus station here, no road to hitch a ride. There isn't even a cheap hotel to unpack my bag if I want a moment to myself.

There are about fifty Wounaan natives standing around the boat landing. They're divided into small groups. Reckless-boy cliques, silent-men cliques, women-washing-clothes cliques. I see four men standing in a group directly in front of me. They aren't welcoming me in any way, but I walk over to them, water still draining from my pack and down the back of my legs.

"Where can I find the *dirigente*?" I ask.

"The *dirigente* is in Yaviza."

"Then, the second in charge?" The *dirigente suplente*?

"He's in Panama."

Nothing ever goes as planned, but I notice that one of the four men leans slightly toward me. Now I have my guide.

After the 1638 Dominican settlement to pacify "wild" Kuna natives failed, the village of Capetí was re-established as a mission for Páparo Indians. By the early 1700s these new residents had been destroyed by disease. Today Capetí is the largest Wounaan community in Darien.

"Who do I ask for permission to spend the night?" I ask this man.

"I'm the *presidente* of the *congreso local*," he says. His name is Aureliano.

"You can put your bags in my house, and we'll talk to the others in the *congreso*."

"There's water in your bag," Aureliano says as I follow him along a path. "You can hang your clothes on our line."

He doesn't understand. The bag floats.

105

A police bunker built with sandbags and camouflage netting crowns the hill behind Capetí. They knocked down the trees and macheted the grass for a clear view of the river. From here I can look over the school and the footpaths winding between village homes and latrines.

A ten-year-old boy walks out of the bunker. A soldier motions for me to leave the area. I can see only his arm sticking out from the shadow below the roofline. The sun shines on his muscles and black skin below the cuff of his T-shirt.

The boy stops in front of me.

"Where are you going?" he asks.

"I'm just looking," I tell him.

"I'll show you the black village," he says.

I wave back to the black arm in the shadow, and then we walk down the hill to a collection of homes with plank walls, metal roofs and sagging front porches.

Three huge black women with giant curlers in their hair are sitting on the porch of a blue house with orange and yellow flowers growing in boxes around the railing.

I ask them if they'll talk with me about their black community living inside the native reserve.

"I can't understand anything you say," one woman shouts at

me across her yard, the pink curlers bobbing on her head.

At first I think that she really doesn't understand me. I repeat my question, but she shouts at me again.

"Talk to the man under the house," she says. "Talk to the man under the house."

What does she mean?

Now *I* don't understand *her*, but then I see the *mestizo* Augustín Alcazar sleeping in a hammock between the house posts.

I came to Capetí hoping to talk with Augustín's brother Victor. He was the guide for Robert Pelton and the American couple when they were kidnapped by Colombian paramilitaries near the village of Paya four months ago.

"Victor is in Panama," Augustín says, waking from his nap.

"I have to urinate," he says, and he crawls from the hammock and walks to the trees. When he returns he's carrying a bench for me to sit in the shade and visit. He says he doesn't know much about *comarca* politics, but everything works fine here.

"They have their land, and I have mine."

He tells me that this was *colono* land long before these "Colombian Indians" settled here. I mention something about early Páparo and Kuna settlements three hundred years ago, but he hasn't heard anything about that. His history goes back as far as he remembers. As far as his dad's and his grandfather's stories.

"Come with me, Martin. Come to my house and take some bananas."

They're my favourite kind. *Manzanitas*. Six inches long, a slightly red peel. They taste like tart apples masquerading as bananas.

Augustín's style is easy for me to appreciate. He's taking a break from work on a Sunday afternoon. He doesn't think that he's poor. He's not looking for an NGO to start a project, or asking anyone for help. His house is complete. It's a bachelor's home where you have to stoop to get through the door. He has one tiny room with a single cot, a table with a propane burner, tools leaning against the entrance wall and the rack of bananas hanging from a rafter. He slips twenty *manzanitas* into my bag, and then dumps in a dozen limes.

"Get out of here!" he shouts at the three black boys who followed us inside.

He takes a swing at them as they grab a few loose bananas and run out the door.

"*Sinvergüenzas!*" he says (*adj.* shameless, brazen. *n.* rascal, scoundrel).

"That's the problem with *them*," he says, "always pushing and stealing things."

I'm not certain who he includes when he refers to *them*.

106

Ovidio lives two doors down from the porch with the giant curlers. He is very black. He has long scars on his chest and shoulders, and extremely tight skin so that I can see the sheets of muscle fibres stretching and sliding under his skin when he moves.

Ovidio's two boys have the start of the same body, but while he looks angry with bloodshot eyes, they just look sullen.

"Go get a bag of sugar," Ovidio says to one son.

"Get in the kitchen and cut up some limes to drink," he tells the other.

They move without enthusiasm. Ovidio and I sit face to face on wood stools crammed tight in his narrow porch. I hear his son cutting limes inside. A few minutes later he walks through the door, passing between us and moving slowly down the path.

"Where are our drinks?" Ovidio asks.

"I'm taking a break," the boy answers. His body turns toward us, but he looks at the ground. These boys don't want to make lemonade for me. Maybe not for their father either.

Ovidio doesn't raise his voice, but his gravity could crush you.

"Get inside and finish," he says slowly, measuring his words.

The boy turns his back to us and begins taking steps further down the path.

"I have a stick," Ovidio warns him. "You know I have a stick."

No answer.

Ovidio looks at me. "Okay," he says, his hands raised in front of him as if he is cradling a basketball in front of his chest. "That's okay. He knows."

Ten minutes later I hear his son working inside. He must have circled around the house. When he appears in the doorway with two tall glasses, he hands us our drinks but avoids eye contact with his father.

Now Ovidio plays my role in the interview game.

"What do *you* think of the *Tierra Colectiva* project?" he asks me.

I tell him that it seems like a good idea. The same as if a group of his family or friends decided to sign a contract to protect their land from been sold off piece by piece.

He's not comfortable with that answer. This whole afternoon experience is a lesson in managing life around an angry man. His words stumble while he decides how to counter my analogy. He begins quoting passages from the Book of Revelations. He mentions 666 and then the Great Beast. When he finds his footing again, he tells me that the greatest problem is that the *Indios* have always crossed back and forth from Colombia.

"The government in Panama makes it too easy for them to legalize their papers," he says. "We don't get that special treatment."

I tell him that the refugee-support workers in Boca de Cupe told me that in the last few years, almost all the immigrants crossing over from Colombia have been black people.

Ovidio glares at me, his lips pressed together. My glass is empty. My shirt is soaked through with sweat.

"Look," he says. "I don't know how long you've been here. Two, maybe three years. Or what you studied before…"

He stops and collects himself again.

He takes our glasses inside to wash them.

This is the debate in Darien. Who has the right to own this land? Do you grant it to those who need it most? Or to those who will be the most beneficial stewards of the forests and rivers? Or to those who can pay the highest price?

Is it a case of deciding who was here first? Who has the earliest claim to the land? And even there, you still have to decide how you will define the contest. Geographically. Racially. Linguistically. Chronologically.

Do you state the obvious—that historically this has been the land of America's pre-Columbian peoples? Or is it important to specify the now-extinct Cueva and Páparo tribes?

Does the presence of escaped black slaves in the sixteenth century validate the demands of today's black residents? Or does the province start fresh with a clean slate and say it is the responsibility of each individual to prove his traditional occupation of that land, and then title it legally through the Land Office?

Even here, in the established Emberá-Wounaan *Comarca*, we have the same problem. Escaped black slaves probably lived in the region before the Chocó arrived. And before the slaves and before the Spaniards, there were other native groups. Were these the ancestors of Kuna or Chocó tribes? Does that matter? And if so, how could it be proven?

You can rule that indigenous peoples were here before all others, but someone will counter that the Chocó arrived late to the region, that perhaps blacks and certain *colono* families can be considered the pioneers and rightful inheritors of the land.

Augustín says that his family has worked the same land for three generations. To him, this is *colono* land, and only the heavy hand of General Omar Torrijos gave it away to the Indians.

Just before I leave, Ovidio says, "Torrijos didn't even come out here and check first. He just believed the Indians. He just gave it to them."

Later in the evening, I ask Aureliano's father about his birthplace and ancestors. He's lying in his hammock when I talk with him. He's sick with a cough and a bad headache. He sips on lemongrass tea and keeps medicinal plant stems and leaves laced behind his ears like little garden plots to help him heal.

At first he fumbles for an answer.

Then, "Oh, hell. I'll tell you the truth. I could tell you something else, but why should I lie about my ancestors?"

Maybe it's only because he is sick, but it sounds as though he has to tear the response out from deep inside a tender part of his soul.

"I'm from Colombia," he says. "We came here when I was just a boy."

107

Capetí is at the heart of the Emberá-Wounaan *Comarca*.

When Panama's Law 22 established the *comarca* boundaries, all of the non-Chocó people living inside the *comarca* who were able to prove right of possession were given title to their land. They can continue to work and live inside the new Chocó homeland. Legally they cannot sell the property without first offering it to the *comarca*, but they can pass it on through inheritance to other family members.

Augustín has no children, but his brother Victor does. Augustín says they'll probably inherit the land from him.

To make matters worse for the Chocó, Colombian refugees allegedly continue moving into the area around Yape and clearing more *comarca* land. Even with all of the police presence in these villages, the Chocó complaints haven't warranted any government response.

The Emberá-Wounaan Reserve may never be a completely Chocó community.

108

The cantina at Capetí is like so many places I've been.

When I step inside at night, music is blasting through broken speakers. Children stand in the doorways staring into the dark room with its low ceiling and two candles burning. In the middle of the dirt floor, a Wounaan man spins reckless circles around and around on his left leg with one hand in the air.

I see Aureliano and twenty-two men crowded against the long counter, waiting. The music is too loud to talk. They stand silent and serious, with glass bottles of *Seco* and a box of milk to mix it with set up beside them like sacraments.

They don't acknowledge me while I finish my beer. I don't think they're angry with me. They're just waiting.

Everyone wants to be that man spinning circles in the centre of the floor.

109

In the dark, Aureliano's wife calls out from her hammock. "Imagine…" she says.

A pause. I have no idea where she plans to go with this thought.

"You've come all the way from Canada. And now you're here. In our home."

I hear in her voice the same amazement I feel sometimes when I'm on the floor eating smoked monkey, or drinking the cacao that we've chewed, spit and dried together.

Imagine that, I think.

I want to hold on to that sense of wonder forever.

110

When I'm ready to leave, I offer Aureliano's wife a few dollars, saying that it can help with the food they've given me. She looks confused as she takes it. She doesn't want to do it. I still haven't found a way to know when to offer and when to just accept.

Aureliano rolls over. With the little strength he can muster, he reaches out his hand. He apologizes for coming home so late.

"The drink made me crazy last night," he says.

111

While I'm waiting for a boat at Capetí, a Wounaan man makes twenty trips from the river to the top of the bank. I can barely keep my footing without anything on my back, but on each climb Humberto carries another hundred-pound sack of flour straight up the muddy slope. He charges fifty cents to unload an entire boat. Later he shoulders a 40-horsepower outboard and he climbs again. A few minutes after that, he pushes by with another motor.

While he's resting between boats, Humberto explains why the income from selling *plátanos* isn't enough to pay his bills.

His hillside plot is near the river between Capetí and Union Chocó. When his product is ready, he'll cut and load four thousand plantains into a dugout for the trip to Yaviza. The buyers pay three dollars for a hundred plantains. That's one hundred and twenty dollars. However, sometimes they'll reject a part of the cargo because it's damaged, or too small or too ripe. He might lose a hundred of them. Maybe three dollars' worth. That leaves him with a hundred and seventeen dollars.

Like most growers, Humberto is cash-poor and he can't afford his own large dugout and outboard motor. He rents these for fifteen dollars to make the trip back and forth. He also buys eighteen gallons of mixed gasoline for the round trip. Another fifty-four dollars, and rising rapidly with international fuel prices tripling in the last few years.

So if all goes perfectly well, Humberto will clear a patch in the forest and burn the slash. He'll plant and clean and later harvest the plantains, and then haul them from the forest to the riverbank, and then by boat to Yaviza. With all the risks and sweat at every stage, the best he can hope to earn is forty-eight dollars.

This is no way to build a nest egg.

Humberto has three children sharing a room in Metetí while they continue their schooling past Capetí's primary grades. All of this is paid for with mountains of *plátanos* and endless trips up and down the muddy slope at Capetí.

112

Nothing works in Union Chocó. The village is a lesson that enthusiasm and good intentions can't compensate for poor planning.

Eight years ago, government engineers built a concrete tank on the Yape River. The tank filled with clean water. Hired workers buried a network of plastic tubes and installed a spigot at every house. However, not a drop of water has ever reached Union Chocó through those pipes. No one can explain why.

Every crumbling house in town boasts a power meter secured to an upright post, but the plan to bring electricity from El Real or Yaviza has been delayed indefinitely.

They used to have a generator. Now they have a shed with three dismantled power plants.

Union Chocó is the administrative centre for the Emberá-Wounaan Reserve, yet nothing works in the village. Traditional knowledge is fading, while a confusing mixture of new materials and knowledge is beginning to take root.

Lacking running water in their homes, women wash clothes in the muddy Tuira River at Union Chocó.

They bought a gas-powered rice mill with *comarca* funds three years ago, but it has never worked. Not even on the first day.

Another agency installed a series of solar-powered street lights throughout the village. The lights have never worked. Only the one farthest from the town centre gives off a dim glow at night. The woman living next to it says it helps her to see if she wakes up at night.

After the *comarca* designated Union Chocó as the capital village, they built administration offices in the village out of cinder blocks, concrete, and zinc laminate roofing. But the representatives prefer to live in Yaviza or Panama City, so the buildings sit empty. The newly elected *cacique* is from El Salto on the Chuqunaque River. He wants to move the administration centre to his village.

They also constructed a massive community building. The *Casa Presidencial*. The outside walls are whitewashed plywood, the windows are screened and it has a traditional *guágara* palm roof. It was designed to accommodate the president if he or she someday decides to stay overnight. I wouldn't want to stay in there. It looks unused and unwelcoming. Just big for no reason. There's a rusty air conditioner in a window, but no place to plug in the cord. The floor is clean except for a pile of guano below the centre post. I can hear bats somewhere high overhead in the dark.

113

Everyone around me has been sick for the last month ... snotty-nosed kids, men with leaves tucked behind their ears, everyone coughing. At night I listen to the hollow rasping of lung infections next to me on the floor.

Now I'm sick too. My head is splitting apart. A nine-year-old boy has attached himself to me and he watches me with concern.

"Didn't you come prepared?" he asks... *preparado?*

I don't know what he means.

"Prepared for what?"

"Didn't you bring medicine?" he asks.

"What medicine?"

"*Mejoral*," he says. It's a cure-all pill in a red cellophane package. Two tiny aspirins promising relief from any ache or pain or fever.

"No," I tell him. "I didn't come *preparado*."

I lie awake on the floor in the afternoon heat, passing in and out of fevers and daydreams. I can hear the village pay phone ringing and ringing, but no one ever answers. The receiver is broken. The phone rings, but when you pick it up you can't hear anything.

It worries me in my sleep.

Fifteen years ago, a week after a friend's suicide and three days before Christmas, I had a dream that my phone was ringing on the bedside table. I bolted straight up in bed, waking the woman sleeping beside me. I fumbled over the desktop, pushing books out of the way until I found the phone. I remember hearing the hissing and popping of long-distance static and then an indecipherable voice starting and stopping behind the wall of noise.

"Who is this?" I called out.

No answer.

"Who is this?"

More static and the muddled voice starting and breaking off with words that I could almost make out. Someone trying to tell me something.

Then I began to wake. I saw my woman's face. I felt her hand on my chest, saw her lips moving and heard her call my name. I heard the empty hum of a dial tone in my ear, and I understood then where I was.

I placed the phone back on the desk that night. I laid my head on the pillow, and I started to cry.

114

Carlos Guaynora touches my shoulder to wake me. It's dark outside. I must have slept all afternoon.

"*Venga a comer*, Martin." Come and eat.

He tells me that the police were searching for me for hours. They thought that I'd given them the slip and headed out into the forest.

115

You know how it is sometimes. You're at the lowest point possible and then suddenly, unexpectedly, you meet the right person.

Carlos Guaynora looks a lot like my uncle who runs a gas station in a Saskatchewan prairie town. My uncle sells used cars and farm machinery, and he has those impossibly high eyebrows and forehead that I connect with prairie honesty. A look of upbeat optimism.

Carlos is a soft-spoken man. When I first arrived in Union Chocó, he was sitting in the shade under a giant mango tree. He carried out another chair for me and brought two glasses of lime *chicha* sweetened with sugar cane syrup. His wife and daughter were behind the house pounding rice with heavy wood pestles to separate the husk from the grain.

"The schools have changed everything," Carlos said. "When I was a kid, I couldn't speak Spanish. Our family avoided *colonos* then, but now we're all mixed together. Even in the *comarca*.

"Everything is changing so fast, and pretty soon no one will remember any of this." When Carlos tells you something, he pauses between each sentence.

"I've been thinking about that a lot. All of those years with my father and grandfather, but I can remember only a few of their stories. I never asked them to teach me about all of the plants and medicines. Now it's too late."

He talks slowly, and it sounds as though he's carefully selecting the right words to use.

"Kids are learning so much these days. But in other ways, we know less and less every generation."

Carlos and I talked for three hours that afternoon. At times we just sat and said nothing. Still it was comfortable. Sometimes that's the way it is when you think you're at a low point.

"Come," he said when the daylight began to fade. "We can eat now."

His wife served us rice and agouti meat and fried plantains with cups of lemongrass tea.

116

In Union Chocó I eat almost every meal with *Dirigente* Carlos.

There isn't a restaurant in town. Sometimes I try to give his family a rest by going to a house that sells sodas and crackers, dried fish and canned goods. I sit in the candlelight with a few other lonely misfits. People who have no one waiting for them at home.

But Carlos finds me in the dark.

"Come, Martin," he says. "The food is ready."

At supper we eat plantains and rice again, this time with brocket venison.

Carlos can see that I'm sick. "I don't think you should paddle alone to La Palma," he says.

He says it without expression. Is it the floods and currents? Or crocodiles, or Colombians? Did he hear some news about guerrillas in the area? He doesn't explain.

Carlos has lost much of his ancestors' Emberá tradition. He lives in a green, two-storey house he built for his family with planks and a metal roof. They run a store through a large window cut into the front wall. He has a propane stovetop and a fridge in the kitchen.

A little more each day, I feel him start to use my presence as an excuse to reach back in time. Every evening meal when we sit down with candles burning and cups of coffee or tea, he sets aside his store and his ambition and all the problems of the day. He tries to take me to those years when he was still a boy living with his parents and grandfather.

"We Emberá can all swim perfectly by age three," he tells me.

I know this is true.

"But when I was nine, our family went up near Paya, and a six-year-old girl disappeared in the river," he says.

"If the river is fine, and someone drowns, the police say it was a heart attack or something like that. But sometimes, like the girl in Paya, the body disappears for three or four days," Carlos says. "We looked everywhere, and then the body appeared in a spot where we had looked before.

"And the body was still fresh," he tells me.

His face is lit by the single candle. A fork in his hand. Forearms resting on the table. His wife sits beside him. At the first two meals together, she would serve the meal and then go outside to work. Later she began to sit close by. Now she joins us and adds details to the story.

"Also a doctor in Yaviza drowned when his boat tipped. They were just crossing the river. They found his body four days later at the edge of town."

"When these things happen, we know that it's the *Madre de Agua*," Carlos says.

117

The Chocó live in a world of spirits—of *jai*—both good and bad. They credit *jai* forces for any event that they can't easily explain. Disasters, good fortune, and especially sickness and unexpected death.

A *haimbaná* (a man or woman who works with *jai*) uses songs to call on spirits to cure or hurt other individuals. Ancestral spirits are the most prevalent and forceful. After Chocó die, their spirits wander the region contacting family members through dreams. If they were good people in earthly life, then they usually do good work as a spirit. These *jai* help a shaman see the truth of a problem. Through them the shaman learns both the cause and cure for a sickness.

Spirits from animals of prey are also powerful, but usually less benign. They are the *jai* from animals killed in the hunt, and they're only too willing to be used to bring sickness to man.

Certain whirlpools are believed to be the home of *Madre de Agua*, the Mother Water mentioned by Carlos. She drags her victims to the river bottom and devours them, only rarely releasing the body back to the surface.

Even trees, rocks and natural forces have *jai*. These spirits can change shape, taking the form of a man or woman, white or black, before tearing off their disguise to become an animal again, or a river current or thunder in a storm.

The anthropologist Reina Torres listed a series of *jai* described to her as monsters by Chocó elders. The *Arripada* is perhaps the most common—a gigantic beast with one hand shaped like a hook to tear open a person's chest and eat their heart.

Arribamia are sorcerers that, anticipating their own death, drink the juice of a *guiban colorado* plant and are transformed into cannibalistic quadrupeds with an enormous head. They hide in the forest and live off the flesh of their own people.

There is also a *Soseré*—a cow with blue horns that lives by a river, attacking Indians and hiding their canoes. And perhaps the saddest spirit in Latin America is the old and wrinkled witch, *Tuluvieja*. She has a face like a sieve, and a single breast hanging long and ugly. Emberá say that she isn't Chocó, that she's *kampunía*, and that she lives in a cave near Rio Sambú, wandering the forest alone. From shame, she wears her hair hanging down in front to cover her ugliness. People accuse her of luring children and stealing them for her own. If a man chases after her to rescue his child, and he wants to use a branch or walk on a fallen log, she spills her breast milk so that he slips and can't save himself by grabbing hold.

When Carlos tells stories like these, he speaks so matter-of-factly that it doesn't seem magical or extraordinary. Just a straightforward account of the known facts.

118

"*En ese tiempo...*" At that time... Almost every story Carlos tells begins with that line.

It's different from a fairy tale's *"Once upon a time,"* which rings with a note of fiction. Instead, the Emberá version is more biblical, or historical. It's as if the storyteller is looking out and pointing to some specific moment and saying, "Yes. Right there at that moment is when and where all of this happened. I know it for a fact."

En ese tiempo... Caragabí built his house and he lived there. Further upriver there were other people living in a *tambo*. Caragabí created a woman for company, and also a brother to live with him in the world.

But Caragabí falls sick. He develops boils and rashes all over his skin. Then leprosy starts and soon he has infections everywhere.

He becomes so ugly that his woman doesn't want to be around him.

They are raising a daughter, and the daughter has to cook for him because the woman is always leaving to drink at the neighbour's *tambo*. One night while she's there she lies down with Caragabí's brother.

The woman comes back just before daylight with scratch marks on her belly, but Caragabí pretends he doesn't notice.

"How did it go?"

"Oh, fine," she answers. "I was just drinking. Nothing more."

"Was the *chicha* good?"

"Oh, yes," she says.

A few days later she tells him that she is going to the *chupata* again.

"Go on then," he says. "Sick like this, it's impossible for me to walk with you."

However, after she leaves, Caragabí takes off his disease as if it was only a shirt he was wearing. His brother stays at home that day because he knows what will happen. Caragabí puts on his *chaquira* bracelets and necklaces and he goes to the *tambo*.

The woman is already there, and when she sees Caragabí she thinks it is his brother.

She goes over and gets close to him.

He asks, "Woman, aren't you worried that you'll make my brother angry?"

"Don't worry about that disgusting man. He won't notice anything."

They climb down from the *tambo* and he is with her until the early morning when he sets off running to arrive before she does. He puts his sickness back on like an old shirt and once again he is a loathsome sight.

When she arrives later after bathing in the river, she's wearing a cloth over her belly because he scratched her during the night. She serves him food, but he refuses it.

"What's your problem?" she asks. "Why are you angry?"

"Have you been sleeping with my brother?" he demands.

"That's not true!" she answers.

"And this…!?"

He pulls off the cloth covering her scratches.

He knocks her down, puts his foot in her mouth and splits and cleaves her open to the ears, turning her mouth into a beak.

"When I leave this time, you're going to cry," he says.

Then he changes her into a *baracoco*. A common potoo. A bird that sits in a tree and stares out at the sun and moon.

I often hear the common potoo just as night comes on. The *baracoco* sings a series of descending notes. The first ones are strong, but the rest of her heartbreaking song trails off at the end. In a nature guidebook, a bird writer paraphrases the call as *poor-me-all-alone*.

AFRAID OF THE DARK

In 1887, the Colombian historian and writer Ernesto Restrepo Tirado travelled up the Tuira River from the Gulf of San Miguel. In his article "*Un Viaje al Darien*," he observed and commented on every aspect of Darien life, from the torment of insects at Boca de Cupe to the exploitation of the "lazy" black population by the "abusive whites" and the "cancerous" influence of Darien's petty government bureaucrats and lawyers.

During the time he spent in indigenous villages, Restrepo Tirado collected stories of native "superstitions" and the apparent success of their cures for venomous snakebites. Overall, however, he was less flattering in his descriptions of native healers.

> There are some shaman (*curanderos*), most of them Chocós, who people both fear and respect because they are terrible men who commit vengeful acts on others. These shamans live comfortable lives, although perhaps with a certain amount of remorse. If someone becomes seriously ill, or is bitten by a snake, the shaman brings the patient to his house where he has a straw bed, food and alcohol. Once the sick person is there, if the shaman sees that the patient is recovering, he gives him some medicine that makes the person sick again so that he continues recovering and falling sick again until the shaman can find another victim to swindle.

120

On my way down the Tuira River, I stop again at Mercadeo and stay at the Emberá home of *los abuelos,* the old ones. My headache is getting worse and I'm sweating from fevers. Something is wrong with a nerve in my neck and I've lost most of the strength in my right arm. I can barely raise my empty hand overhead.

In the afternoon while I'm resting on the floor, grandmother asks me, "*Hermanito* [little brother], do you have any medicine for my eyes?"

She has cataracts. She spends hours every day squinting over their cooking fire and wiping tears away.

"I don't think there is medicine for that," I say.

She is almost blind. For twenty years she's cared for her paraplegic husband. She pulls him up from the floor in the morning and props him against a post. When he has to defecate, she drags him to the edge of the platform and back again to the post after she cleans him.

In the afternoon when I go to town, she washes my dirty laundry by hand. Now everything smells like fresh soap and lemons.

121

When I return to the *abuelos'* house, Luis Rivera Garcia is drinking coffee with the old woman.

"*Hermano,*" he says, offering his hand in greeting as I climb up the *tumé*.

Luis is a *colono* from western Panama. He's probably in his fifties or sixties. You just can't tell for certain because even though he looks old and wiry, he hops around the floor like a school kid.

Luis has seventy hectares of land on an empty stretch of the Tuira River, but he's building a large house in Mercadeo to bring his nineteen-year-old Kuna wife and their two children to live. He wants his son and daughter to go to school.

"Oh, this is good coffee," Luis says. "It's wonderful under the thatched roof. It cools so much better than the metal ones."

The old woman nods her head.

"It breathes," he says, fanning the air with his free hand.

When the *abuelos'* ten-year-old grandson Luis arrives, Luis and Luis immediately launch into a conversation.

It's the same everywhere in Panama. When two people with the same name meet, they begin a ritual interaction in which they address each other as *tocayo* (namesake).

"*Como va, tocayo?*" How's it going, *tocayo?*

"Fine, *tocayo*. And you, *tocayo*, how is everything for you?"

"Oh, it's so hot, *tocayo*. But thank you for asking. And *tocayo*, there is something that I was wanting to ask you…"

They go on and on with this conversation that has absolutely no purpose other than to insert the word "*tocayo*." It drives me nuts to listen, but I also know that for some reason it feels good when you are with your own *tocayo*.

At the end of the evening, Luis Garcia rolls out his bedding right beside mine. I'm still sick, and I just need one night of good sleep. And it's such a big floor, but perhaps he believes that I'd be lonely with too much space around me at night.

Luis looks like every truck driver I've met in oil field camps in northern Canada. Scrappy men, all bones and sinew. They work long hours and then shake the rafters at night with their snoring. I assume that Luis will do the same, but I can't politely do anything about it, so I search in my bag for earplugs.

"I love sleeping on a *gira* floor," Luis announces as he settles down next to me.

"*La gira bendiga al cuerpo*," he says. The *gira* blesses the body.

He says things like that. He's full of that truck-stop sort of wisdom and confidence. As he lays his head down on a rolled towel, he pushes his hat forward over his eyes. He's unshaven. He's still wearing his work clothes. I can smell the sweat and the wood shavings from his day in the sun.

Los abuelos, *the grandparents, at Mercadeo rest in the afternoon heat. They sleep on a floor made from the open shell of a gira tree.*

I'm about to put in the earplugs when I hear Luis give two short breaths and then fall asleep. I hear his breathing shift. He develops a tiny *puff, puff* with each exhale. The sound of dolphins. The breath of a sleeping child and a clean conscience. A body blessed by a *gira* floor.

122

I paddle on through the overcast day. I drink water and the fever sweats it out. I stop briefly at Luis Garcia's homestead along the river, and I talk with his young Kuna wife and her father.

Two hours later, I see a fishing camp with three natives, and then I pass by the site where the butterflies comforted me.

123

travel: v., 1 make a journey. 2 withstand a journey without adverse effects.
ORIGIN variant of *travail*

travail: n., 1 painful or laborious effort. 2 labour pains.; v., undergo such effort.
ORIGIN Old French, from Latin *trepalium*, an instrument of torture.

124

I don't have a clear description of the entrance to the Lirial lagoon or the route into the village of Lirial. The government maps are inaccurate with mislabelled rivers, few details, and villages marked miles from their actual location. In Mercadeo, Luis tried to give directions, but mostly he described other entrances and lagoons. He talked on and on about an inlet, side branches, the best place to fish, the swamp where he killed a seven-foot caiman and a curassow turkey, and other sidebar information.

Then, *"Pero eso no es."* But this isn't the one you want. He did that all afternoon.

Now the tide is turning and I still haven't reached the channel. Or maybe I passed it and didn't realize what it was. All I know for certain is that the day is ending, and I should have stopped at the fish camp or the butterfly landing to spend the night. This stretch of river has become my nemesis.

After tying the dugout to a mangrove root, I take off my clothes. I drag myself and a small pack up the riverbank using broken branches and tree roots to keep from sinking into the mud.

The highest patch of ground is soggy, but it looks as though it will stay a few inches above the high tide mark tonight so that I can sleep. That's the plan, but barely five minutes later, three black men approach in a fibreglass fishing boat. *Colombianos.* They must have been watching me from the far side of the river. They arrive just as I'm sorting out my bag of food.

"Awwooo!" the driver calls out, as he turns off the motor.

I respond the same.

He gestures with his hand, the palm turning upward, fingers spread. The *what-the-hell-are-you-doing-here?* gesture.

I respond with the same hand movement, and I point at his boat with my lips, as if it's strange for me to come upon a fishing boat in these waters.

"*A donde va?*" he asks. Where are you going?

"*Aquí no más.*" Just here, no further, I answer.

"And you?" I ask. "Where are you going?"

He seems a little taken aback at the inferred equal status.

"We're fishing," he answers, nodding his head toward the coolers and fishnets.

The other two men are either uninterested or they're fugitives. They keep their heads bowed. I never see their faces, only their hat brims and ragged clothes.

"*Que tenga suerte,*" I say, wishing them luck with the fishing.

They motor off against the current.

I avoided answering their questions. Wounaan style. Autemio style.

But when they leave, I also lose my only possible ride into Lirial. My gut tells me I shouldn't have anything to do with these three. They feel like trouble. But it's less than an hour before dark. I have nowhere to turn or run, and now they know where I am.

I spent the entire day without meeting another boat on the river until this final moment when I really want to be invisible and forgotten.

I wish there was a *gira* floor to bless my body tonight.

125

On my last night in Mercadeo the *dirigente*, Cachoro, said, "There are Colombians in the Laguna Lirial. They'll see you, and they'll think you have money. They'll try to rob you and kill you."

There was only one candle burning. I couldn't see Cachoro's face clearly.

He also said, "And no matter what happens, don't try to sleep in your *piragua*. A *lagarto* [a caiman or alligator] or a crocodile will tip it over and eat you. Get some long poles and sharpen them…"

He stopped.

"You don't carry…?" He squeezed an imaginary trigger with his finger.

I shook my head from side to side.

"Okay, get some long, strong poles, and use a machete to sharpen them.

"*Bueno*," he said. Good.

It was settled.

In Theodore Mendez's book on Darien, he writes that you have to drive the spear right into that soft spot in the *lagarto's* armpit.

Bueno.

126

It's all those things that I can't touch or see that frighten me most. Fear of everything I don't know. Things that might or might not be waiting for me in the shadows. Fear of death. Fear of the dark. Fear of noises I can't identify.

Fear hobbles me on this trip. It's fuelled by all the warnings I've heard and read. It's trapped in my head now, so that every tiny noise develops a life of its own. I can taste it in my mouth tonight. It's causing this kink in my neck, a dull ache that keeps me awake.

I'm sweating and soaked through in my nylon tent. I wish that a breeze would rustle the trees and drown out these unknowable water noises. These clicks and pops. The low roar from a jet overhead that sounds like a jaguar. Branches snapping. The sound of voices. Whose voices? I'm far from any village or any pathway, so why do I hear machetes and rifles scraping over a mangrove root?

I'm on the highest patch of the mud flat, but the river is still rising, inching higher and higher, until it's lapping at the doorway of the tent. This is just how an alligator or a crocodile wants his supper. He'll charge out with his jaws open, chomp down on the tent with his jagged teeth and crush my body, grinding back and forth while dragging me into the water.

This isn't like swamping a dugout canoe in a racing flood current at night. There isn't anything to confront. No wild animal, no thieves in the night or a Colombian guerrilla. There's only my fear and my unbridled imagination. Everything inside conspiring to destroy me.

Now I hear boots trampling the ground outside. I can't get this madness under control. I fall apart in the tent, trembling and weeping. I can't find my glasses or even my shirt. I pull on my pants. I've lost the flashlight, but I grab my machete. I tear open the tent zipper and burst through the doorway into the mud and shallow water. Mosquitoes cover my body and face. I raise my machete overhead to attack, to cut someone down, anyone, anything. I try to roar. I let go with everything I have left, but it gets caught in my throat and warbles.

I try a second time to roar like a beast. Still nothing. And nothing answers. Only the mosquitoes in my ears. My heart pounding in my head. Mangroves clicking, more water noises. Everything the same as before.

I fall to my knees in the mud. My tent is full of insects.

I've heard that alligators and crocodiles prefer to wait for their prey to enter the water before attacking. I have a sharp pole in the dugout, but I'd never be able to find a reptile's armpit in the dark. It seems impossible to me, and I wonder if Cachoro and Mendez were serious, or if it's just a joke that Darien natives play on gringos. I think about that while I'm still kneeling in the mud.

I'm so fucking tired of being afraid.
 I don't know what beast I was trying to imitate. Is there some sorry animal that tries to protect itself that way? At first crying and curling into a ball, and then suddenly rearing up and shouting? Is there such a freak?
 And FARC guerrillas, and those so-called *maleantes*, bad people … what would they think of my roar? How would they respond to a gringo warrior exploding from his tent, waving a machete overhead, tears streaming down his cheeks?
 What would they think?

I really want to go home.
 I've felt that way for twenty years. I want a good night's sleep. I want a hot bath and a family Christmas. But I was hoping that I would sail home.
 I wanted to return someday from an epic journey. Not crying like a baby and helplessly weeping in the mud. Desperate for not writing. No well-told story. No lines of poetry. No art. No passion. No battle between good and evil, with scenes so horrible that they mark me with a sadness that never fully leaves my eyes.
 I think every traveller wants a version of that. From there, we believe, with the wisdom that comes from hardship, maybe we'll finally be able to work our way home again.

127

At mid-morning, I launch the dugout with the ebb tide, but I never find the entrance to Lirial. The few promising channels I enter all end in closed mangroves, and so I return to the Tuira and enjoy the long paddle through the day.
 It's raining hard and beautiful when I reach Cavimál at midnight.

I scare a snake when I step on the porch, and I hear the familiar sound of termites in the crossbeams. I use the rainwater bucket to rinse the mud off my body. I make a pot of tea, and I sit down in the mouldy hammock.

It's already hard to remember the night in the mangroves, but I'm happy to be where I am. Life can be like that. Just tidewater rising and falling in the bay, ebbing then flooding eighteen feet every six hours, and it doesn't have a damned thing to do with any of us or our plans.

128

A swarm of bees descends on my house in the late afternoon, filling the porch and over the gardens. I walk away and down the hill to where Otilio is dragging drift logs and old coconuts to the tidal flats.

"There's *una plaga* of bees on my house," I say.

"Where?" he asks.

"All over. Inside and out." I point at them through the mango trees.

"*Africanas*," he whispers. He puts his finger to his lips and he crouches low as if we can hide.

"Quiet," he says, motioning palms down with both hands.

"They'll go away, or if they build a nest we can buy a gallon of diesel and burn it down at night."

I love Otilio's pragmatic straddling between tradition and modern ways. It's a balance that few people can accomplish so gracefully.

Sometimes at night I hear him shout out from his house.

"Autemio! Temio! Temio!"

He shouts a long string of words in Wounaan, but he mixes in enough Spanish so that I can understand.

"Get up, Autemio! The tide is right for fishing ... for setting your shrimp net in the mangroves and catching *corvina* at the point."

Autemio and Diana set shrimp nets across a mangrove channel to earn extra money for the outboard motor.

"Get up! Now's the time to make money to pay for the motor. Get up!"

Only silence.

Otilio starts over again.

"Autemio! Temio! Temio!"

129

My *tocayo* has fallen sick since we last saw each other. His last name is Martínez. Technically that's not a *tocayo*, but we use the ritual whenever we meet.

I hardly recognize him this morning. He's sitting on his porch, built out over the water, when I paddle past Puntita.

"*Tocayo*, how are you?" I ask.

He used to look so healthy, walking his three-hundred-pound pig Nena (Babe) along the trails, scavenging for food. But now his face is twisted out of shape. One eye is swollen shut and his mouth is contorted. He can't even form words clearly.

"*Tocayo*, what has happened?" I ask.

"*Tocayo*, I'm sick," he says. He tells me it is *derrame*, a hemorrhage … maybe a stroke.

"I was in the hospital. I died for an hour before they could revive me."

I wonder if that's possible, but he does look as though he died a while back and hasn't fully recovered. And the pig is gone. Martínez had to sell Nena to pay his bills.

"Where's your woman, *tocayo*?" he asks. Kathy has been gone for almost a year now.

"She's in America," I say. I really don't want to talk about her.

"When will she be here, *tocayo*?"

"*Tocayo*, I tell you the truth. She'll never come back. She's gone forever."

He doesn't want to see me living like him.

"I'm all alone," he says. "No one to look after me."

It isn't just loneliness. That isn't the word. It's something more profound and tragic. It's loneliness with a failing body and a broken heart that might never heal.

If the *baracoco* bird sang right now, we would both fall inconsolably to the ground.

I wish that I'd taken his photo a month ago. I want to say, "Look, *tocayo*. Here's a picture of you and your fine pig."

And she was a beautiful, fat pig.

Martínez used to laugh and throw ripe plantains or spoiled vegetables to her. Babe would grunt and squeal and shove her snout into the pile to eat like only pigs can eat.

"Look at her! Look at her!" Martínez would shout as I paddled by.

130

I wait another two days for Bill and Autemio to produce the two hundred dollars or at least another explanation, but eventually I have to ask.

"How goes the battle?"

"It goes," Autemio answers. "Do you want some smoked fish, Martin?" he asks.

He mentions that ants have been destroying my tomatoes and peppers and corn.

I can tell the money topic won't surface if I leave it to him.

"And the motor?" I ask. "Is it running well?"

"Perfectly," he answers. "It's still brand new. We look after it in every way."

"And the payment?" I ask. "Have you been able to save any money from fishing?"

"You'll have to ask Bill," he answers. They both do this with motor and money questions. They send me back and forth.

When Bill arrives, he says, "Aii, Martin. We did really well, and for a while we had over two hundred dollars. But then we bought ice and small fish from the vendor for twenty cents per pound. We bought gas and made the trip up to Tucutí where you can sell the same fish for forty cents."

"And fast you can pay off the motor in this way," Autemio says. "All at once."

However, since the buyers in Tucutí didn't have money, they paid the Tovars with sacks of unmilled rice. The boys tell me that they were able to sell "most" of the fish. They got the rice "at a good price," and in this way it's possible to "make money at both ends."

"And?" I ask.

"We spread the rice out to dry. Then we spent some money to mill three bags to sell it at the market. But there wasn't much sun, so it took a long time to dry."

"... and maybe we waited too long," Autemio says. "Because now everyone has rice and the buyers don't want any more."

"We have the rice," he says, pointing at the sacks piled in the corner. I think he wants me to take five hundred pounds of rice as a motor payment.

"How much money is left?" I ask.

No one answers.

131

I feel safe at Cavimál. Or, I feel safer at Cavimál now than I did at the start of this trip, and safer than I do at other places.

It must have something to do with the familiarity of a place and people. At night, I recognize the sound of mangoes and coconuts falling from the trees in a light breeze. I know that the pig will be under the floor, and that Autemio's dog will dig through the compost scraps after midnight.

We gain some confidence through familiarity. We come to know the people in our small circle, not just through interviews or business transactions, but by working with them in the field, resolving disagreements, and staying for the full cycle of seasons.

The real concerns still remain. And the truth is that there isn't any place in Darien that is completely secure for a foreigner to stay for a long period. But over time in one place, the shadows don't seem so foreboding.

For the last four months, the Colombian who sells pirated music CDs in La Palma has tried to convince me to stop my upriver trips. The first time we met, Fernando was resting on a sidewalk bench in the evening, reading a Spanish translation of Chekhov. Across the street, the butcher shop sells the coldest beer in La Palma.

"Martin," Fernando says later, as we sit on the bench with our cans of beer. "If you won't listen to me, then at least you should talk to my friend in Metetí. Maybe he will change your mind."

132

Alexis Ortiz has a soft handshake. When you grip his hand it feels as though there isn't any solid shape under the flesh. Like uncooked pork sausages.

He tells me twice that he isn't afraid to live in Metetí. He would just like to have back that year and two months he lost.

133

On October 23, 1999, Alexis wasn't feeling well. He decided to stay home rather than go to his night class at the local college. He brought home food for his six-year-old daughter, Katherine, and they were watching a video when three men armed with automatic weapons barged into his house.

A month before Alexis's abduction, another worker from the region had been kidnapped by Colombian FARC guerrillas. A month before that, another man was shot dead by the same group when he resisted.

The intruders told Alexis that they were border police, but they didn't fool Alexis. He tried unsuccessfully to hide the keys to his truck. When they forced him to drive, he pretended the vehicle ran out of fuel, but they'd played this game before.

Because of a heart condition, Alexis fainted three times during the drive to Lajas Blancas along the Chuqunaque River. From there they continued to the outskirts of Puerto Peñita, where the guerrillas stole a pair of rubber boots for him to wear. They used a boat to cross the river, and then they disappeared into the forest, at night, in the rains of October.

134

Today Alexis walks with a limp. He wears a gold necklace with a lucky horseshoe pendant. He flirts with schoolgirls when they come into his family's store, but he's normally quiet and soft-spoken.

At first he hesitates to tell me his story. He wants to know if there's something in it for him. He says that he'd like to get something back for the year and two months. He never says "fourteen months." It's always "a year and two months."

"What would you like to do?" I ask.

"I've thought about writing a book," he says.

"Have you started on it?"

He opens a cardboard box and pulls out a file folder with twenty-two handwritten pages.

"I'd like people to know how it was. How it felt."

He keeps the folder in his hands.

"I was thinking," he says, scanning his right hand across the face of the folder as if tracing the title on an imaginary book.

"*Secuestrado en Darién. Una Experiencia Vivida.*"

Kidnapped in Darien. A First-Hand Account.

The guerrillas forced Alexis to march for fourteen days after his capture. At that stage, he met a guerrilla captain who used a radio telephone to call Metetí. Alexis's father insisted that they had very little money, but the captain mocked him, and he threatened to kill Alexis if they couldn't come up with a million dollars. From there, the group marched another two days to a new camp where they tied Alexis's hands and feet and put him in a cage built from tree branches. They kept him there for two months.

Only for *necesidades* could Alexis leave the cage. A guard would tie a rope to Alexis and stand beside him while Alexis tried to defecate. He became constipated from the tension. He developed dysentery and blood in his stool. His hemorrhoids grew more painful until he didn't want to eat because he knew it would only cause more pain and bleeding.

"But you don't want to die," Alexis tells me. "If you die, then they win. If you die, they'll still collect the ransom. They win in every way. You can't let them break your spirit.

"What you have to do," he tells me this later in the evening when he comes to visit at my rented room. "You have to forget about your home, your daughter, your family and friends. You can't think about them. You just have to say that it's in God's hands.

"I tell myself," Alexis says, "if *He* is on my side, then who can be against me?"

Alexis doesn't cry when he says these things, or when he talks about his daughter and how the guerrilla captain threatened his family.

At the toughest moment, he turns to look at me. His eyes are brimming to the top, but not a tear rolls out. He won't cry. He says that he's not able to cry anymore.

His journal notes describe each march through the mountains. The second one lasted a month and eight days. The next was twenty days. Then another for a month and thirteen days.

Guerrillas died from snakebites. They had to move camp when they heard a jaguar roar a little closer to them each night. After Colombian government troops or paramilitaries fired on the guerrillas, they moved on again. Alexis ached. His hemorrhoids bled. They hiked endlessly. Sometimes in daylight. Sometimes at night. When they reached a new camp, the guards tied him up or locked him in the cage.

Rotting branches sometimes crashed down around their camp, and on one night a tree collapsed on the two hostage cages built side by side. It killed one prisoner and pinned Alexis, breaking both of his legs.

A year and two months after his abduction, after his family had sold everything they'd built and saved from twenty years working in Darien, FARC guerrillas led Alexis out of the forest to freedom at Punta Cocalita on the Pacific coast of Panama.

Alexis hobbled into the clearing, supporting his broken body with crutches made from a tree branch.

135

When Alexis arrived back in Panama, he spent four days in Santo Tomás hospital in Panama City.

The government offered Alexis a counselling program, but he said he was fine. He returned to Metetí, and three months later he registered for more college courses.

"What's different about you today from how you were before the kidnapping?" I ask him.

I don't know if he blocks out those memories, or if he's willing to talk about it with a stranger.

He says, "My heart is harder now. It's like steel. I don't feel the pain or the joy as much as I used to."

He thinks that maybe this is a bad thing, but it's how his heart is coping. He believes that it will never change and that he'll die this way.

He's thirty-one years old.

136

I've become mired in politics.

I wanted to write a poem to Darien. I thought I was going to describe the sound of *corvina* fish growling at the full moon and the soft puff of two dolphins swimming at night while I lie awake on the floor at Cavimál. I wanted to paint the skies, the morning half-light in the mangroves, clouds snaking through the valleys, and the lush green of Colombian mountains in the evening.

I was hoping to be that wide-eyed traveller, always amazed, always in love with the forest and rivers and the stories told at night by a fire.

Instead I've pushed forward, asked questions and pulled back layers. But now it feels as if I've lost touch with the beauty and colours and poetry of the place.

137

On the evening before I left the *abuelos'* home in Mercadeo, grandfather watched me load my basket of food.

"*Hermano*," he called to me. Brother.

"What is that fruit?" he asked.

"A tomato," I said, judging by the shape he made with his thumb and two fingers.

"Oh, yes," he answered, nodding his head. "It's very beautiful."

CALEDONIA

138

From the boat docks at Colón, a sailor can walk across the railroad tracks to the main street, past the bus depot, the bars and brothels, fried-chicken stands and crumbling apartment balconies with rolls of barbed wire cascading down like jungle vines. He can buy hardware at Wing Fat's *ferretería*, spare engine belts and motor oil at Champion Auto *refacciónes*, fresh produce at Pepe's *frutería*, bread and sticky buns at *panadería* Carmelita, medicine without a prescription at a dozen pharmacies and lottery tickets at sidewalk stands on any corner. It is everything that a transient sailor could possibly want. But Colón changes after dark. It takes on a sharper edge, and when the sun is setting, most gringos scramble back across the tracks to the safety of the so-called Colón Yacht Club where there is a large round bar and an international crowd of sailors telling the same stories you'll hear in any sailor's port of call.

One evening, while I was lingering on the main street after daylight had started to slip away, two black schoolgirls with pigtails skipped up beside me and talked to me while looking in the other direction. We acted like secret agents, passing information while pretending to be just standing casually in the street.

"Some bad men are waiting for you at the end of the block," one girl said while playing a hand-clapping game with her school friend. "They have knives and they're going to take your money."

I didn't look down the street toward my welcoming party. I thanked the girls without turning to face them, and I headed off to the docks along a different route.

139

Hernán won't want to take me on his boat. He's a sad poet from Venezuela, and he usually sails alone. Single-handed sailors are often lonely and sad, but most of them prefer life that way. Sailing poets take that preference even further. Still, when I hear that Hernán is going to sail through the San Blas Islands on his way to Colombia, I hurry down to the dinghy docks to wait for him.

It begins to pour, but the rain is warm and tropical. I've been waiting for almost an hour by the time I see him cross the railroad tracks, bags of groceries in his hands and a small pack hanging from his shoulder.

He's wearing a long red raincoat, and by the way he walks, the lightness of his steps, it looks as though he's happily lost in thought.

"Stocking up for the next leg of your trip?" I ask in Spanish.

He must see the grey cloud of my own melancholia. It makes him comfortable. We stand in the rain and he lets his guard down as we begin talking. He doesn't realize that this is an ambush.

We talk about writing, and then sailing, and then the fish and birds and animals we've seen in Panama. He says a few words about the hardships of sailing alone, and I tell him about *Ishmael* and my experiences in Darien. He's interested and asks more. He still doesn't suspect anything.

It's only later, when I'm soaked through to my skin and I know the hook is set well and we are thick in an intimate conversation about poetry and the taste of ocean salt on a woman's body that I ask him if I can hitch a ride as far as the island of Mulatúpo on his way to Colombia.

"Oh, *coyño*," he says. I don't know the exact translation of that word. In slang expressions it refers to a woman's vagina, but Hernán also uses it as "friend" or "dear" or "brother." He calls other men by that name after he decides that he likes them.

"My boat is very small," he explains. "It's only thirty feet."

I don't say anything at first. I use my own sad-poet eyes to respond.

"I'm actually much more comfortable travelling alone," he says. "I usually prefer it that way."

"I know what you mean," I answer, and I pause and nod my head in agreement, hoping that my kindred spirit will put him at ease. "I'm exactly the same," I tell him.

I feel sorry for him right now, for the pain I'm causing in his peaceful world. He rocks back and forth from one skinny leg to the next. Just minutes ago we were talking from the core of our loneliness and desire. It will be impossible for him to close the door on me so easily.

"You get used to that control of your boat, and the tiny space around you," I say to him. "You have to be so careful who you invite in, even for just a short leg. We're exactly the same."

140

Hernán and I sail *Sirius* through the first afternoon, all through the night and most of the next day. He sails and I rest. I sail and he goes below. Sometimes we talk, or we silently share the cockpit and look out to sea, but we leave plenty of room for each other to breathe.

After each watch, I curl up damp and salty on the downwind bunk, savouring the delicious phlegm of exhaustion in my mouth.

141

At the anchorage at Holandés Key we're surrounded by coral atolls and coconut trees. I lie down on the deck in the shade of the boom, and I can hear Hernán talking to three Kuna men who have paddled

Hernán, the poet from Venezuela, sleeps in the cockpit of his sailboat Sirius *while the wind blows us toward the San Blas Islands. He didn't want to take me along at first. "I'm actually much more comfortable travelling alone," he said to me. "I usually prefer it that way."*

over from their fishing net. Hernán wants to trade his old *Playboy* magazines for their weavings and carvings.

They thumb through a few pages.

"Do you have any *National Geographic*s?" the oldest one asks.

Each leg of a trip swallows me so completely that after a short time in a new world it can feel as though I've been there for years. It was just yesterday that we left Colón, yet I can hardly remember it now. Colón, the main street, the filthy marina water—all of these are lost somewhere in my distant past.

I'm only half-awake in the gentle roll of protected water, hypnotized by the slap of a slack halyard against the mast.

I have to tighten that down, I think. And then I fall asleep.

142

"You're from Canada?" Presci asks me. He is the youngest of the three Kuna brothers waiting for me onshore. He's more boy than man.

Their family lives alone on the tiny atoll, guarding the coconuts from thieves.

"You're Canadian?" he asks again. Hernán must have told him while I was asleep on the deck.

"Yes, I am."

"You know Bryan Adams?" he asks.

"I don't know him personally," I answer.

I can see that Presci is disappointed. He's been waiting all afternoon to talk to me.

"But I saw him in concert," I say. I never did, but I lie about it and Presci looks happier.

"It was great," I tell him. "Bryan played 'Cuts Like a Knife' and 'Everything I Do.'" Those are the only two Bryan Adams songs I can remember.

"And the song from Robin Hood?" Presci asks.

"He closed the show with that one."

Presci nods. Can he imagine what a concert would be like? Has he seen a Bryan Adams video somewhere?

"Do you live near him?" he asks.

"About six hours away by bus," I answer. Once you start telling lies, each one leads to another.

This isn't what I expected when I rowed to shore. From *Sirius* I could see the cane-walled huts, the *ulu* dugouts pulled up on shore, a cooking fire outside, red-skirted Kuna women walking through the coconut groves.

Presci brings out a battered guitar with the neck repaired using a block of wood, four screws and a thick coat of glue. Walking through the house, we duck under the hammocks and leave our footprints across the smoothly swept sand floor. The extended family gathers outside. I play a Bob Dylan tune and two John Prine songs. Presci sings a love song he wrote in the Kuna language about a man who went away on a ship. The sailor is sad and lonely, and in the song he cries to be back with his woman.

It's a beautiful song. Presci's voice is rich and full for such a young man. His brothers and father sit beside us. The women sit on another log across from us. Their forearms and calves are bound tight with laced beads in reds and blues and yellows and greens. They each wear a gold ring pierced through their nasal septum, and while Presci sings, they look away expressionless as if nothing is happening.

I wonder what his family thinks of his music. And how does he know so much about Bryan Adams? There's no electricity out here. Only coconuts and sand.

143

Five days later at Mulatúpo Island, Hernán and I make *café con leche*. We have another bowl of soggy corn flakes with warm milk for our last breakfast together.

I can tell that he'll be glad to have his small space back to himself, but I think that sometimes he'll miss my company. On late night

At Mulatúpo Island Kuna children and adults swim and paddle out to Sirius *until there is a revolving group of thirty or more passengers constantly aboard. Hernán brews pot after pot of tea and makes snacks with honey, sausages, or melted cheese on crackers.*

watches. Or when thirty Kuna kids swim wildly out to *Sirius* and clamber aboard the boat for the afternoon as they did when we first anchored here. Moments like that.

144

On shore yesterday, Mulatúpo's *saíla*, the village leader, threatened to fine us for arriving unannounced at his island. He'd been drinking all day and stared at us glassy-eyed. It was a Sunday. We could see a line of Kuna men in a similar condition sitting on his back porch. We weren't welcome here, he told us. He ordered us to get off Mulatúpo and return in the morning to pay a visitors tax.

In the morning, however, we decide that we aren't enthusiastic about a repeat visit. After sharing breakfast, I flag down a motorized dugout on its way to Caledonia Island. Hernán hauls up his mainsail and sails off the anchor.

My ride passes close to Tubualá Island. We skirt along the edge of a sea-level islet with an airstrip for small planes that carry the lobsters caught by Kuna fishermen to the market in Panama City. It feels good to be choosing my path again. Just as Caledonia appears in the distance, the driver turns the throttle down to an idle. Our bow drops, and the boat dies in the water, rocking with the following wake.

At first I think that there is a problem with the outboard, but the driver leans toward me to talk.

"*Su misión?*" he asks.

He's worried about bringing me unannounced to Caledonia.

The Kuna prefer it when you follow protocol. You're supposed to go through proper channels and request prior permission to visit each village, but before today I really didn't know where I wanted to hike. It has only been during this last week on *Sirius*, talking to Kuna on the islands of Holandés and Mulatúpo, that my plans have taken shape.

"I'm going to Caledonia where the Scots built their colony and where Balboa was killed," I tell him. "I want to hire a guide to take me across the mountains and back into Darien's Chuqunaque Valley on the other side."

He nods. He nods at the part where I say I'm going to leave San Blas.

"You're going back to Panama City?"

"That's right. Eventually," I answer. "I'm taking the hard route to Panama City."

"Okay."

Kuna don't usually invite outsiders to live in their communities. To visit might be acceptable, but to stay is another thing. They like to know that you're definitely going to leave.

The driver opens the throttle again and a bow spray arcs out. We cut a trail over glassy waters with a clear view of the coral below.

145

At Caledonia, the concrete pier is only a foot above sea level. The island isn't much higher. Dugouts and driftwood lie scattered on the shore, and rock jetties radiate out with lopsided latrines perched at the end of each one.

A Kuna official saw my white face approaching in the distance and he's waiting for me on the dock.

"Come with me," he says when I step out of the boat.

"Who are you?" I ask.

"I'm the school director."

"Is this part of your job?"

He doesn't answer.

I follow him down a soft sand road between tightly spaced houses built with vertical sticks.

It's 9 a.m. and I'm already sweating. My packs are so big and clumsy. I don't know why I'm dragging around so much stuff.

A man sells clothes, fabric, cooking oil, sugar, pots, utensils and hardware from a cargo boat tied to a dock at Caledonia Island.

We stop outside the community hall.

"You'll state your mission here," he tells me before we step out of the tropical sun and through the entrance.

It's cool inside. Benches spread out like pews in a church with enough room for at least three hundred parishioners to pray. I can see five men lounging in hammocks and sixteen more on the benches. Three women kneel by a pot, their gold nose rings bright against their brown skin. One of them ladles a drink into a cup. A man acts as the *vocero*, the spokesman, relaying messages between the *saíla* and any foreigner arriving with a request.

In a moment, everything has changed again. Hernán and *Sirius* brought me here, but now they've also faded to history. I'm *here. Now. Completely.* I'm the outsider, and it's a familiar discomfort. An old suit of clothing, well-worn and ready for anything.

"State your case," the school director tells me. "Tell them why you're here."

Even in the worst-case scenario, I know that there will be a story to tell. I'll come away with a more complete picture, and a taste of Darien that will linger. And I'll slow down and remember everything. I'll jot down notes. I won't forget anything this time.

146

Caledonia. A Scottish name for a village of Kuna natives in Latin America. How does that happen?

On March 12, 1698, a Scottish company posted a proposal folio in every coffee house in Edinburgh, Leith and Glasgow.

> To Settle a Colony in the Indies
> Everyone who goes on the first expedition shall receive and possess fifty acres of plantable land and fifty-foot square of ground at least in the chief city or town, and an ordinary

house built thereupon by the colony at the end of three years.

Every councillor shall have double. If anyone shall die the profit shall descend to his wife and nearest relations. The family and blood relations shall be transported at the expense of the Company.

The Government shall bestow rewards for special service…

At the time of the folio, King William III had just signed the Treaty of Ryswick to end the decade-long War of the Grand Alliance against France in Ireland, the Netherlands, Spain and the Holy Roman Empire. Thousands of Scottish soldiers returned home to find there was no hero's welcome waiting for them. There was no work, and it was the second of seven bad years in which snows came early and remained late on the fields so that food rotted in the ground and livestock suffered. Some of the men turned to begging or thieving. Others signed contracts to sail to America, or sent their children to the tobacco fields of Virginia as indentured labour.

In their misery, they found the colony proposal intoxicating. The response to the call for volunteers was overwhelming. The company selected mostly single men for this first wave of colonization, although a few officers took their wives. Those who remained behind in Scotland, both men and women, emptied their pockets to invest in the company and enthusiastically sent their sons to take part.

147

Near the end of the same year, three ships sailed to Darien with two small tenders and a cargo load of 1,200 Scots—minus the forty-three men and one woman who died during the voyage.

They arrived in Darien, planning to build New Edinburgh in the rainforest. The ships were loaded with barrels and tons of goods, useful and otherwise. An incomplete list includes:

300 tons of biscuits

200 slaughtered oxen
70 tons of stalled beef
15 tons of pork
so much stockfish that they couldn't estimate the quantity
20 tons of prunes
5,000 gallons of brandy
1,700 gallons of rum
1,700 gallons of strong claret
5,000 gallons of vinegar (to wash down the decks and avoid dysentery)

So far so good. However, their list of trading goods raises some doubts about their chances for success:

1,440 Scotch bonnets delivered as a first instalment on the contract for an even larger order
1,500 English Bibles
2,808 catechisms
2,000 reams of paper
29 barrels of white-clay tobacco pipes (27,000 pipes in all)
14,000 needles
3,000 candlesticks
25,000 pairs of shoes, pumps and slippers (these items were in response to a pirate's account of the barefoot natives in Darien)
a mountain of serge, dyed "one-fourth part black, one-fourth part blue, one-fourth part of several sorts of red, and one-fourth part of several sorts of cloth colours"
tartan hose, stockings, and boxes with four thousand periwigs, bob-wigs, and campaign wigs (it's not clear whether these were to trade with natives or for the Scots to replenish their personal supply)
many items that aren't easily identifiable today, including the gross of "Meikle Hair Buttons" and the hundred "Wombles" of three sizes

148

By now I should be accustomed to the questions. I should have polished my story to put everyone at ease.

Cual es su misión? My mission?
Explica su caso. State your case.
Que es lo que quiere? What is it that you want?

I can see the *saíla's* hat brim, and his trouser legs, and his bare feet over the edge of the hammock, but I can't see his face in the shadows.

I wonder what they will do with me if they decide my trip is unacceptable. There is no easy way out. Hernán has left with *Sirius*, and they can't just take me to the mainland and dump me since that's where my trail destination begins.

I start to say something about crossing the mountains, but the *vocero* interrupts me. He sips from a cup of cacao and then offers it to me.

I repeat his style, sipping from the plastic cup. I'm the only person standing. Everyone watches me sip chocolate and then wipe the sweat from my forehead.

I start again.

"Wait," the *vocero* says. "Here it is a custom to first drink the cacao. Then talk."

Low laughter all around me.

"And you're supposed to drink it down all at once. Not with little sips."

I drain the cup.

If they have a chance to laugh at you, and you're not offended, then you're usually well on your way. I return the cup to the man next to me, and the others in line pass it hand to hand to the woman with the ladle.

While I resume my story, the chocolate brigade continues. The woman with the pot fills a cup. The same man sips from it before passing it hand to hand for the next man to drink down in a gulp. There's only one cup, and the first man takes a sip every time.

I explain my plans and why the route from their village is the one I most want to follow. I also ask for a guide by the name of Auboydí. Earlier, two men in Mulatúpo told me that he is an honest man. They said that he's old, but that he knows the mountains well.

The *saíla* listens. Even now, growing accustomed to the dim light, I still can't find his face in the shadows. He speaks quietly to the man next to him who, in turn, announces that Auboydí is the man sitting on the bench beside me.

This is how it happens sometimes.

Another man suggests that my guide is too old to make the trip.

"What are you offering?" Auboydí asks me in Kuna dialect, rubbing his thumb and two fingers together and ignoring the question about his age.

"I want to leave in the morning," I say. "My time in Panama is almost finished, and I don't know how long it will take to cross the mountains and descend the Chuqunaque River."

"A hundred dollars," he says, answering his own question. "That includes my grandson Leo to help."

This is just perfect. The school director says that I'll be left at the first Chocó village on the other side of the mountains.

"Two days," Auboydí says, holding up two fingers.

I like him already. It will probably take longer. He doesn't know how slowly I walk with a full pack, taking photos and asking questions along the way.

The other men in the room start an emotional debate. I can't understand what they're saying, and my guide isn't interested. There's a job to do. He's short, wiry and bowlegged with square shoulders. He grabs my expedition pack and pushes out into the street.

I think he wants to show the others that this weight is nothing for a man of his strength.

149

When Scotland formed the Company of Scotland Trading to Africa and the Indies, they tried to keep their planned colony destination a secret from England. Between meetings, the board of directors and their chief organizer, William Paterson, locked away their collection of charts, maps and journals. The company included Africa in their title mostly to divert the attention of their chief trading rivals. The only location they seriously considered was Darien, where they envisioned building a Scottish colony to control the commercial hub of the shipping world.

Paterson, the son of a Dumfriesshire farmer, was the only member of the company who had been anywhere near Darien. He had left Scotland when he was nineteen and had sailed to the Caribbean. While he was living in Jamaica he likely heard stories from buccaneers and former pirates—Henry Morgan, William Dampier, Bartholomew Sharpe and most likely the pirate/surgeon Lionel Wafer, who had lived three months with Kuna Indians. Paterson had heard enough to spark his interest, but he had never actually seen or set foot in Darien.

He returned to Scotland with considerable wealth, and his new business ventures flourished. England appointed him as one of the first directors of the new Bank of England, and he could have lived out his days in comfort and respectability if the pirate stories and half-truths weren't still fresh in his mind. He found it impossible to settle and enjoy his success. After a petty quarrel, he resigned his post at the bank, and in 1696, he convinced the Company of Scotland to accept his Darien colony proposal.

150

In the afternoon, Auboydí's grandson Leo invites me to paddle out onto the clear Caribbean waters in his dugout. When we approach the reef, we dive into the sea and let the boat drift while we snorkel and spearfish.

I want to say that "we" hunt and spear four small lobsters and seven fish, but the truth is that I catch only one fish. I'm more of a line-fisherman, and it takes me a long time to spear the first fish. I knock it loose in the boat, but it's pretty small. I'm not sure if Leo is laughing or if he accidentally swallowed seawater. However, the women at home laugh openly when they see the little fish. It's a beautiful laugh. I'm not sure why it feels so good in this house, with this family, but everything is perfect. Considering the spreading tropical rash on my legs and butt and armpits, I'm as comfortable as I can hope to be. Unfortunately it doesn't last.

In the afternoon, a Kuna elder arrives and motions for me to step outside.

"*Saíla* has decided that you'll cross with me," Aristotle says. "And we'll take another man, Alfonso, and his gun."

Aris looks as though he might be in his late fifties, probably fifteen years younger than Auboydí. He tells me that he wants to guide the trip and use his pay to continue on to visit a sick relative in Panama City. Unlike Auboydí, he speaks good Spanish. He even knows a selection of English words from the days when he washed cars in the American Canal Zone. During conversations he inserts these individual words as if they are complete thoughts.

"Clean," Aristotle says, polishing a coin with his shirt sleeve.

I'm not sure about the politics at work here, and no one seems willing to explain the sudden change. Auboydí and Leo stand next to me, but they don't answer when I suggest I might talk with the *saíla*. They look away. A door has just closed, and I can't interpret how I'm supposed to respond.

I want to state my case once more to the *saíla*, but since I don't speak Kuna dialect, when we arrive at the community hall, Aristotle speaks for me. This translation arrangement begins without a plan. Aris just begins to speak. He talks and talks without ever having consulted with me. I don't know what he's saying, and I'm realizing that he doesn't have any motivation to present my case well.

When Aris stops, there's only silence. It doesn't feel good.

The *saíla's* face is still lost in the shadows. I don't have a clue what he looks like, but when he speaks his first Spanish word, there is no misunderstanding the tone.

He says, "*Salga.*"

"Leave. Get off our island. You can't stay here. You'll fly out from Tubualá in the morning. You can't make your trip across our land."

"*Salga.*" Leave.

"I don't understand," I say.

Sometimes I stutter when I'm nervous. My tongue trips and it makes me even more nervous. I don't want to end the trip with another door slamming in my face.

I take a breath, and I pause.

"I accept your decision," I say to the shadow, as if we've just negotiated an agreement. "I'll be glad to cross with Aristotle and Alfonso. I thank you for your decision," I say, pretending that I didn't understand him.

Aris and I turn to go. I'm sure that the *saíla* recognizes what I'm doing.

Please, let's just pretend I didn't hear the order.

We walk out into the tropical heat and no one calls us from behind. The sun beats down and reflects back up from the white sand around us.

"Let's get your bags," Aris says. "We have room in my house."

151

In the evening, Aristotle returns home with a new plan.

"We can't leave tomorrow," he says.

Because of the solar eclipse today, the *saíla* has ruled that it's better to wait another day. He has also decided that Aristotle can't accompany me all the way to the highway. They'll have to cross the mountains, and then backtrack quickly to help repair the community airstrip.

"Also, *saíla* says that your visitors tax will be twenty-five dollars," Aris tells me.

The village chief is working me, but I still believe I'm in the best possible place. There are no police barring my route, and it appears the village has forgiven the *salga* order. I just want to go on my way with two guides and let the rest of the village forget I was ever here.

That night, Aris and I walk across the island to meet Alfonso, the second guide. I can't tell how old he is. He has three candles burning in his hut. His eyes look very old, but his skin is smooth and tight. He must weigh all of ninety pounds. He doesn't seem to know any Spanish, but he shows me his single-load 28-gauge. He's very proud of his shotgun. It should be in a museum, but instead he keeps it alive by rubbing oil on the metal whenever he handles it.

I've been trekking back and forth across the province for over a year now, but this is the Darien crossing I really want to make. Panama's border police closed down some of my earlier plans. I've also misjudged certain trips and made mistakes. I've paddled down rivers and hiked through forests, but I know that the journey won't feel complete without this one isthmus crossing. I want to start here at Caledonia, near the ruins of the Scottish colony and the original Spanish settlement of Acla, where Balboa was executed. I want to hike from the Caribbean to Pacific tidal waters following a similar route used by Balboa when he first crossed the isthmus and claimed the South Sea for King Ferdinand of Spain.

This is where two centuries of expeditions have been launched. From here, pirates and buccaneers crossed from Caledonia to raid the gold mines at Cana. British, French and American teams all searched in vain for a low passage through these mountains to build a sea-level canal. And decades later, Richard Marsh dragged his hired men across the same Sucurtí River route in his search for the white Indians.

Twenty years ago I probably would have bypassed this journey and instead attempted to complete the stretch between Boca de Cupe and the first dirt road in Colombia. I would have slipped past the Panamanian police and crept through the forest. I would have travelled as fast as possible and avoided any unnecessary contact with locals in case they might want to turn me over to the guerrillas for ransom money. Today, however, stealth missions and fearful adrenalin don't have the same draw for me as they once did. Risk is still a necessary part of my trip, but not a goal in itself.

I've come to believe that a sprint across the troubled Darien Gap to Colombia would be mostly an exotic thrill ride. A sort of gladiator sport with extremely high stakes and providing little chance of learning about anything other than my ability to respond to calamity. It's likely a game best left to younger men who are still convinced of their own immortality.

152

The San Blas Islands are so low-lying that if you approach on a sailboat it looks as though coconut trees are growing straight out of the water.

As the population increases, villagers have to haul sand and rocks in their dugouts from the mainland to extend the island perimeter. The land area spreads, but the elevation stays the same. Even with the breakwater rocks along the shore, water sometimes seeps up through the ground, and during high tide in the afternoon three inches of seawater cover the sand floor in Aristotle's home.

153

When Scotland's ships, filled with new colonists, arrived on the isthmus on November 3, 1698, two native canoes paddled out to greet them. The Kuna unstrung their bows and waved a white flag, and the Scots invited them onboard.

Chief Andreas wore a silver cone over his penis and a large golden disc from his nose. His wife and sister were dressed in white linen mantels. They had strings of beads wrapped up and down their arms and hanging around their neck, and each had a golden crescent hanging from her nose. Another chief and his second were just returning after killing the Spaniards and priests who had been living on Golden Isle.

Even after the Scots explained their settlement plans, the Kuna chiefs invited them to stay. Most likely the Kuna hoped to use the visitors as temporary allies against the Spanish.

It was an ideal beginning for the Scots. The sea was full of fish. The skies were clear and the rivers were running. The Kunas' acceptance of their proposal should have been all the advantage they needed.

Unfortunately, the colonists and the company council were able to create enough problems on their own. The first setback was their inventory of trade goods. The Kuna had no use for Meikle hair buttons, tartan hose and periwigs. Even more crippling was the lack of a political structure. The Scots had no clear hierarchy of control. The company had appointed a committee of councillors, but no permanent chairman. They decided to cycle the chair position amongst all members, changing at the end of each week. It was impossible to make the arrangement work. They fought over tiny details and each member spent the better part of his week undoing the work of his predecessor.

On arrival, the ships' captains—all of whom were also councillors—attempted to assert their maritime authority on land, even when they disagreed amongst themselves. Using their control of provisions to enforce their decisions, they selected a mangrove swamp for the townsite. The colonists wasted two months in that futile effort before the council issued a new order to move to higher ground and start over. The councillors squabbled endlessly. The colonists divided into factions. Every necessary project, including construction of the fort, was bogged down by infighting. After months in Darien, no work parties had been organized for planting crops or gathering and preserving meat and fish during these dry months. When heavy rains began six months later, they washed away any chance of success.

It rains hard on Darien's Caribbean coast. Close to two hundred inches can fall in a year. Thunder shakes the ground. Lightning splits open the sky. Water floods the rivers and turns the earth to mud and mangrove swamps.

With no substantial harvest to carry them through, the colonists settled down with old ship biscuits and rotting meat. By the end of April three hundred graves hugged the shoreline.

154

The colonists stared out through the rain and prayed for new supplies and healthy men to arrive from Scotland. Days dragged into weeks, and then on March 18, a merchant ship from Jamaica arrived with devastating news. England was against them. King William had ruled that the colony was jeopardizing relations with Spain, and he forbade all English merchants from trading with the Scots in Darien.

This was more bad news than the sick men could bear. They assumed that this also meant England would never defend them against a Spanish attack. Almost without exception, the colonists insisted that they should admit defeat and return to Scotland. Paterson and his friend Thomas Drummond pleaded for calm and patience, but Paterson could barely stand on his feet. His wife had already died months earlier, and yet he was still protesting when a group of men loaded him on a stretcher and carried him onto the waiting ship.

On June 19, using whatever healthy men they could assemble, they pulled up anchors on the four ships to evacuate the colony. But their trials were far from over.

The Spanish fleet attacked one ship, killing the captain and 130 men before they could limp away to safety in Jamaica. Another ship came apart at sea and a few survivors washed up on a Caribbean island. The ship *Caledonia* reached New York on August 3, 1699, but only after the captain "hove 105 corpses overboard on the trip … and still another 11 died since I came here already."

Eleven days later, the crippled *Unicorn* limped into the harbour with only a hundred of the original 250 men still on board.

Of the original 1,200 colonists, 750 were dead. Paterson was barely alive and now wasting away in New York.

"He looks more like a skeleton than a man," a survivor wrote later. "The grief has broke Mr. Paterson's heart and brain."

155

I am hoping that Aristotle, Alfonso and I can slip out of Caledonia without a sound. Just the faint ripple from a carved *ulu* in Caribbean water.

This one-day delay makes me nervous.

In the early morning, with the sky just waking and the faint light and the water still morning grey, I see thirty-eight dugouts cutting across the bay. On every San Blas island, the Kuna rise early and drink their own chocolate before crossing to the mainland to plant and hunt and harvest or fish. I want to be an anonymous part of those thirty-eight *ulus* fanning out before sunrise. I don't want someone to shout, "Hey! Where's the gringo going!?"

A police patrol boat arrives just before dark and ties up at the dock. I can't believe the bad timing, and I know that they'll stop my trip if they hear about it.

Fortunately the Kuna share information only when it's absolutely necessary. Also, there's no electricity in Caledonia. When it's dark, it's very dark. The paths are thick black, and people walk the sand paths with only sporadic flashes of light to keep their bearings and to warn other walkers.

The community hall is full tonight with about two hundred Kunas in the warm glow of candlelight. I see mostly women, but Aris is also in there. He tells me later that it's a Catholic service.

The evangelical minister on the island tells me that there aren't any Catholics in Caledonia. I ask him about the gathering, and he smiles. He smiles even wider and shakes his head when I tell him that we've been delayed a day because of the eclipse.

156

Auboydí's grandson Leo finds me at the pastor's house and he invites me back to his family's home to eat a big eel he cooked on the fire.

Leo is acting goofy tonight. I can barely see his face in the dark. I can't smell alcohol, but he's either drunk or dangerously happy.

Auboydí arrives later with the women, returning from the Catholic gathering ... if that's really what it was. Then the children arrive. Where were they? Everyone seems disproportionately happy.

Auboydí's grandchildren ask me to teach them English words. They absorb everything and immediately begin using the phrases. When I attempt to speak the Kuna phrases they've taught me, the women burst out laughing again.

"That's fine," I say. "I'm glad I can make you laugh."

I don't fully understand why their laughter sounds so beautiful and rich to me. Total abandon. I would love to stay with this family for a long while. Let them laugh at me for weeks and months.

I squat on their sand floor around the cooking fire, surrounded by their extended family—elders, women and children, and everyone leaning forward while I share English phrases that Leo wants to learn.

"I want to kiss you," I say.

"I love you," I tell him.

And then he asks me to teach him how to say "father-in-law."

Auboydí watches closely as my mouth and lips shape these words.

"I want to kiss you," Leo says a dozen times. His siblings join him and they repeat the words louder and clearer each round until they're shouting and laughing.

Auboydí nods his head. His grandchildren are fast learners.

Leo masters the three lines. He's still giddy, and now he's smiling so intensely that it makes me nervous.

"I love you," he says again. Practising once more.

Then he walks off into the night to visit his girlfriend, the evangelical minister's daughter.

157

Most young Kuna women I've seen are slim, with a flat bum, beautiful legs and a slightly swollen belly.

There is a candle burning on the table at Aristotle's house. One couple is asleep in the queen-sized bed with a wood headboard propped up on rocks above the flood-water line. The rest of us—fluctuating between twelve and fifteen each night—sleep in hammocks hanging from the rafters.

There is a chair beside my hammock. When the woman approaches, she sits down next to me and the candle casts a warm light on her face and body. Laced beads in primary colors on her forearms and calves. A soft fuzz on her neck. Her black hair cut short with bangs parted to the sides and a squared line at the back. I'm drawn to her collarbone and the shadows it forms.

She doesn't say anything. She just stares at me. Her skirt wrap rides high so that I see her thighs pressed together, much whiter than the rest of her visible body.

158

Paterson's arrival in New York should have ended the Scottish disaster, but in Scotland the next four ships were already loaded with new colonists and provisions. Fortunately the same wind that held them in Scotland's Clyde River was also driving another ship across the Atlantic carrying the one councillor still healthy enough to travel and letters from other survivors. As soon as the councillor's ship reached Bristol, he posted a hasty message to London, which in turn went by coach to Edinburgh and arrived before the ships could sail. However, the company's greatest handicap at that point was their unflagging patriotic optimism. Even with councillor M'kye's testimony in hand, the directors refused to believe that the colony had collapsed. In the absence of real news during the last half-year, they'd created a wonderful image of a thriving Scottish community in Darien, complete with a church, planted fields and a solid fort with cannons in place. It seemed so real that it had to be true.

Instead of acting quickly, the directors sat on the news for three days before finally sending a message to the waiting ships stating that there was a "rumour" circulating that the colony had been abandoned, "…altogether malicious and false … but though there be nothing in it, yet wee think it fitt that yow keep to yourselves…"

The message advised the captains to wait until the arrival of the councillor in order to hear his full report. They were that close to putting an end to their losses, but then the wind suddenly shifted. With everyone impatient and hungry for a better life in the New World, the ships weighed anchor and sailed out for the tropics and the fifty acres of plantable land for each man.

With M'kye's arrival a few short days later, the Company of Scotland finally realized the full extent of the colony disaster. They started organizing another ship with proper supplies to sustain the volunteers and appointed a chairman, Captain Alexander Campbell of Fonab, to lead the council.

For that brief moment in history, the colony came together. When Fonab arrived in Darien, two and a half months behind the second group of volunteers, he found the colony already bitterly divided. He immediately took charge. He freed the colonists who had been jailed because of new leadership squabbles, and he organized work parties to prepare the colony's military defence.

When Kuna natives warned Fonab that Spanish soldiers had established a camp nearby, he led a group of two hundred men on a three-day march to drive off the Spaniards and destroy their stockade. However, a few days later, when Spain's naval fleet began to land more troops and artillery on all sides of the Punta Escoces, the colonists had to retreat into the unfinished fort. As exhilarating as it had been, their brief taste of success was over.

The Spaniards were better armed and supplied, and the fort offered little protection. A fire destroyed the roof over their heads. It wasn't safe to walk to the river, so they drank from stagnant puddles. They had to survive on worm-riddled ship supplies, with hundreds of men becoming sick and feverish and a growing number of them dying each day.

On March 30, 1700—a month and a half after the siege had begun and seventeen months since the first colony ships had arrived in Caledonia Bay—the Scots surrendered to the Spanish general Don Juan Pimienta.

He allowed them fourteen days to stock food and water for their voyage back. More men died as they were carried onboard and others while waiting to set sail. They were so weak that they had to ask the Spaniards to tow one of their ships clear of the bay.

Not one of the four ships ever reached Scotland. The first was wrecked on the Cuban coast. The second leaked so heavily that it turned and ran for Cartagena, where it was sold for next to nothing.

A hurricane in Charleston, Carolina, destroyed the third ship. The same storm drove the fourth up onto a breakwater, sinking the vessel and drowning more than a hundred men.

Of the second expedition's 1,300 men, 940 died during their short-lived adventure.

159

Aris makes a show of spitting on the dirt floor in every house we enter. He sits down in the centre of the room. He looks around at his hosts and sometimes he looks at me. Then he leans down and spits on their floor.

Unprompted he tells me later that this is a healthy thing to do. The heart, lungs, blood … everything rids itself of waste and disease, and it all ends up in the phlegm to be spat out.

To not spit would be unhealthy.

He tells me that when he washed cars in the Panama Canal Zone, the Americans posted signs that read "Do Not Spit."

This didn't make any sense to Aristotle.

160

Thunder shakes us at 3 a.m. Rain beats down on the thatched roof and it rains for the rest of the night. It soothes me.

I wish I were lying in the big queen bed with a loving Kuna woman and her white thighs. We'd lie awake listening to the storm outside.

It's too wet to work today, I'd whisper to her in the early morning hours.

161

Last night we made a plan to leave at 5 a.m.

I get up at five, and no one else is moving. I dress in the dark and sit in my hammock. The police patrol boat is still at Caledonia's dock. I can't hide away for a full day on this tiny island. Someone will say something, and the police don't want gringos wandering through the mountains.

When Aristotle and his family join me in the kitchen later, we drink two cups of chocolate instead of one. I spit on his floor for good measure, but the family seems uneasy about that. I wonder if I'm supposed to spit before or after eating. Or not in the kitchen. Or only in the afternoon. I'm not sure.

Alfonso paddles in the bow. I paddle in the centre, and Aris mostly steers in the stern. Thirty *ulus* fanning out this morning across the glassy water, gliding silently to the mainland. One outboard-powered boat cuts across the water toward us.

Not now. Not now. Don't stop me now.

I keep my head down, and the boat passes by at a distance.

The San Blas mountain range towers up from the shoreline with misty clouds hanging in the forest between the highest peaks. I can't see any low passage through the chain of mountains. We'll have to climb up and over to reach the Darien lowlands.

I'm happy to be here, to move into some place and situation unknown and unpredictable to me. I'm happy to be walking with two aging Kuna guides.

ACROSS THE DIVIDE

162

All great Darien journeys begin or end on the coast near Caledonia.

Balboa's two great crossings began here. He also ended his life nearby, on the executioner's block at Acla.

Pirates would anchor in the bay while they marched across the isthmus to attack the gold mines at Cana. The Scots chose it, and named it for their ill-fated colony. Even the con men and investment schemers, such as the Irishman Dr. Edward Cullen, usually referred to Caledonia when they presented their fictitious reports and maps to investors.

In 1850, returning empty-handed and disappointed from the gold fields in California, Cullen slipped into Darien on his return trip through Panama. He wanted to investigate the abandoned gold mines at Cana, but in the end he was too sick to travel anywhere. Instead, while he rested in Darien at the house of a white settler, he asked a lot of questions. On his return to England, he presented a report claiming that he'd travelled back and forth across the province. To add some colour and detail to his description, he stated that he had paddled up the Sabanas River and climbed a tree where he "enjoyed a view of both Atlantic and Pacific, so narrow is the isthmus here."

Cullen's only interest was the gold mines at Cana, but by suggesting that there was a low pass to the Caribbean, he inadvertently set off an international race to claim control of a Darien canal route.

When Cullen realized what he'd done, his entrepreurial instincts took over. Instead of correcting the mistake, he embellished the story. He quickly returned to Panama, this time insisting that he had hiked across from the Sabanas River to Punta Escoces in six hours. He wrote in the margins of his report: "No high ground. No difficulties."

In the second edition of Cullen's *The Isthmus of Darien Ship Canal,* he included a title-page drawing of a wide canal running straight across the isthmus through lowlands lined with palm trees, and an insignificant mountain pass that was hardly worth mentioning.

The British sent Lionel Gisborne, a government civil engineer, to complete a survey and verify Cullen's claim. However, Gisborne had no experience in the tropics. Cullen had agreed to accompany him, but the doctor temporarily disappeared, forcing Gisborne and his assistants to proceed alone. Without guides, the survey crew became lost in the mountains soon after beginning their hike from the Caribbean coast. When the Kuna discovered the foreigners, they ordered them to leave.

Gisborne's Pacific experience wasn't any more productive. He damaged his equipment before he could even begin to survey. He never walked any real distance from either coast of the isthmus. However, like Cullen, rather than admit defeat, Gisborne followed the time-honoured Darien tradition. He climbed a tree and claimed to be able to see across a long valley to the point where he had ended the survey on the opposite coast.

His maps were much more detailed than Cullen's, but they were just as inaccurate.

163

With Gisborne's stamp of approval, Caledonia once again became the staging ground for a Darien expedition. Although Britain, France and the United States signed an agreement to cooperate on the project, both the British and the Americans began independently hatching plans to race across ahead of their partners. Britain sent a ship to the Golfo de San Miguel to find the path from the Pacific.

Almost simultaneously, an equally secretive American navy sailed a three-masted man-of-war to Caledonia to stage a short sprint from the opposite side.

From the deck of the USS *Cyane* anchored at Caledonia, Lt. Isaac Strain and his twenty-six hand-picked men gathered at the ship's rail to study the towering San Blas mountains. It looked nothing like Cullen and Gisborne's descriptions.

To make their situation worse, the Kuna at Caledonia weren't enthusiastic about foreigners making expeditions through their land. They told Strain that the maps were inaccurate and that there was no low pass through the mountains. However, Strain had already assumed that the natives would hide Cullen's route from him, so when they refused to act as guides he wasn't overly disappointed. The international partners—including the original surveyors and mapmakers—were only a few days away, but Strain had no intention of sharing the glory of this first crossing. He gathered his men and announced that they would leave immediately, and that he would lead them through the proposed canal route on his own.

One hundred and fifty years later, when Aristotle, Alfonso and I reach the mainland shore at Caledonia, we pull the *ulu* up onto the protected side of the point and tie it off in a swampy inlet. We walk the hundred feet to the exposed sandy beach where a row of dugouts are pulled up on shore with their paddles stored inside on the floor. There isn't an outboard motor in sight.

We begin walking through the fringe of coconut trees and then turn onto a path heading inland. Aris points to a mound of earth covered in thick vegetation on the side of the path.

"There was a fort there," he says. Does he mean Acla? "We know where these places are, but we keep it to ourselves."

164

The mid-1800s were good years for explorers and adventurers. Every ambitious nation had heroic individuals scaling mountains, and armies of men pushing back the frontier.

The United States was flexing its new muscles. Britain's navy still ruled the seas and controlled an empire that wrapped around the planet. Darwin set off on a three-masted bark as the crew's naturalist for a five-year circumnavigation. A British steamer crossed the Atlantic in fifteen days. On land, the US was building thousands of miles of railroads across the continent. Davy Crockett's biography was a bestseller, and America declared war on Mexico, eventually acquiring Texas, New Mexico, California, Utah, Nevada, Arizona and parts of Colorado and Wyoming.

By the end of the 1840s, the California gold rush lured thousands of money-hungry men to sail down America's east coast to Panama where they crossed the isthmus by horse and foot, or later by the American-built railroad, before heading north again by ship. France was at the earliest stage of its project to build the Suez Canal. And then Cullen released his report.

At that moment in history, every nation was competing for a piece of the international shipping and transport pie, either through control of marine ports or ownership of railroads. Even though Britain was stretched thin with fighting in Turkey, Russia, Burma, Afghanistan and New Zealand, they recognized the important role Panama would play in the future. After sending Gisborne to complete his survey, they signed the agreement with the US and France, and then tried to gain an advantage with their early expedition from the Pacific coast.

Unfortunately, the surveys and maps had been faked by their authors. The covert operation was a total failure, with the British sailors hiking a long distance in the wrong direction. Four of them were killed, apparently by Kuna natives, and the remaining men backtracked, desperate and exhausted, with another man dying shortly after reaching the ship.

165

At Caledonia, the mountains roll all the way down to the coast like the folds of a long skirt resting on the shoreline.

Aris, Alfonso and I start hiking along the trail at nine o'clock in the morning. Ten minutes later we begin a gradual climbing grade. We pass through a clearing with an empty communal house and five huts where forty Kuna Indians live and work during their harvest season each year. From there the trail steepens as it climbs from the feet of the *cordillera* (mountain range) and onto the slope of the continental divide.

When I ask Aris the name of these mountains, he tells me that they call them *las montañas*. They're the only ones he knows.

We splash back and forth through a narrow creek as we climb. Sometimes there is a trail. Sometimes it seems as though Alfonso has never been here before. I think that I was expecting a series of maintained pathways and signposts, and that my guides would steer us along the route that crossed the divide most efficiently to the Sucurtí River on the far side. It doesn't look as though anyone has walked this way in years.

I clean my glasses and wipe the sweat from my forehead. I'm glad that my guides are old men.

Forty minutes into the hike, my left shoe falls apart. Two-thirds of the sole peels away from the boot.

We're just branching off from the stream and starting to climb straight up the hillside. My shoes and socks are full of river sand and pebbles, but I don't want to turn back to Caledonia and face the *saíla* again. I wrap the long laces and a thin vine twice around the middle to hold the boot together.

There's nothing graceful about the way we're climbing. We pull on trees and exposed roots to keep from sliding backwards. Twice I stop to retie the shoe as the sole separates completely. Alfonso doesn't seem worried about my footwear. He probably assumes that my feet are tough like his. How could he imagine how tender a gringo's feet are?

At a little after 11 a.m., only two hours into the hike, Aris tells me that we've reached the top of the pass. I assume that this is just the first stage before the next valley and at least one more pass to climb before we reach the Pacific watershed.

In the summer of 2001, American writer Todd Balf tried to follow Strain's expedition route while researching his book *The Darkest Jungle*. He had wanted to cross at the same mountain pass used by the American navy expedition, but instead he settled for another route that the natives at Mulatúpo Island insisted upon. They told Balf that the other trail was overgrown and likely impassable.

During their hike from Mulatúpo to the village of Mortí, they slashed through vines and undergrowth. They hiked for three backbreaking days just to reach the top of the continental divide. Even their descent to Mortí turned into a slog. For most of two days they had to walk in the river "swamping through silty bottoms and water up to our waists."

Strain's expedition followed a slightly lower pass, but because of wrong turns and false starts, his group needed about the same amount of time to reach the Pacific slope. By stubbornly pushing themselves onward and higher, most of Strain's men reached the summit together. Unfortunately, a five-man scout group—including two experienced woodsmen and the doctor with his supply of medicines—became separated and lost, and eventually had to return to the ship.

After another ten minutes of walking through open forest, Alfonso points at a thin trickle of clear water.

"That's the Sucurtí River," Aris says.

Hiking steadily for little more than two hours from the Caribbean coast, we've already reached a tiny stream that will build and swell into rapids and chutes until the mountains ease and the water turns muddy and joins the Chuqunaque for the trip to the Pacific Ocean. It's all downhill from here.

Near the headwaters of the Sucurtí River, the water is clear and refreshing, and tiny red-headed sardines nip at my flesh whenever I swim in a protected eddy.

Alfonso is scouting ahead. Aris and I slow down and he asks me questions about geography and population statistics from around the world.

"How many people in Miami?" he asks.

"And Alabama?" When he pronounces the state, it comes out like *Hálabama*.

"*Donde está Pérsica?*" he asks. Where is Persia?

"Is Mexico a part of the United States?"

And then, "How many *departamentos* in Argentina?" he asks.

I once flew to Argentina to work for a week in Buenos Aires and in the far south of the country, but I don't know how many *departamentos*, or states, there are in Argentina.

"You don't know?" he says.

He seems puzzled by that.

Lieutenant Strain, having no knowledge of the region, followed a difficult route across the mountains. Todd Balf, wanting to duplicate Strain's early experience, chose a path with similar conditions. The route chosen by Alfonso is probably the lowest pass over the divide. It makes good sense to cross here. Very likely Balboa hiked through here on his second expedition to the South Sea. He would have needed to find the path of least resistance in order to transport his supplies from Acla to the Pacific watershed. According to the Spanish chronicler Andagoya, even with the well-chosen route, five hundred or more Indian slaves died while carrying timbers, sails, anchors and iron—everything necessary to build two ships on the Sabanas or Chuqunaque rivers.

Alfonso's route likely uses the same pass used by the seventeenth-century English pirates William Dampier, Lionel Wafer and John Coxon, who led three hundred to four hundred men across. From the summit they would have diverged from our path and followed a bearing more to the east as they hiked for nine days to attack the fort at El Real in 1680.

Invariably, the pirates used local natives to guide them on their expeditions. In his memoirs, William Dampier reflected on their decisions, saying that "if a Party of 500 or 600 Men, or more, were minded to travel from the North to the South-Seas, they may do it without asking leave of the Indians; though it be much better to be Friends with them."

A year later, during their twenty-three-day return trip across Panama, Dampier's group followed their Kuna guides around the many locations where Spanish troops were waiting for the pirates.

166

On the US Navy expedition each man strapped on a fifty-pound pack with a blanket, ten days' worth of provisions, a single change of clothes, a cartridge box with forty rounds of ammunition and a carbine that weighed ten pounds on its own. Strain wanted his men to travel quickly. He dropped his original plan to survey the route because he didn't want to carry the equipment or spend time maintaining it. He left behind the sextants, barometers, chronometers and miles of survey line. They carried only one axe and one fish hook for the entire team.

Based on Cullen's claim to have strolled across in six hours, Strain felt confident that his men could make the trip in a matter of days, or even hours. Their only focus was to sprint across ahead of their French and British partners.

Strain was thirty-three years old. Earlier in his career he'd launched an expedition that was planned as a two-year survey of uncharted regions in Paraguay, Colombia and Brazil. That trip fell apart after six months. Later, after being chosen to lead what was going to be the most extensive geodesic survey work ever attempted in the US, he resigned his position at the last moment, just as the work was scheduled to begin.

Now he found himself in a situation where he might be able to redeem his reputation.

The French and English ships with Cullen and Gisborne and the chief survey official from New Granada were due to arrive within three days. For Strain, the temptation to pre-empt the international team was too much to bear. It must have felt as though a fat, juicy mango was dangling from a low branch in front of him, crying out to be plucked.

167

El Perro y el Machango (The Dog and the Agouti), a Kuna story:

One time a dog saw a *machango* eating a nut in a tree. The dog asked for the nut and the *machango* dropped it down to him, but the dog couldn't open the nut. The *machango* watched the dog and then told him that with his mouth he could never open it. Instead, to open the nut he would have to look for a rock, and then place the nut between his balls and the rock.

The *machango* said that he would help him break the nut, and the dog accepted his offer. The *machango* came down from the tree, and he swung the rock so hard against the dog's testicles that the dog passed out from pain.

The *machango* ran a long way and climbed an avocado tree. When the dog recovered consciousness, he followed the *machango's* trail and found him on a branch eating a piece of the fruit.

The dog couldn't climb the tree, so the *machango* called out, "Friend, do you want some fruit?"

The dog answered that he did.

"Wait a minute while I find the sweetest one here."

He picked the avocado and told the dog to sit on the ground with his mouth facing upward while he dropped the fruit. When the dog did this, the *machango* dropped the avocado and it wedged into the dog's throat. The dog immediately began to jump and thrash about to knock the fruit loose. While this was happening, the *machango* came down from the tree and ran into a small cave.

After the dog worked the avocado loose, he went looking for the *machango* again. When he found the cave, he saw that the entrance was too narrow for him to enter. He tried to poke his nose inside, but the *machango* threw ashes in his face.

Now with his eyes filled with dust and ash, he couldn't see when the *machango* ran out of the cave and slipped away.

Blinded like this, the dog could never return to look for the *machango* again.

This is a curious tale to hear from a Kuna Indian for a few reasons. One obvious point is that agoutis have hoof-like claws that aren't effective for climbing trees. It might be possible if there was a long, gradual branch to use like a ramp. But then the dog might be able to follow.

The other puzzling premise is that the *machango* outwits the dog. A Kuna hunter can often catch an agouti without carrying a firearm if he has a hunting dog. Agoutis are territorial animals. At night, if they are caught in a beam of light, they often freeze in position making them an easy target. At other times they'll try to escape, but they will run in a circle, around and around within the confines of their home territory.

168

At the river Didú, we stop at an abandoned hut to spend the night.

The first sign that we have a problem occurs while I'm pulling a blanket out of my backpack.

"Do you have any meat?" Aris asks me.

I know that Alfonso has only one pound of sugar and a few packages of flavoured drink crystals in his basket. Aristotle is unpacking his own belongings. He has already pulled out two sheets for his bed, a spare shirt and a Bible. To me, the pile looks about the same size as his basket's inside dimensions.

The original deal I made with Auboydí and his grandson Leo included an agreement that they would bring a cooking pot and food for the three of us.

"No, I didn't bring anything," I say, looking at his face and trying to understand our situation. I'm beginning to suspect that we'll be travelling hungry and potless across Darien.

Aristotle turns to look at Alfonso. They both look down and continue arranging their bedsheets as if it's important to straighten out the wrinkles before nightfall.

All day long they've probably assumed that my green pack is full of food. They likely can't imagine how anyone can carry such a big bag and not have fresh meat, chocolate, rice and more sugar for their drinks.

We work silently for another ten minutes until we're certain that our beds are made.

"You're sure you don't have any meat?" he asks again, in case I've forgotten about some fresh cuts I had packed in a hurry this morning.

I explain the deal I'd made with the *saíla* and Auboydí, and how I assumed that the deal had stayed the same when we transferred guides.

It's starting to grow dark. Aris tells me to start a fire and cut some green plantains from the skinny tree growing near the hut. The two of them walk into the forest for a conference. I start a fire and after the flames die down, I put six hard plantains directly on the coals to cook for fifteen minutes.

Cooking them this way makes it a little easier to separate the peel from the fruit, but it doesn't soften them or make them any sweeter or more palatable in any way. They're still hard and dry and tasteless. The only flavour comes from the charcoal smears from my black fingers.

> For some of them look'd on us very scurvily, throwing green Plantains to us, as we sat cringing and shivering, as you would Bones to a Dog. This was but sorry Food; yet we were forc'd to be contented with it.
>
> —Pirate/surgeon Lionel Wafer while in the hands of a Kuna tribe, 1681

169

At night it rains. Then it pauses, followed by a downpour. Again and again.

The floor of the hut is four feet off the ground, and there is just enough thatched roof remaining that we can stay dry on the *gira* planks.

During the night, a few minutes before each burst of rain, Alfonso begins talking out loud in the dark. He speaks in Kuna dialect, and sometimes Aris answers from across the floor. Other times it seems as though Alfonso is talking to the approaching storm.

After midnight I finally fall asleep, waking during the claps of thunder and drifting off in the lulls. On the far corner of the floor, Alfonso has started a fire. He pulls his shirt tight around his shoulders. His body is just bones and angles. I can hear the river rising, rushing through the trees close to our hut. Alfonso sets his last six cigarettes on a board near the fire to dry the paper and tobacco.

I can't understand what he mumbles to himself. He doesn't sound happy.

Aris might be awake, but he doesn't answer.

On the flank of *las montañas*, tucked into the folds of the *cordillera's* skirt, you realize that the thunder is really more than just one speaker's voice. When you're right in the middle, you can hear giants jousting back and forth from one ridge to the next.

One voice shouts something to the other, shaking the floor of the hut. Then they pause until the second voice rumbles the ground with his answer from the cliff across the valley. Enormous words. Not necessarily angry. Just heavy, heavy words splitting the night open so that I can't breathe. And when it happens that one voice doesn't wait for its turn, and their words piggyback on top of each other, the voices crash down the valleys and shudder my body with an explosion as if half the earth has torn away from the planet.

I never sleep after that happens. Not with this mountain range hanging over my head.

170

During William Dampier's return trip through Darien in 1681, the pirate/surgeon Lionel Wafer burned his leg to the bone while drying gunpowder over a fire. With his injury, he couldn't walk. The pirates left him and four sick men behind with the Kuna Indians.

Wafer spent three and a half months with the Kuna—sometimes treated as a guest, and other times as a prisoner, starving and afraid for his life.

When Wafer was ready to travel, the five men tried to escape to the coast. On the trail, they took a wrong turn, became lost, and then decided to camp in a fork between two rivers. That night a storm caused a flood that nearly swept them to their deaths. Here is his description, as published in 1699 in *A New Voyage and Description of the Isthmus of America*:

> … but not long after the Sun-set, it fell a Raining as if Heaven and Earth would meet: which storm was accompanied with horrid Claps of Thunder, and such flashes of Lightning, of a Sulphurous smell, that we were almost stifled in the open Air.
>
> Thus it continued till 12 a Clock at Night … we could hear the Rivers roaring on both sides us; … but t'was so dark, that we could see nothing but the Fire we had made, except when a flash of Lightning came … the water approaching us; which in less than half an hour carried away our Fire … everyman seeking some means to save himself from the threatening Deluge. We also fought for small trees to Climb; … I very opportunely met with a large Cotton Tree which … was become rotten, and hollow on one side; having a hole in it at about the height of 4 foot from the ground. I immediately got up into it … When I awoke, I found my knees in the Water and the Water was running as swift as if 'twere in the middle of the River… ; Which made it so dreadful and terrible, that I forgot my Hunger, and was wholly taken up with praying to God to spare my life.

171

With the first light in a rainforest, the atmosphere is thick and magical. I'm only half-awake, at that point where anything is possible. I open my eyes and look around the floor and into the forest without moving my head.

I'm at Didú, in the abandoned hut across the divide. Skinny Alfonso is sitting by the fire. He already has six more plantains charring in the flames. He's smoking one of his last cigarettes, the imported French brand that the Kuna prefer.

A *colono* from the province of Chiriquí has his house not far downriver from here. The problem, Alfonso says, is that the house and trail are on the far side of the river. With last night's rains and flooding, the water has risen over ten feet and now it's impossible to cross. Aris sits up on his sheet. His hair is a mess. He looks tired and disappointed.

The original plan had been to hike the long trip to the highway together. When the *saíla* decided that Aris couldn't go to Panama City, the two guides decided it would be enough to deliver me to Chocolatál, the first Chocó village on the Sucurtí River. Now they've shortened their destination to the first Chocó family higher up on the river.

Alfonso says something in Kuna to me, and then he pretends to laugh casually as if he surprised himself with his own joke.

Aris translates.

"He says that it's too bad about the rain and flood. I guess we'll have to go back to Caledonia," Aris tells me. "But he was only joking."

172

At Didú, the sun shines on our fork in the river. I see a blue Morpho butterfly fluttering in the shadows.

Alfonso suggests that we leave our packs while we scout for an alternative trail on this side of the river. I leave my tattered shoes to dry in the sun, and I walk in my sandals. After an hour and a half, they also fall apart.

We're not going to find a trail over here. I know it, and so do Aris and Alfonso. The mountains on this side grow steep and irregular, while they're gradual and consistent on the other bank. Alfonso is somewhere ahead with his shotgun and machete. I talk to Aris, and then I turn back to the camp, sliding barefoot down muddy banks and stabbing my toes with thorns.

Near our camp, there is a river eddy in a circle of rocks with a flat stone where I can sit naked in the water. Stray sunlight leaks through the canopy. I take my time shaving. I sit cleaning my cuts and pulling out slivers and thorns. Little red-tailed sardines (*Astyanax ruberrimus*) attack me relentlessly, nipping at my body. Their mouths are no larger than the nub end of a pencil. Are they carnivores? Some type of frustrated piranha?

In some ways it seems ridiculous to shave out here. Why should I shave now? I've never particularly enjoyed dragging a blade across my chin. Even at home I shave only once or twice each week and let my face go scruffy between. But still I do it. I think that I refuse to grow a beard because I love that momentary sense of youth as I rinse my chin and cheeks and neck after each close shave. I love being with a woman and feeling my smooth face on her body, her softness against my new skin.

As well, on a trip like this, shaving takes on an added significance. There's something about respecting an unwritten code of discipline at those moments when it's tempting to let go of your daily rituals. We're stuck in the jungle. We have no food. My guides want to go back, and I'm not sure if I can finish the trip alone.

Shaving is a way of saying that nothing is tremendously wrong.

Nothing will stop me from being human and feeling strong and capable. By satisfying a petty vanity, a traveller denies his desperation. We say to ourselves, *Now that I'm clean-shaven, what next?*

Lt. Strain recognized the importance of discipline and ritual on his journey. Some of his men were volunteers, not soldiers or sailors. Even though the group believed it would be a quick dash across, Strain insisted on following the rules of military hierarchy.

From the first day, his men built two camps and two separate fires at night. One for officers, and another for sailors and volunteers. When decisions had to be made, Strain gathered his officers to hear their opinions while the other men waited on the sideline. When he ordered his men to stay away from the Kuna plantations they found along the route, they respected his decision, even when their own provisions were gone.

On our second night at Didú, we cook the last green plantains in the fire. Before we lie down to sleep, I tell Aris that we'll try to cross over to the *colono*'s house tomorrow. I tell him that if it doesn't work out, they can return to Caledonia and I'll finish the trip on my own.

173

After Strain lost his scouting party, the group was down to twenty-two men. Nothing they saw matched up with Cullen's map.

On the sixth day, they arrived at the village of Sucurtí, but like all of the previous settlements, the Kuna had burned their own homes and destroyed any remaining dugouts before disappearing into the forest.

Earlier at Caledonia the Kunas had vaguely agreed to let the Americans pass through unharmed, but now the smouldering remains put Strain and his men on edge. They rotated watches at night and kept their campfires burning.

Strain had planned for the trip to last a few days or a week at the most. Their provisions were almost gone now, and they still had to make the return hike over the mountains to Caledonia.

That afternoon, to the Americans' surprise, five Kunas appeared at the edge of the village. Inexplicably they now offered to lead the expedition across the isthmus to the Sabanas River, telling Strain that the trip would take another three days.

The Americans struggled to keep up. The natives travelled light, and they were accustomed to the climate. After a gruelling day and a half, a second group of Kuna men appeared and argued with the guides, forcing them to hand over control. In the morning, the new Kuna guides arrived and led the Americans across the Chuqunaque River and further into the forest. Two hours later, they went on ahead and were never seen again.

Strain's men were exhausted. Earlier, one member had been stung by a scorpion and was now delirious. Everyone was starving. Most of them suffered from a foot fungus that made it painful to walk. They were plagued with botfly larvae forming lumps under their skin, and a parasite that caused a searing pain in the epidermis of the head of the penis, but they weren't prepared to turn around and hike back to Caledonia in shame.

Although they were beginning to have doubts concerning the accuracy of their maps, they had even less faith in the Kunas' advice. What Strain didn't realize was that if they continued a few short miles along the same direction, they would intersect the open trail slashed through the forest by the British expedition a month earlier. Tragically, after Strain met with his officers, they voted to abandon their cross-country route and instead follow the large river they'd crossed in the morning.

174

For Strain's men, in spite of the sandflies and mosquitoes, the first four days along the Chuqunaque were good ones. They cut a trail and hiked five to ten miles each day. They caught fish and shot birds to eat. Now that the Kuna had completely abandoned them, Strain allowed his men to fill themselves with bananas and other fruits from Kuna plantations.

Strain still believed that Darien Harbour could appear at any moment. He thought it was possible that this river was the Sabanas or one of its tributaries. Cullen and Gisborne had never mentioned the Chuqunaque River, and it wasn't marked on their maps. In fact, Cullen and Gisborne didn't even know it existed. They'd never hiked anywhere near it.

In a small coastal forest, it's usually a sound plan to travel downriver to reach the coast, but the serpentine Chuqunaque is an exception to the rule. The river bends and snakes and doubles back ten to twenty miles for every mile it makes good. Even worse for the Americans, all the curves and oxbows made it impossible to realize that the river runs almost parallel to the two coasts.

When Strain attempted to save time by cutting across from one bend to the next, they became lost in the bogs. It took two days for them to slash their way back to the riverbank. During that stretch they weren't able to fish for food or enjoy the open patch of sky that the river offered. They named the two forest camps Camp Noche Triste (Sad Night) and Camp Sorrowful.

By the time they regained the river's edge, they had passed the final Kuna settlement and there were no more plantations. A few days later, an inexperienced expedition member accidentally broke their only fish hook. Now two weeks into the expedition and completely out of provisions, Strain drew on his experience from South America and taught his men to collect the tiny nuts from *trupa* palm trees. Sometimes they climbed the tree to gather nuts. When they had less energy, they would cut it down with their axe, or shoot the nuts out with their rifles.

On the fourteenth night, while Strain's men built two more fires and nursed their wounds and their hungry bellies, five major vessels anchored in Caledonia Bay. There were nine hundred men and two hundred convicts onboard to help clear trails. The map-makers, Cullen and Gisborne, had also arrived, but it immediately became obvious that they had no idea how to proceed and that their drawings were worthless. Cullen was confined to his quarters onboard. Gisborne accepted some limited responsibility for his mistakes and he was allowed to negotiate with an English-speaking Kuna who offered to lead him across Darien through the lowest mountain passage.

Once again, Darien responded in its usual fashion to foreign expeditions.

The British advance team had suffered and some had died on their solo attempt. Strain's men, after deciding to cross quickly without native guides and advice, had already spent two weeks in the forest. They were lost and starving and completely unaware that their ordeal had barely begun.

In contrast, Gisborne crossed from Caledonia to the Pacific tidewaters on the Rio Sabanas in less than six days. Because he was travelling with a Kuna guide, native villages welcomed him and he slept in their homes and ate their food.

On the same night that Gisborne arrived at the British supply tent on the Sabanas, Strain's group harvested a quantity of a plant they thought was pussley. One member assured the others that it was regularly fed to hogs in the US, and it would certainly be fine for them too. Soon after supper, everyone, including Strain, was wracked with violent fits of vomiting.

Maybe if they had realized that Gisborne had already walked across the isthmus and that there was no hero's welcome waiting for them, they would have limped back to Caledonia. Instead, after a long night of retching, Strain decided that their only chance for success was to split into two groups. He would push ahead with three strong men to reach Darien Harbour and return with food and supplies for the others.

175

It rained in the mountains above Didú again last night.

Aris and Alfonso don't tell me with words, but I know they don't want to hike any further. In the morning, instead of grabbing their baskets, they pace back and forth in the hut. Aris hops down to the ground and he finds a large, empty sardine can buried in the dirt. He washes it in the river before setting it over our fire to cook the one cup of rice he had brought along.

After we eat, I suggest that we should start walking.

Around noon, the hillside forces us to the edge of the Sucurtí River. There is a gravel bar on our side and then a rocky island followed by a fast, deep channel along the opposite bank.

This looks like the best crossing point I've seen in the last two days, but Aris and Alfonso shake their heads slowly. They look at the water and say that we should wait for the river to drop.

I'm the only one who really wants to continue. They've already spent three days, not all of them travelling, but it will take at least another long one to return to Caledonia. The money I offered doesn't seem quite so impressive spread over four or five days.

When we were walking this morning, Alfonso pointed at my shoes.

"He says that it's too bad about your shoes. If you had good shoes we might be able to go faster," Aris translated.

But I know that I'm not slowing them down. And speed isn't the problem. They walk up and down the gravel bar while I carry my pack to the upstream point of the island. Alfonso lies down for a nap. Aris tries to look busy.

At 2:30, Aris says we should wait a little longer.

Alfonso walks over and points at my pack.

"He says that it's too bad you have such a big pack. It will make it difficult to cross the river," Aris translates.

"If we wait, it's only going to get worse," I say.

I don't have to tell them this. They already know it. We can see the dark rain trailing from the clouds upriver.

I take off all my clothes except for my shoes and glasses. I inch out into the river from the uppermost part of the island until the water is pulling at my thighs and legs. I make a gesture to demonstrate how I'll dive out at an angle with my pack and ferry across to the other bank.

"I'm going to go with my pack," I tell Aris. "I'll cut a vine or a branch to help you across."

Neither of them looks enthusiastic. Alfonso walks away as if he doesn't understand. Aris ambles downriver with his head bowed, feigning indifference. He stops near the bottom of the island, probably getting in position to fish out my body if I drown.

My pack is bulky, but everything is sealed inside, so I know that it floats.

But why don't they want to cross, I wonder? What is the real reason? Do they just want me to send them home? Or is it really that dangerous?

It's only about forty feet across to the other bank. The water looks deep enough that I won't hit any rocks, but if I get swept past Aris, the Sucurtí becomes wide and chaotic with frothing whitewater racing over shallow rocks.

I tighten the strap on my glasses, grab my pack, and then I ease into the river until the current begins dragging my feet through the gravel. When I lunge upstream at an angle, the water immediately sucks me downriver in the channel. I begin clawing at the water with my one free hand. The bank races by in front of me, and it feels as though I'm getting nowhere. I bounce off a hidden boulder with my leg, and I lose a hundred and fifty feet and sweep past Aris before I can grab a branch on the far bank and pull myself on shore.

Just one cut on my shin. I wave to Aris at the end of the island.

"Is there a trail?" he shouts.

They still want to turn around. If I can't find a trail here, I know that Alfonso can ... if I can convince him to swim across.

"What do you think?" Aris shouts over the noise of the river.

"It looks good," I answer back.

176

I don't know how old my two guides are.

At Caledonia, Aris told me that he was seventy-two years old. I was amazed at how strong he was and the tightness of his facial skin. Alfonso's hands and posture look older, but his skin is even smoother.

Yesterday Aris revised his story and told me that he was sixty-two. This morning while we were hiking, he told me his birth year and we calculated that he's actually sixty years old. He's regaining his youth after just a short hike in the forest.

177

Aris holds his basket overhead with one hand. When he walks into the channel, the current sweeps him away and he sinks down until the water stops just below his frightened eyes. I reach out with a long, hooked branch. He stretches out his swimming hand, dipping completely under for a brief second before he snags the branch and I pull him in.

Alfonso has skinny, bandy legs, with a gentle outward curve at the knees. Earlier Aris told me that Alfonso is much younger than he is.

When Alfonso enters the water, he walks straight in holding his precious shotgun in the air. He watched both of us cross, but he looks suddenly shocked as the current carries him away.

He locks his eyes on mine as if to say, *I'm counting on you.* I reach out with the branch and hook him under his gun arm. He trusts me completely. He doesn't even grab hold of the branch. I pull him in close, and as his body begins to roll off the fork, Aris reaches out from the shore and grabs him.

Alfonso doesn't understand Spanish. I know only a few words and phrases in Kuna, but he refuses to believe that another adult cannot speak his language. He sometimes stands close in front of me and says something in Kuna. He pronounces the words slowly and patiently.

"*No entiendo,*" I say. I don't understand. "*No hablo la lengua Kuna.*"

But he doesn't accept that. Or, like me, he doesn't understand.

Instead, he repeats the phrase slowly, again and again. He doesn't give up until I repeat the words back to him.

A slow smile spreads across his face.

178

At the *colono*'s home site, there is nothing left but rotting posts and a battered aluminum pot.

We don't stop. We hike until the light fades, then use our machetes to clear a patch in the forest. Aris cuts palm branches for our mattress, and we lie down side by side as the world grows dark.

They don't even suggest that we light a fire.

We don't have anything to cook. So why light a fire? I suppose that's what they're thinking. But when a foreigner sleeps in the forest at night, he usually feels more comfortable with a roaring fire, sparks spitting up into the canopy. We cling to the belief that the fire will keep us safe.

If a jaguar is waiting to pounce, we hope that it won't have the courage to enter our protective circle of light.

179

Before we fall asleep, I say to Aris, "You've grown up in these forests. Even when you were a boy, you slept on the ground and travelled through the jungle."

How should I phrase this without sounding feeble?

"Weren't there times when you were worried about things?" I ask. "You know, frightened of animals with teeth … that might bite you?"

He doesn't understand.

"...that might bite you late at night," I say, cupping my fingers like claws.

He's still puzzled. It doesn't make sense to him.

"*Cosas peligrosas*," I say. Dangerous things. "That might come at you in the night and start biting you with their teeth."

"Oh," Aris says. Now he understands.

"Yes, yes. Sometimes, when we would go into the darkest forests, far away from our homes, *jejénes* and *zancudos* would come in plagues at night, thick like clouds."

He's talking about no-see-ums. Tiny biting flies, sandflies and mosquitoes.

"Yes," he assures me. "Sometimes these creatures would arrive at night, and then, *Pica! Pica! Pica!* they would start biting us," he says, using one hand to demonstrate a mosquito biting his face and body.

"And we would rub and rub our faces and ears like this," he explains. "And yes, this would frighten us. Especially when we were young boys."

These two old men, they're not afraid of anything.

I lie down to sleep. I feel the breeze from bat wings as they shift and flutter right in front of my nose. I pull the sheet over my head and fall deep asleep, like I have never slept while travelling by myself in these forests.

180

To quote from *Mammals of Central America and Southeast Mexico* by Fiona Reid:

> Jaguar (Spanish: *tigre, jaguar*. Kuna: *achubarbat*): Head and body length up to 4 feet 3 inches. Length of tail up to 22 inches. Weight up to 160 pounds. Much larger and heavier

than other spotted cats. Favours undisturbed evergreen forest in the lowlands and foothills, but is also found in deciduous forests, mangroves, and grasslands.

Habits: Usually active at night. Small prey are killed by a smack of the forepaw. Large prey are killed with bites on the neck or head which crush the spinal cord or break the skull; prey is then dragged into cover and eaten…

Vampire Bats (Spanish: *murciélago vampiro*): The only mammals to feed exclusively on blood of live animals. They do not drink water and do not take solid food. To feed, they make a small incision with the razor-sharp incisor teeth, and blood is lapped up, not sucked. Anticoagulants in the saliva inhibit blood-clotting. The bats usually feed at a wound until they are bloated with blood and take only one meal per night.

181

A Kuna story:

A jaguar lived on the edge of a river. He was the only one who had fire. Everyone else lived without it. They had to eat their food uncooked.

One day those without fire decided they should find a way to get it for themselves. They asked the jaguar if he would share his fire, but he refused to help. Since he had always been the most powerful of all of them, they were afraid to argue, and instead they gathered together to make a plan. They knew that on rainy nights the jaguar built a fire under his hammock to warm his body while he slept. They made a plan and sent the *lagartija*—a tiny iguana—to the jaguar's camp.

It was raining hard that night, and the *lagartija* had to swim across the river current.

"What are you doing here?" the big cat asked the tiny iguana.

"I've come to do a favour for you. I'll tend your fire while you sleep," he answered.

Because of the rain, all the fires had fizzled out except for the one under the cat's hammock. The *lagartija* added a few branches to the fire, and the jaguar never suspected any trickery.

Later, when the iguana saw that the jaguar had fallen asleep, he began urinating on the flames to put them out. However, before he could finish, the jaguar awoke.

"Why are you putting out the fire?"

"Brother jaguar, I'm tending it well. The cold and rain make it difficult to keep it burning. That's all."

The tired cat believed him and he fell back to sleep.

This time the iguana worked quickly, urinating all over the fire. He saved just one burning branch before extinguishing the rest of the embers. Then he tucked the branch into his head comb, and he swam back across the river.

By the time the cold air woke the jaguar, the river was running fast and swollen. Even though he could see the fire burning on the other bank, he couldn't swim across to steal it back.

Ever since that day, the jaguar has had to eat his meat raw.

182

Strain chose three strong men for his lead team. The remaining eighteen were left behind with the understanding that they would rest for a day and then follow Strain's trail. Everyone assumed that the first village would be only a few days away. A week at the most.

The front four men marched eighteen miles on the first day. However, the second group was much weaker, and they needed four days to cover the same distance. When they arrived, they found an optimistic note from Strain predicting his fast descent and return with supplies.

The group cheered after they read the lieutenant's letter. They named the location Hospital Camp, and they collapsed exhausted and full of hope. Every falling tree sounded like a signal shot from Strain's gun. For ten days they watched the river, expecting him to paddle into view at any moment.

Finally, on February 26, thirty-eight days since beginning the journey, and two weeks since Strain had gone ahead, they broke camp and stumbled along the trail for a few miles before collapsing at a new location.

They called the second site Hospital Camp No. 2.

The Americans suffered with fevers, body aches, chills and sweats. Probably these were symptoms from malaria, stomach parasites or yellow fever. Their clothes were torn and shredded. Boots had fallen apart. Their skin was always damp from sweat and swamps and from sleeping on the ground. Infections, skin fungus and insects burrowing under their skin made life even worse.

They lived on birds and an occasional monkey they shot to go with the *trupa* palm nuts. Without the nuts they would have died long ago, but the heavy fibres were blocking their intestines, and the acid from the nuts had completely destroyed the enamel on their teeth.

Days turned to weeks, and it seemed impossible that anybody would rescue them. They began to accept that something had gone wrong for Strain and the scout group. Likely the four men had drowned or they would have returned by now.

183

The painful lumps on their legs and arms that the men called *gusanos del monte*—mountain worms—were larva-stage botflies.

A mature botfly is a large, stocky, hairy insect that resembles a bumblebee with orange legs, brown wings and a metallic abdomen. It grows to a half-inch or longer in length and lives a very short life. Once it pupates, it never feeds again. Its only aim is to propagate, which it accomplishes by capturing another insect, such as a mosquito, and holding its wings while attaching fifteen to thirty eggs onto the abdomen of the insect.

If the mosquito lands on you to feed, it acts as a vector. The warmth of your body stimulates the eggs to hatch, and the first-stage larvae emerge from the eggs and burrow through your skin at the bite, or at a hair follicle or a wound. The burrowing lasts five to sixty minutes, but usually you won't notice a thing.

As it grows, the larva faces headfirst into your body with two oral hooks pointing into the meat to tear at tissues while it feeds. The curved spines along the side of its body anchor it to your flesh, and a small breathing spiracle from the posterior end protrudes through a pinhole in your skin.

If you find a botfly larva growing under your skin, you can deal with it in three ways.

You can smother it by spreading petroleum jelly over the breathing hole. Then place a large circular patch of tape over that, and seal it with superglue. In the morning you'll still have to put pressure all around the lump and squeeze the body out through the hole. Remember to keep your head back because sometimes the larva will shoot five or six feet into the air.

Alternatively you can restrict the breathing by placing a thick slab of meat over the hole and hope that the larva will be lured to crawl through your skin and into the fresh steak.

And finally, the simplest option is to just leave it alone and watch it develop. From a tiny egg, the larva will grow and feed on your tissue. After six weeks, a fully developed maggot will squirm free of your body and drop voluntarily to the forest floor.

184

In the morning we reach the abandoned village of Sucurtí where Strain's expedition met the first Kuna guides and began their cross-country hike westward.

Alfonso knows these forests well because he lived here when he was a boy. We continue following the river and find some bananas to eat. Our steps feel lighter, and Alfonso hikes ahead while Aris and I meander along behind.

"What is the English word for *caigo*?" he asks.

"To fall down," I say. "I fall down."

I repeat the words a few times and Aris tries them out, stopping to ask me if it sounds right.

"Oh, and Asunción? Where is that?" he asks.

"In Paraguay," I tell him. "Near Argentina."

"Oh, and what language do they speak there?"

"Spanish, just like almost everywhere in Central America and South America, except for Brazil and Belize, and a few countries beside Venezuela," I tell him.

"Paraguay is in Central America?" he asks.

"No, in South America, between Brazil and Argentina."

"Then which is bigger in population and size, Paraguay or Argentina?"

"Argentina wins both times," I tell him.

We walk a little faster to catch Alfonso.

"And *Pérsica*?" he asks a few minutes later.

"What about Persia?"

I don't know why he asks about Persia so often.

"Which is bigger, Persia or Argentina?"

185

An hour after the abandoned Sucurtí village site, we reach another clearing where a young Chocó native is dismantling the pole frame from an old house along the edge of the river. His six-year-old daughter is round and healthy. She's dragging palms and branches onto a pile. These two don't look lost or hungry.

We see them as we enter the clearing, but they can't hear us over the noise of the river rapids. Alfonso stops at the edge of the trees. Aris says something to him. Alfonso nods and slips a shell into the shotgun before putting it casually on his shoulder. Then we begin walking again into the clearing.

We talk a little louder as we approach. We make sure that the man hears us long before we arrive.

186

When you want to cross through a forest, the trip is often limited by the amount of supplies you can carry to sustain you over time.

For José Luis, the Chocó native we came upon that day, the forest is a generous provider. He built his house from the trees. He uses forest soil and compost to plant rice and corn, root crops and plantains. He knows the best pools to fish. His son and two daughters are healthy. His wife's breasts are full and large like round melons.

We've lived on small fish and rice for almost a week. Everyone in the family at Asnatí watches while Rosa cleans a large rat that José Luis killed with his machete.

José Luis keeps a small shed with baskets for chickens to roost and lay eggs. He has a *piragua*, paddles, an axe and an adze. He has a hunting dog, a wood-roller press to squeeze juice from sugar cane, and a grinder for his corn and cacao.

He and his family planted and built all of this with their hands, piece by piece. Everyday, José accomplishes something, and his family knows that he's here to stay. Not just someone passing through, trying on the lifestyle like a costume at a party.

187

Near the beginning of Strain's expedition, before the group had divided into two, the lieutenant shot an iguana near the riverbank. A landsman named Holmes dove into the water to retrieve the animal before it could sink. Unfortunately the river was deeper than he expected, and he lost a boot while swimming back to the edge. Other men dove in to search for it, but with the current and the silty water, they came back empty-handed.

Even with the moccasin that Holmes made, he likely took more than his share of thorns and puncture wounds while they marched through the forest.

Weeks later, on March 4, forty-four days into the expedition and twenty days since Strain had gone ahead for help, Holmes became the first in the group to die. His foot had become infected and had started decomposing. They didn't have medicine or even proper food to sustain him.

On that same day, earlier in the morning, three desperate men from the group slipped into the forest to hide until Holmes was buried. They had planned to wait until the others were gone before digging out the body, feeding on his flesh, and then hiking back to Caledonia. However, while hiding, they became lost and began firing their guns and begging the others to rescue them.

By that time, everyone was certain that the scout team had died. It seemed impossible that they could be gone for three weeks without having reached a village and returned. Midshipman William Truxton, Strain's appointed leader for the second group, was torn between following his orders to advance downriver, and his belief that their only hope lay in returning to the Kuna plantations and crossing back to the Caribbean coast.

On March 5, 1855, at Hospital Camp No. 2, he wrote a letter and left it in an open space along the river.

> Dear Strain: This is Holmes's grave. He died yesterday, March 4, partly from disease and partly from starvation. The rapidly failing strength of my party, combined with the earnest solicitation of the officers and men, and your long-continued absence, have induced me to turn back to the ship. If you can come up with provisions soon, for God's sake try to overtake us, for we are all nearly starving.
> —W.T. Truxton

188

Contrary to the rear group's consensus, Strain and his three partners were still alive. But only barely. They had hiked along the river until the forest became too thick. They built rafts and nearly drowned in the rapids. Their bodies wasted away until they were little more than naked skeletons. Strain had no pants, not even underwear. He was wearing the remains of a shirt, a tattered Panama hat and a wrap of leather around one foot. His legs were torn by thorns and blistered from the sun.

Somehow he found the strength to force his men forward each day. At times, one of them would fall down to the ground and refuse to clear the path, lying prostrate beside his machete and weeping like a child.

On March 4, the day Holmes died, it was Strain's thirty-fourth birthday. All day Strain and another man paddled the raft while the other two, afraid of drowning, hiked along the river's edge.

At the end of the day, while they were eating the remains of a dead iguana they'd found in the forest, Strain noticed the first sign of the Pacific tide on the river.

"Oh captain! Here's tide! Here's tide!" one of his men shouted when he saw the upstream ripple.

Strain couldn't sleep that night until he had carried a burning stick down to the river at 11 p.m. to watch the tide shift a second time.

189

Alfonso and Aris are used to stable Kuna homes built on sand. They toss back and forth when they sleep, and the Chocó house sways on its posts all night.

I actually don't know when Alfonso sleeps. After everyone else is asleep, and it has been quiet for hours, he'll say something to Aris. Aris might grunt, or answer "yes" or "no," or sometimes he doesn't say anything at all. It doesn't seem to matter to Alfonso.

When I wake early in the morning, they've already packed their baskets and they're sharing the last cigarette.

I pay them twice as much as our agreement and I give Alfonso my machete and the leather sheath. They didn't have to continue past the *colono*'s house, but they never hesitated that morning. They were likely afraid that I would die on my own.

When I give the machete to Alfonso, he takes my hand and he holds it and begins talking earnestly to me about things in Kuna dialect. I understand only his gestures when he uses the other hand to point toward heaven, and the Spanish words that have no Kuna equivalent. He says that God sees all, and that He knows all. And that God is always with us, in the forests, and at Caledonia and in cities far away. He says that God walks with us on our journeys, and that I am always welcome back at his home in Caledonia.

I didn't expect such an outpouring from Alfonso. He rarely says a word. As lonely as I have been for such a long time, I have tears in

Aristotle (left) and Alfonso with his precious 28-gauge shotgun prepare to return to Caledonia after guiding me across the San Blas Mountains.

my eyes when I watch him walk to the edge of the river to cross—bandy legs, baggy underwear and no pants, my machete in one hand and his shotgun resting on his shoulder.

Here is a man who knows who he is.

190

Eight-year-old Luzneri uses a cockroach and rice from last night's dishes to lure sardines into a basket in the river. She takes the first five sardines to the beach, breaking their necks between her thumb and fingers, and then scoops in more rice and a cockroach for a second round.

I fish in the day with José Luis. He hunts with his dog for two nights without any luck. He seems nervous about something. He says that he wishes he had meat and coffee to offer me. I tell him that I wish I had meat and coffee to offer them.

At night, Rosa puts hard corn in a pot over the fire. She leaves it to cook until the kernels begin to smoke and burn black before she pours in water to boil for twenty-five minutes. Afterwards she sweetens it with sugar cane juice, and then serves the corn coffee in large cups.

191

I had a dream last night. It was a long dream and it has left me exhausted. Every tiny detail remains disturbingly clear this morning.

For two years I had been hiding in my bachelor apartment watching movies while my parents believed I was writing a serious work of literature. For some reason, the landlord kicked me out of the apartment and I moved onto an old sofa in the basement, watching pirated DVDs of Hollywood movies on phony trademark electronics.

In the final dream sequence, I was the only one in a studio audience that understood that the football scene, set on a city street corner, was just a staged event.

"It's fake!" I was shouting foul at a phony football game, on a mock television show, in my dream. No one else in the audience seemed to care.

192

After reaching the upper limits of the Pacific tide, Strain expected to find a village at every turn. They stopped collecting nuts, and for the next three days they ate almost nothing. However, it wasn't until the fifth day, only three miles from Yaviza that they finally met a group of local boatmen who carried the men the rest of the way to town.

Strain weighed only seventy-five pounds by that time. He was covered in sores and boils, bites and infections, with no pants or underwear or boots.

Even in his emaciated condition, Strain never rested or let go of the command. In the first twenty-four hours, he organized a rescue mission to travel upriver with his strongest crew member, and he hired another large *piragua* and group of men to paddle a day and a night with him to the Golfo de San Miguel. Unfortunately the British navy vessel that was supposed to be waiting had sailed to Panama City for supplies. Strain left his two men there to recover, and he paddled with the hired men back to Yaviza.

The upriver rescue team returned a day later. They'd found Holmes's grave and Truxton's note, but the hired paddlers had been unenthusiastic. They pilfered the rescue provisions and refused to continue. On the return trip, they found an expedition member named Parks who had become separated from the others. He had been wandering lost for eleven days and was mostly incoherent. When they reached Yaviza, Parks lay down to rest, and he died two hours later.

With no reliable paddlers for hire in Yaviza, Strain began another descent of the Tuira. He had just tied off to a tree at the end of the ebb tide when the British rescue team arrived in a paddle-box boat. Strain gratefully joined them as they pushed upriver eighteen miles past Yaviza before launching the canoes again.

The eighteen men in the rear group had abandoned any hope of rescue. When Holmes died, there were seventeen left. After Parks disappeared in the forest, the remaining sixteen men shouldered their packs and began the retreat.

They were sick and wasted away to bones. They had been marching for forty-five days, and now they could barely walk. They had no fish hook. Their rifles were mostly useless or discarded. Even if some of them reached the Kuna plantations in two or three weeks, they would need a miracle to climb the Sucurtí and cross the continental divide.

Next to die was the New Granadian diplomat on the trip. They gave his few belongings and a lock of his hair to his junior officer, Polanco. Then Polanco collapsed on the following day. He was still alive and conscious when the remainder of the group voted unanimously that the life of one man who couldn't survive many hours shouldn't be put before the well-being of the remaining fourteen.

Polanco tried to follow, but his legs wouldn't carry him. As the men marched forward they could hear him shrieking and begging them not to abandon him.

Two days later, another man named Lombard pleaded that the group allow him to die in peace. Again they voted, and let him remain behind. They built a fire for Lombard and left him with a hatchet, a knife and a pot in case he might survive until a rescue party found him. Lombard sat calmly leaning against a tree as each man passed by, "bidding him an affectionate farewell with streaming eyes and took his place in the file in marching order."

Now there were thirteen in the group. Of that number, perhaps only three or four were more alive than dead. The progress they made each day was hardly worth measuring. On the eighteenth day of the retreat, sixty-four days since the start of the expedition, they left behind a man named Vermilyea with his kit of essentials. That should have been his grave, but perhaps the fear of dying alone in Darien gave him new strength, and an hour later he regained the group and began plodding along behind.

This was going to be the final day for most of the men. So far they had pushed stubbornly forward, but many of them wouldn't be able to get to their feet in the morning. When the few stronger men had moved on, there would be no one left to gather palm nuts or shoot birds for their food. They might continue breathing for another day. Likely their final act would be to lie on the forest floor and wonder how a disaster of this size could have happened in such a tiny piece of rainforest.

193

It feels good to have a paddle in my hands again.

At the first stretch of whitewater, José Luis tells me to sit down. He says that he'll take me to the village of Chocolatál today. I think that he wants it to be clear that he's providing a service and I should let him do the work. But I love paddling a Chocó canoe.

In a calm section of the river, José Luis stops paddling. He sits down in the stern and rests the shaft across his thighs.

"How much did you pay the Kuna guides?" he asks me.

"Thirteen dollars per day for each man," I tell him.

"Only thirteen dollars?" he asks.

He knows that is about twice a labourer's daily rate.

"How much are you going to pay me?" he asks.

José Luis wanted to go to Chocolatál to buy cooking oil and sugar, but he didn't have any money.

"Well, you can return today if we both paddle and get there early. I'll pay you twenty-five dollars," I say.

He looks disappointed.

"I'll give you thirty," I say.

We drift for a few more minutes, and I begin to paddle. José Luis keeps his paddle on his lap. Sometimes he puts the blade in the water to steer.

"Make it thirty-five," he says a short while later.

"Okay," I answer.

I think he was expecting a lot more. Now he mostly sits in the stern and steers with his paddle. I stand in the bow and paddle, slow and steady. On the way, we surprise a large *poncho*, a capybara, at the edge of the river. José Luis has his rifle, but he doesn't reach for it.

"Isn't the meat good to eat?" I ask.

"Some people eat it," he says, not explaining why he doesn't want it.

We drink three cups each from his plastic bottle of corn *chicha*, and I paddle the rest of the way.

194

On the Caribbean side of the divide, the village of Caledonia and the surrounding land aren't so different from three hundred years ago when the pirate Wafer stayed with the Kuna. A few families have outboard motors, but most villagers use crudely carved paddles. They have no electricity in the village. They hunt iguanas, deer and peccaries on the mainland, and they plant crops with a sharpened stick. The mountains are covered in a dense forest. However, descending the Sucurtí is nothing like travelling through the Kuna Yala. The lower we go on the river, the more logged patches, grazing cattle and mixed-blood settlers we find.

While the Kuna will consider development proposals from outside their community, they jealously guard their autonomous homeland along the Caribbean coast. When you read their history, their occasional violent actions sometimes sound unjust or unwarranted. You realize that they can resort to anything when they feel it is necessary—ambushes, evicting a long-term resident, chopping foreign officials into pieces and throwing them into the sea. They don't usually offer explanations. They make a decision, and that is enough.

Kuna women shop on the cargo boat at Caledonia Island's dock.

Perhaps there might be more diplomatic ways to guard their independence, but after sailing through the 365 San Blas Islands, or hiking across the divide, I can appreciate how effective they've been in keeping their land for themselves. Keeping it Kuna. Any economy like our own, based almost solely on market factors, would long ago have paved these islands and forests, covered them with chrome and glass, and built a larger canal through Cullen's imaginary pass.

195

The geological forces shaping the isthmus didn't create a convenient canal route through Darien, but this didn't discourage one group of ambitious scientists and politicians. Already in the 1930s and '40s the Panama Canal was undersized for the volume of international shipping. It was also too small for the US Navy's new aircraft carriers that were under construction. During World War II, when the Americans realized that the gated locks were easy targets for an enemy, they started searching for solutions.

With the image of the raw power unleashed in 1945 on Hiroshima and Nagasaki still fresh, Washington created Project Plowshare to search for non-military uses for nuclear technology. They developed proposals to excavate new harbours and mines, and others for oil and gas production, electricity production, pest control and food preservation. Out of all of these, the hottest proposal was a plan to blast a sea-level canal straight through the isthmus between Caledonia and the Gulf of San Miguel.

The scheme called for 275 piggybacked nuclear explosions, each charge twenty to two thousand times more powerful than the bomb dropped on Hiroshima. In theory, at the same time the explosion cut a trench three hundred feet deep and twelve hundred feet wide, it would also toss the material off to the surrounding forest and eliminate the cost of transporting the waste.

The Caledonia route was singled out as a favourite. The distance across was one of the shortest, and since it involved moving relatively few people—mostly Kuna and Chocó natives—the savings would be significant.

During the early stages, when US scientists and engineers were enthusiastic believers, they suggested that they could limit evacuations to communities within five miles of the site. Kuna representatives listened to the proposal and allowed US scientists to study weather and water conditions in San Blas. It wasn't until years later, in 1966, when the Americans shipped in heavy equipment to begin clearing a wide swath through the forest, that the Kuna ended their cooperation. The Kuna *cacique* Yabiliquiña travelled to Panama City to protest at the foreign minister's office, telling the press, "We are and will continue to be happy without a sea-level canal in San Blas," he said.

By the mid- and late 1960s—ten years or more into the project—a few nagging reports admitted that they had no idea for how long, or at what rate, radiation would continue leaking into the land and sea from excavated materials. Other government-directed investigations suggested that there could be a general shock in the region comparable to a level 8 earthquake on the Richter scale— triggering severe landslides in the existing canal, damage to buildings as far away as Venezuela and Ecuador, and as many as six thousand broken windows from San José, Costa Rica, to Bogotá, Colombia. Still more international concern over uncontrolled nuclear fallout developed after a 1965 underground test explosion in Nevada created a radioactive cloud that drifted across the Canadian border.

Even at that point, White House aides and Project Plowshare officials stated that it was only superstitious Latin Americans and the public's hysterical anti-nuclear attitude holding back their project. It still took another four years for the White House to accept the verdict. In 1970, after fourteen years and tens of millions of dollars spent on studies, Richard Nixon's administration finally closed the book and declared the canal unfeasible.

196

When José Luis and I arrive at the river landing, an Emberá named William greets us.

He says, "This used to be Chocolatál."

Everyone left seven years ago because of a rumoured guerrilla attack approaching. William's father and his extended family are the only ones who have returned. They found other non-native people working their land, but they convinced the squatters to move upriver. The surrounding forest and planting fields that used to support thirty families are now owned by five outside individuals. Most of it has been logged and turned into cattle pasture.

I count out three tens and a five to pay José Luis. He folds the bills and walks over to a house to spend five dollars on two pounds of sugar, a bottle of cooking oil and a package of cigarettes.

197

On March 23, 1854, at the end of the US expedition's sixty-fourth day, the last thirteen surviving men were spread out like war casualties on the banks of the Chuqunaque River. Some were doubled up with stomach pain, others propped up against trees. They still lit two separate fires, but now the camps were only a few paces apart.

Just as the light was fading, Maury, the second-in-charge, thought he heard a rifle shot. By now however, after more than two months in the forest, they refused to be fooled by another rotting tree crashing down to the ground.

John Maury was one of the few men who were strong enough to continue the march. Despite the group's indifference, he used a precious slug to fire his rifle in response.

Moments later, with the light almost gone, Maury shouted.

"I see boats and Indians!"

Then, "I see white men!"

Then finally, "I see Strain! I see Strain!"

198

I paddle downriver and fish with William in the late afternoon.

I lose six grasshoppers before he tells me to stand sideways in the *piragua* to gain extra distance to swing the handline across my chest when they strike.

It's just starting to grow dark when he gives me the advice, and then I catch my only fish.

"Your fish is the biggest one," he says.

There are nine of them. It looks to me as though they're all between nine and ten inches long.

199

When you walk barefoot between the three houses in Chocolatál, mud and manure squeeze between your toes.

At night, William's mother quietly asks me if I know about problems with sleep. She says that she's tired in the day, but at night she can't sleep.

I know that two years ago, an armed group attacked her village and a stray bullet killed her eleven-year-old niece. I wonder if scenes like that are part of the problem.

She says that it helps her relax if she drinks coffee in the evening.

As everyone settles down at night to sleep, another son climbs up the *tumé*. He walks into a small side room with vertical cane walls. He lights a candle and turns on a battery-powered stereo, tuning into a channel from Bocas del Toro playing the Panamanian *cantadera* accordion music.

He turns it up loud just as everyone goes to bed. It's the most noise I've heard since the marina bar in Colón. Around midnight, the channel fades until there's only static with garbled voices in the background.

At 12:30 a.m. the father walks across the floor and urinates off the edge. He stops at his son's room where the radio still pops and crackles. He looks at the curtain hanging across the doorway, then bows his head and crawls into bed.

I feel the faint breeze again from a bat darting in front of my face. It feels very close. I even hear the wings flap as it adjusts while hunting for insects. I have blood on my ear from scraping a thorn bush this afternoon, and so I pull the sheet over my head.

A horse tied outside brays and flaps his lips. Pigs squeal, rubbing against the posts and shaking the house. The radio hisses and pops. At 3 a.m. a rooster crows under the floor. I start to laugh because that's all I can do. I think that I might understand something about sleep problems after all.

In the morning, William's mother hands me fresh pan bread for my trip. She says that her daughter-in-law brought her a cup of coffee last night, and that she slept well and feels better today.

200

In the early morning, a powered dugout stops at the landing and offers to carry me further downriver.

By choosing the route used by Balboa and the early English and French pirates to cross the mountains, and following the Sucurtí and Chuqunaque rivers where Strain and his men struggled miserably week after week, I wanted to recreate some of the flavour of the historic events along the route. I hoped that it would help breathe life into the stories. But even with the minor mishaps during my hike across—little or no food for the first days, the river flooding, bumping over rocks while swimming through rapids, and sleeping on the jungle floor after sighting jaguar tracks earlier in the day—I'm realizing that the most I can hope to gain is a sense of place and people: the sounds of the forest at night, the howler monkeys roaring at the approach of a rainstorm, the force of the river current, the insects and bats, and the flight of a capped heron across the river with her long occipital feathers trailing proudly behind.

Skimming over the Chuqunaque River in a powered dugout, I watch the tangle of wetlands, forests and bogs slip by. It would have been utter madness to hike along the edge of the river. Even today there are no trails or settlers living on this stretch of the Sucurtí.

Strain's expedition didn't have the luxury of an outboard motor or even a *piragua*. Whereas we use a chainsaw to clear out a logjam in the afternoon, Strain's lead group flipped their raft and almost drowned in similar conditions. On this same stretch of the Chuqunaque where I sit cramped in a boat with a crew of loggers for eleven hours, Strain's rear group wandered lost and starving for fifty-three days before the rescue team found them.

Of the twenty-seven men who began the American navy expedition in 1854, five were separated and returned to the ship after only two days. Four men died while the rear group was retreating. Three more died shortly after their rescue. Many of the remaining men suffered from bronchial infections, and likely most of them lost all of their teeth from the acid in the palm nuts.

When Strain reached America, he secluded himself in a small cottage to write his version of the expedition—to counter the reports that Gisborne and Cullen were preparing at the same time.

201

The downriver boat leaves me at Lajas Blancas landing just as the sky becomes dark. The air is thick with mosquitoes and sandflies. There is a rough, muddy road from here leading to the highway, but no vehicles could get through today. I walk for over an hour in the dark until I reach the first Chocó home where a man called Edilberto invites me to spend the night with his family under their mosquito net.

In the morning I travel by horseback for two hours with Edilberto along a forest trail to a neighbour's house. From there I catch a ride on a farm trailer loaded with sacks of rice and pulled by an old tractor. It's a long, slow trip to the highway, and I reach Meteti by nightfall.

In town I buy a cheap pair of sandals for a dollar to replace my battered shoes, and I drink two ice-cold beers at the bar before renting a plywood room with a single bed at the motel owned by Alexis Ortiz's father.

I was planning to go out for one more beer after my shower, but I change my mind and stay inside. I lie down on the bed, and for the first time in so many months, maybe even years, I am at peace. It feels as though I've done what I came to do. And I think that maybe I'm ready to return to Cavimál, to gather together my collection of notebooks and maps into a small pack with a change of clothes, and to finally find my way home again.

I fall deep into sleep and dreams, and I don't wake until the roosters begin calling in the early hours of the morning.

202

In 1857, three years after the American expedition, Lt. Strain signed on for another tour of duty aboard the *Cyane* in Panama. Until then, he had actively avoided any contact with the tropics as well as with his former sailing vessel.

American writer Todd Balf speculates that perhaps Strain returned in response to a report that a surgeon aboard a US frigate had found Cullen's pass through the mountains. The surgeon claimed that he had advanced as far upriver as he could from the Golfo de San Miguel, and that after climbing a tree (it's always done the same way) he'd been able to sight the Caribbean Sea through a low passage.

This was in the days before aircraft and satellite imagery. Cullen was still insisting that the surveyors had completely missed his route. Strain must have wrestled with doubts.

The lieutenant arrived in Aspinwall—present-day Colón—on May 14, 1857.

That evening, instead of going directly to his ship, he checked into one of the city's best hotels. He was scheduled to report on the following day to the *Cyane*. However, the next morning a navy commander sent a message to Washington stating that Strain had died in his hotel room during the night and that carpenters were building a coffin. He offered no explanation or details.

They buried the lieutenant at three o'clock in the afternoon. A few British and American officers attended. Probably all of them would have been strangers to Strain.

EPILOGUE

203

At Cavimál, when Bill sees me walking toward his house, he grabs a towel and begins looking for his shampoo.

The Tovar brothers still owe me three hundred dollars for the motor and another one hundred and fifty for my boat that they've been using for the last ten months.

"I'm going to bathe down by the well," Bill says after I tell him that I want to finish our business.

"Autemio will be here in a few minutes," he says. "My wife will cook some rice and shrimp. And we'll make a pot of coffee."

"You drink coffee, Martin?" he asks. Then, "Oh, here comes Autemio."

They know that this is my last day, and that I'm going to leave in the morning. Rufino warned me about this when I first arrived. Lots of promises, but very few payments.

"Martin wants to talk," Bill says as Autemio and Diana climb the *tumé* and join us in his house.

Autemio looks at me, then back at Bill. He answers in Wounaan dialect, talking steadily for over a minute. Then, in Spanish, he says, "Well, talk then."

Diana giggles.

I wish this wasn't such a battle.

"I want to finish our deal before I go to La Palma this afternoon," I say.

"We're going to town too," Bill says. "You can come with us."

Autemio's cousin is also there. He begins picking up the chickens, weighing each one separately and writing numbers on a piece of paper. Diana says that she doesn't want to sell the chickens. They have three small pigs, but Autemio tells me the meat is very cheap in town right now.

To make the last payment, it will take everything they have.

Bill offers me a plate of food.

"Sit down, Martin. You can relax here for a while."

Autemio assured me yesterday that they already had the cash in hand to pay for the motor. Now they want to deal with business after they take the boat to town and sell this morning's catch of shrimp. I stand in front of the *tumé*. If they go now, I don't know when they'll be back.

"I'd like you to pay for the motor now," I say.

I've finally brought everything to a head. Autemio could probably explain that this isn't how business is done in Darien, but I want to settle before the very last second arrives without any options.

They set down their shrimp coolers and walk over to Otilio's house where they talk and argue for twenty-five minutes. I hear Otilio lecturing them, and I hear the sound of coins being counted. When they return, Bill offers me a stack of fives, tens and singles, along with eighteen dollars' worth of quarters. They're still sixty dollars short for the motor, but at least it's clear where we stand.

I know that they hope I'll accept this, and that I'll also leave the boat behind for free. I wrestle with that in my head. I could do it. Even though I'm flat broke, I could put my flights on a credit card and borrow money from family until I find work back in Canada. But I'm already selling the new motor for half of what I paid. I've let them use it and the boat for the last year to earn the payments, and so I decide to stick to our deal.

I take the boat to sell in town. They tell me they'll do everything possible to find the last sixty dollars.

204

When I paddle past Puntita, I see Martínez standing under his house, stabbing a tree branch at the floor joists. He's in worse condition than before.

"*Tocayo!*" I call out.

His legs and arms are shaking. His cheeks have sunk into this face. One eye is closed, and he can barely talk.

"There's a snake," he says. It's hard to understand his words.

"It's in the house. I want to kill it, but the stick is so heavy."

The branch isn't so big, but Martínez is very sick. I take the stick from him and jam it into a corner until we hear something drop to the ground and move into the tall grass.

Martínez is still alone. He's almost happy to be able to pity me.

"Without a woman, a man is nothing," he says.

These are the only words that roll easily off his clumsy tongue and lips. It's as if he's been rehearsing the line all day for months.

Martínez tells me that a native woman from Rio Balsas is coming to stay with him.

"In Colombia it's so easy to have a woman," he tells me. "But you have to be careful about diseases."

We talk about women. About how we could move to Colombia and the women would see us as desirable men—a gringo who lives alone, my body failing, losing my hair, no money left in my pockets, selling my possessions to buy a ticket home; and my *tocayo*, all bent and twisted and weak, with his garbled speech and his right eye swollen shut.

Martínez leans on a paddle for support. We both need a bath.

205

Autemio counts out the final sixty dollars in coins and small bills. They sold their shrimp. They killed the rooster and four chickens, and they took one of the three pigs to La Palma.

He tells me that they've already started carving a smaller dugout to replace the one I sold.

For a brief moment he crosses over from his Wounaan habits to something else.

He says, "No one else would have given us this deal, Martin. It was a lot of work, but now we have a motor."

From Autemio, those are words of deep appreciation.

For the last year and a half, Autemio has coveted my multi-tool with the knife blades, pliers and assorted screwdrivers. Now I take the tool and its sheath from my belt and set them on the table beside him.

Autemio nods. He doesn't even look at it. As if I'm returning an overdue loan. After I'm gone, he'll open it. He'll oil the hinge and sharpen the blades. In a few days it will seem as if it has always belonged to him.

There's no need for thanks. He flatters me with his silence.

206

In the afternoon I pack my books and the few belongings I'll take back to Canada. I organize the rest to leave for the Tovars. I sweep the floor for the last time, and I'm sitting outside on the porch when Otilio comes to visit at sunset.

He relaxes in the blue cloth hammock. It smells like mould, but he likes using it anyway. He'll be happy that I'm leaving it behind.

I tell him that a scorpion stung me while I was clearing a campsite on the Tuira last month. That's all I say. I don't mention that I made hissing noises to stop the pain, that I tied a little tourniquet around the finger to slow the poison, and that I worried I might die alone in the forest.

"Did you kill it and squeeze the guts on the wound?" he asks.

"No, I didn't know about that," I say.

Otilio looks across the gulf at the mountains bathed in warm light at the end of another Darien day.

His bare feet. His sad eyes. His full lips pursed as he rocks so slightly back and forth, deep in thought.

I wonder what he is remembering.

ACKNOWLEDGMENTS

Initially, when I began the journey through Darien, I didn't fully understand what I had started. After five years of travel, research and an endless series of drafts and revisions, it was Silas White and Vici Johnstone at Harbour Publishing, and my editor, Meg Taylor, who saw the story hidden amongst the few hundred pages of personal narrative. This book might never have happened without them.

Anna Comfort, Erin Schopfer and all the staff at Harbour Publishing used their skills in art and design to create a beautiful book. Ruth Gaskill provided positive input far beyond her copy edit, and John Lightfoot tracked down the location of every village, island and river bend to produce a remarkable map of the region. Julie Velázquez-Runk and Stanley Heckadon-Moreno at the Smithsonian Institute for Tropical Research were helpful sounding boards at the earliest stage, and Rogelio Cansarí was an invaluable bridge between traditional Emberá and the outside world.

On my return to Canada after years of sailing in Central America, there were many friends and family who gave me shelter, encouragement and a clean well-lit place to write. When I arrived sick with dengue fever at the airport, my brother Don and his family took me in. Ragnar Ingibergsson in Edmonton opened his door with friendship, employment and my own room for the first months back in a northern winter.

My parents, Doreen and Gerald in Victoria, offered unconditional support, a lot of food and their sunny balcony as my summer writing desk.

Tim and Gayle Schauerte gave me work to pay my bills and never flinched when I imposed my writer's schedule on the construction timetable for their dream home. Kristen Scott and Kika and Sierra Mueller always left the key under their mat, and Thomás Ritchie begrudgingly allowed me to commandeer his beach *cabina* in Costa Rica when I needed it.

Others who helped immeasurably include my loving woman Tova Krentzman, relentlessly tough and supportive at the same time. Also, my younger brother Paul, in too many ways to mention, but mostly as my guiding example and as my imagined ideal reading audience. Kathleen "Kathy" Torres sailed *Ishmael* when I rested. She climbed the mast, did everything that needed doing, and helped bring me to Darien. Her largest gift was her insistence that if I was going to "fuck up everything else in life," I had better see this book through to the end.

I won't be able to list all of the people in Darien who fed, sheltered, guided and befriended me. Amongst those who stand in the forefront are the Kuna guides Aris and Alfonso from Caledonia Island, Rufino and Poncha in Puntita, and the Venezuelan poet Hernán who took me aboard his sailboat *Sirius*. *Los abuelos*—the grandparents at Mercadeo—and all of the native villages along the upper Balsas River showed me limitless patience and generosity. In particular, former *cacique suplente* Manuel Ortega and his wife Tranquilina welcomed me into their family. I owe Manuel more than I can ever repay. Without him, I would never have travelled as far.

Geronimo and Isabel in Manené told their stories well. *Cacique* Clementino Berrugati opened village doors for me wherever he could. In the *comarca* along the Rio Tuira, Carlos Guaynora and his family in Union Chocó shared their quiet spirit and peace of mind when I needed it most.

And finally, I offer my heartfelt thanks to all of the Tovar family living on their small hill at Cavimál—for the coconuts, mangoes and pineapples I lived on, and mostly for giving me a sense of *home* when I was so far adrift. In particular, I want to thank Otilio who welcomed me with open arms from the first day that I stepped on his shore; and Autemio and Diana, who were my brother and sister and very much my teachers of life skills in Darien.

Without any one of these people, and many more not listed, the story would not be complete.

GLOSSARY

It might have been simpler to have translated all of these terms into English, but I think that would steal some of the flavour from the story. It's like watching a foreign-language film when it's dubbed rather than subtitled. You want to understand the conversations, but you also want to hear the ambient sound and the music of the language. Here's an example:

Chocó houses have no walls, and they are built on raised platforms, five to eight feet above the ground. A *tumé* is a notched log used as a ladder by the family to climb up to their home. However, the word *"tumé"* is simpler than a long English explanation, and it's more accurate than the single word "ladder." Moreover, it's a part of daily conversation in Darien. When a family decides they don't want to invite more company in the evening, the father doesn't say to his son, "Turn that notched log on its side." He simply says, "Roll over the *tumé*."

Written language is still being developed for Darien native dialects. Most of the Emberá and Wounaan words are written using Spanish phonetics. The accent mark of a letter doesn't change the vowel sound; it only indicates an accented syllable.

Vowel pronunciations:

a   like *a* in *father*

e   like *é* in *café*

i   like *i* in *machine*

o   like *o* in *piano* (but only half as long, and without the *w* sound usually heard at the end of the English vowel)

u   like *u* in *rule*, or *oo* in *food*

Also, the phonetic symbol **x** (usually to represent the letter *j*) is an extremely hard *h*. It can be likened to the *ch* in the Scottish *loch*, or the German *achtung*.

abuelo: *(a-bwé-lo) Spanish*, grandfather, old man. **abuela**: grandmother, old woman.

alcaldía: *(al-cal-dí-a) Spanish*, mayoral office; elected district representative.

Ankoré: *(an-ko-ré) Emberá*, God, used to indicate various Emberá god figures, or to represent the Emberá interpretation of the Christian god.

arriera: *(a-ri-é-ra) Spanish*, leafcutter ant.

bohío: *(bo-í-o) Spanish*, rustic dwelling, shack, hut.

bueno: *(bwé-no) Spanish, adj* good, fair, right; *adv, as interj* right! all right! Okay!

cabecera: *(ka-be-sé-ra) Spanish*, headwaters of a river. Often used by Chocó in Darien to refer to the upper forests in the mountains along the border with Colombia. The expression is often accompanied by a sweeping arm gesture and pointing towards the mountains; it can infer a place that is untamed, full of wild game and *cimarrónes*, and is beyond the reach of non-Chocó people.

cacique: *(ka-sí-ke) Spanish*, chief.

Caragabí: *(ka-ra-ga-bí) Emberá*, son of Tatzitzetze, he becomes supreme god and master of the Emberá world after overpowering his father.

casa: *(ká-sa) Spanish*, house, dwelling.

cédula: *(sé-dju-la) Spanish*, document, identity card.

-cito/cita or –ito/ita: *Spanish*, diminutives. Thus, a *casita* would be a "little house"; *Martincito* would be "little Marty."

chicha: *(chí-cha) Spanish*, fermented corn alcohol drink.

Chocó: *(cho-có)* a generic term referring to three native rainforest tribes in western Colombia and Panama's Darien province: Emberá, Wounaan and Chocó subtribes (Katió, Cholo, Citara, Andagueda and others). Although their tribes and languages are distinct, Emberá and Wounaan worked together in Darien to establish the Emberá-Wounaan Comarca in 1983. While the term Chocó is still commonly used, most natives prefer their individual tribal names.

cholo: *(chó-lo) Spanish*, Indian from Colombia.

chupata: *(chu-pá-ta) Spanish/Emberá*, party where alcohol is served.

cimarrón: *(si-ma-rrón) Spanish*, *adj* wild, untamed; *n* Emberá who has turned away from all outside contact, gone wild; escaped black slave.

colono: *(ko-ló-no) Spanish*, settler, tenant farmer; in Darien, a farmer or agriculturist who has immigrated from another Panamanian province.

comarca: *(ko-már-ka) Spanish*, Indian land reserve; homeland region.

Cueva: *(kwé-bva) Spanish*, tribal name. The indigenous group controlling most, or all, of present-day Darien at the time of the first Spanish contact. Within ten years, the Cueva had been largely destroyed by Spanish violence and European diseases, and later through enslavement by black *cimarrónes*.

curandero: *(kú-ran-dé-ro) Spanish*, healer, shaman.

dirigente: *(di-ri-jén-te) Spanish*, political leader. In Darien's Emberá and Wounaan communities, village leaders are appointed or elected and they normally hold their position for at least three years.

Emberá: *(em-be-rá)* tribal name. An indigenous group living in Darien and western Colombia. Also known as Chocó, Katió and Chamí. Today they still fish and hunt, but they are primarily a farming people, planting maize, rice, plantains and sugar cane while also occasionally raising domesticated animals. There is intermarriage between Chocó tribes, and multiracial marriage is becoming more common every year.

ferretería: *(fer-re-te-rí-a) Spanish,* hardware store.

frontera: *(fron-té-ra) Spanish,* frontier; border; borderland (also figuratively).

frutería: *(fru-te-rí-a) Spanish,* fruit or produce shop.

gentserá: *(xen-se-rá) Emberá,* name of large black ant created when Caragabí punishes a woman (Gentserá) who has been hiding the water source from the rest of mankind.

golfo: *(gól-fo) Spanish,* gulf.

guayuco: *(wai-yú-ko) Emberá,* loincloth.

haimbaná, or **jaibaná:** *(xai-ba-ná) Emberá,* shaman or *brujo.*

hermano: *(er-má-no) Spanish,* brother; *adj* similar, matched.

hombre: *(óm-bre) Spanish,* man.

jagua: *(xá-ua) Spanish,* purplish-black dye from the *sabdur* plant (*Genipa americana*), used by Chocó natives to paint their skin for traditional ceremonies.

jai, or **hai:** *(xai) Emberá,* spirit(s) or devil(s), usually in the form of animals or deceased family members.

jejénes: *(he-xén-es) Spanish,* no-see-ums, sand flies.

jenjené: *(xen-xen-é) Emberá,* the tree of life, an immense tree cut down by Caragabí to form ocean, rivers, fish and animals.

kampunía: *(kam-pu-ní-a) Emberá,* any non-native person.

Kuna: *(kú-na)* tribal name; indigenous group formerly controlling all of Darien, but now living mostly throughout the 365 San Blas Islands and a narrow strip along the Caribbean coast.

ladino: *(la-dí-no) Spanish, adj* cunning, shrewd. *n* half-breed; non-Indian.

lagarto: *(la-gár-to) Spanish,* alligator, lizard; shopkeeper who charges high prices.

laguna: *(la-gú-na) Spanish,* pool; *(near coast)* lagoon.

Latino: *(la-tí-no) Spanish,* Latin; Latin-American *(usually indicating a non-indigenous resident born in Latin America).*

maleante: *(mal-e-án-te) Spanish, adj* wicked, villainous; malefactor, unsavoury character.
misión: *(mi-si-ón) Spanish*, mission (intent); missionary work.
mogote: *(mo-gó-te) Spanish*, hummock, a piece of ground rising above a marsh.
moreno: *(mo-ré-no) Spanish, adj* dark, dark-haired, black *(person); n* a black person.
nene or **nena**: *(né-ne, né-na) Spanish*, baby, small child, dear; Babe (as a name for a large pig).
panadería: *(pa-na-de-rí-a) Spanish*, bakery.
piragua: *(pi-rá-wa) Spanish*, pirogue; a long, narrow dugout canoe carved from a single tree trunk.
plaga: *(plá-ga) Spanish*, blight, plague; *(fig)* scourge.
playa: *(plaí-ya) Spanish*, shore; beach. Also used as a descriptive noun referring to the upper river regions where water flows pure and clear over sand and rocks, as opposed to the muddy currents in the lower reaches.
punta: *(pún-ta) Spanish*, end, tip, point; headland.
refacciónes: *(re-fak-si-ón-es) Spanish*, repairs; spare parts.
rio: *(rí-o) Spanish*, river.
saíla: *(sa-í-la) Kuna*, person with highest authority in the community, chief.
suplente: *(su-plén-te) Spanish*, substitute; reserve; replacement. In Chocó village politics, the appointed *suplente* serves as the second-in-command with the village *dirigente* to resolve village issues.
tambo: *(tám-bo) Spanish*, trading post; country inn; large, round home with conical roof.
Tatzitzetze: *Chocó*, the name signifies "father of all." He is the creator of the Chocó universe, and for a period of time he remained the supreme god of the world. Eventually he was overthrown by his son Caragabí.
Tierra Colectiva: *Spanish*, a native land-rights project designed to gain collective title for all land traditionally used by Emberá and

Wounaan people living outside the Emberá-Wounaan Reserve established in 1983.

Tierra Firme: *(Ti-ér-ra Fír-me) Spanish-Latin,* solid ground; used to refer to the mainland continent claimed by the Spanish in the sixteenth century (the present-day American continents).

tocayo: *(to-kái-yo) Spanish,* namesake.

tumé: *(tu-mé) Emberá,* notched log used as a ladder to climb to the floor of a native home raised up on posts.

ulu: *(ú-lu) Kuna,* dugout canoe.

Wounaan: (also Waunana, Nonama) *(wou-nán)* tribal name. A rainforest people who often intermarry with Emberá even though their tribes and languages are distinct. Every year, intermarriage with white *colonos* or immigrant black Colombians becomes more common.

yuca: *(yú-ca) Spanish,* a root crop traditionally grown by indigenous people in the New World. It is the American version of the cassava and manioc root grown in the West Indies; considered to be a "sweet" cassava, with relatively low toxicity in comparison to the larger types; by simply cooking *yuca,* the root is rendered safe for consumption.

zancudos: *(san-kú-dos) Spanish,* mosquitoes.

SELECTED SOURCES

Indigenous History and Culture

Gasteazoro, Carlos Manuel. *La Historia de Panamá en sus Textos: Tomo 1 (1501–1903)*. Panama: Editorial Universitaria, 1999.
Howe, James. *A People Who Would Not Kneel: Panama, the United States, and the San Blas Kuna*. Washington, DC: Smithsonian, 1998.
Kane, Stephanie C. *The Phantom Gringo Boat: Shamanic Discourse and Development in Panama*. Washington, DC: Smithsonian, 1994.
Marsh, Richard O. *White Indians of Darien*. New York: G.P. Putnam's Sons, 1934.
Ocharan, Mauro. *Notas Histórico-Religiosas Sobre el Darién Sur*. Colón: Taller de Evangelización Diócesis de Colón–Kuna Yala, n.d.
Pardo, Mauricio. *Zrõarã Neburãz: Historia de los Antiguos Literatura Oral Emberá—Según Floresmiro Dogiramá*. Bogotá: Centro Jorge Eliécer Gaitán, 1984.
Torres Araúz, Reina. *Panamá Indígena*. Panama: Insituto Nacionál de Cultura Patrimonio Historico, 1980.
Ventocilla, Jorge, et al. *Plants and Animals in the Life of the Kuna*. Austin: University of Texas Press, 1995.
Wassen, Henry. "Cuentos de los Indios Chocós: Recojidos por Erland Nordenskold Durante su Expedición al Istmo de Panamá en 1927." *Journal de la Société del Américanistes* 24 (1933): 103–107.
———. "Mitos y Cuentos de los Indios Cuna: 1932–33." *Journal de la Société del Américanistes* 26 (1934): 1–35.
———. "Contributions to Cuna Ethnography: Results of an Expedition to Panama and Colombia, 1947." *Etnologiska Studier* 16 (1949): 7–139.

Isthmus Geology and Evolution

Coates, Anthony G., ed. *Central America: A Natural and Cultural History*. New Haven: Yale University Press, 1997.

Heckadon-Moreno, Stanley, ed. *Panamá: Puente Biológico.* Panama: Instituto Smithsonian de Investigaciones Tropicales, 2001.
Jackson, Jeremy B.C., et al., eds. *Evolution and Environment in Tropical America.* Chicago: University of Chicago Press, 1996.
Jaen Suarez, Omar. *Geografia de Panamá: Estudio Introductorio y Antologia.* Panama: Biblioteca de la Cultura Panameña, 1981.
Krichner, John. *A Neotropical Companion: An Introduction to the Animals, Plants, and Ecosystems of the New World Tropics.* Princeton: Princeton University Press, 1997.
Reid, Fiona A. *A Field Guide to the Mammals of Central America and Southeast Mexico.* New York: Oxford University Press, 1997.

Spanish Colonial History

Andagoya, Pascual de. *Narrative of the Proceedings of Pedrarias Dávila in the Provinces of Tierra Firma or Castillo del Oro, 1514–1526.* Translated and reprinted. New York: Burt Franklin Publisher, 1965.
Anderson, Charles L. G. *Life and letters of Vasco Nuñez de Balboa, including the conquest and settlement of Darien and Panama, the odyssey of the discovery of the South sea, a ... civilization on the continent of America.* 1941. Reprinted, Westport, CT: Greenwood Press, 1970.
Castillero Calvo, Alfredo. *Conquista, Evangelización, y Resistencia: Triunfo ó Fracaso de la Política Indigenista.* Panama: Impresora de la Nación, 1995.
Dampier, William. *A New Voyage Round The World.* London: James Knapton, 1697.
Fernández de Oviedo, Gonzalo. *A Natural History of the West Indies.* 1526. Translated and reprinted. Chapel Hill: The University of North Carolina Press, 1959.
———. *Writing from the Edge of the World: The Memoirs of Darien, 1514–1527.* Translated by G.F. Dille. Tuscaloosa: University of Alabama Press, 2006.
Mendez, Teodoro E. *El Darién: Imagen y Proyecciones.* Panama: Instituto Nacional de Cultura, 1979.
Mercado Sousa, Elsa. *El Hombre y La Tierra En Panama (Siglo XVI): Según Las Primeras Fuentes.* Madrid, 1959.
Mosquera, José E. *Las Guerras y Conflictos del Darién.* Medellín: Editorial Lealon, 2002.
Wafer, Lionel. *A New Voyage and Description of the Isthmus of America.* 1699. Reprinted, New York: Burt Franklin, 1970.
Wassen, Henry, ed. "Anonymous Spanish Manuscript from 1739 on the Province of Darien." *Etnologiska Studier* 10 (1940): 80–146.

Caledonia, Routes Across the Continental Divide, and General Information

Balf, Todd. *The Darkest Jungle: The True Story of the Darien Expedition and America's Ill-Fated Race to Connect the Seas.* New York: Crown, 2003.

Bannister, S., ed. *The Writings of William Paterson: Founder of the Bank of England.* London: Effingham Wilson, 1858.

Borland, Rev. Francis. *Memoirs of Darien.* Glasgow: Hugh Brown, 1715.

Bushby, Karl. Goliath Expedition website: http://goliath.mail2web.com.

Cullen, Edward. *The Isthmus of Darien Ship Canal.* 1852. London: Effingham Wilson, 1853.

Gisborne, Lionel. *Journal of the Expedition of Inquiry for the Junction of the Atlantic and Pacific Oceans.* London: Saunders and Standford, 1853.

Headley, J.T. "Darien Exploring Expedition, Under Command of Lieut. Isaac C. Strain." *Harper's New Monthly Magazine* 10, no. 58 (March 1855): 433–458; no. 59 (April 1855): 600–615; no. 60 (May 1855): 745–764.

Lindsay-Poland, John. *Emperors in the Jungle: The Hidden History of the US in Panama.* Durham, NC: Duke University Press, 2003.

Mankins, Nancy. *Hostage: The Incredible True Story of the Kidnapping of Three American Missionaries.* Nashville: W Publishing Group, 2001.

Prebble, John. *The Darien Disaster: A Scots Colony in the New World, 1698–1700.* New York: Holt, Rinehart & Winston, 1968.

Torres Araúz, Reina. *Human Ecology of Route 17 (Sasardi-Morti Region), Darién, Panama.* Columbus, Ohio: Battelle Memorial Institute, 1970.

World Bank. *Panama Poverty Assessment: Priorities and Strategies for Poverty Reduction.* Volume 1, Main Report. Human Development Department, June 28, 1999.

ABOUT THE AUTHOR

T. Krentzman photo

Martin Douglas Mitchinson has spent much of the past twenty-five years in Latin America, seven of those aboard his 36' ketch, *Ishmael*. To pay for his travels he has worked as a carpenter, diamond driller, newspaper reporter, freelance writer and photographer, oil-rig roughneck in northern Canada and crew member on yacht deliveries.

His photography and writing have been published in magazines, calendars and newspapers. Mitchinson's articles document his wide ranging travels, including his reflections on oil field work in a northern winter, and time on the road with a ragtag circus in Honduras. *The Darien Gap* is his first book.

Mitchinson presently lives in a cabin north of Powell River on the Sunshine Coast of British Columbia.